Twentieth century type designers

This book is for return on or before the last date shown below

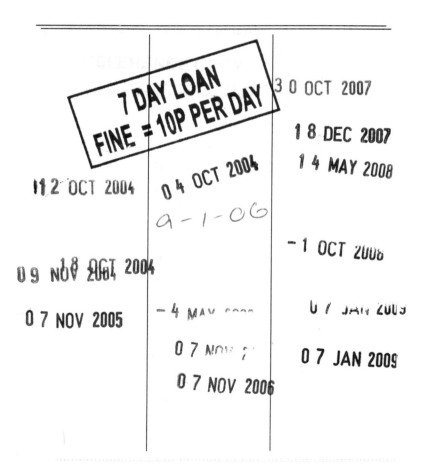

Sebastian Carter

Twentieth century

New Edition

type designers

Lund Humphries

First published in Great Britain in 1987 by
Trefoil Publications Ltd, London

This paperback edition first published in Great Britain
in 2002 by
Lund Humphries
Gower House, Croft Road,
Aldershot, Hampshire, GU11 3HR

ISBN 0 85331 851 4

Library of Congress Control Number: 2002100643

Text design by Sebastian Carter
Cover design by Philip Lewis
Typeset by Goodfellow & Egan Phototypesetting, Cambridge
Printed in China by Midas Printing Ltd

Contents

Foreword

The first edition of this book appeared in 1987, and two years later it was possible to reprint it unaltered, without so far as I know incurring universal contempt. The development of type design was progressing rather faster than in the era of hot metal, but in a way which could be encompassed in a short book. Admittedly this book was one with a conservative viewpoint, which turned a blind eye to the wilder shores of the advertising world, and concentrated on text faces and a few of the more restrained display founts.

Since then, there has been a rapid growth in the ownership of personal computers equipped with sophisticated software for designing typefaces on screen. The design of type is no longer largely in the hands of big manufacturers, but has been democratised among a number of small 'kitchen-table type foundries', to use Matthew Carter's phrase. The resulting explosion of type designs, and the speed with which they appear on the market, means that I am even less able than I was in the first edition to cover the entire field without making the book unduly huge and indigestible, and likely to be out of date not only in a year's time but even before it is published.

Accordingly, while I have left the earlier historical sections of the book largely intact, adding a few terminal dates and some information and documentation which have appeared since 1987, I have substantially revised the later parts in the light of recent developments. Here I cannot pretend to describe fully the embarrassment of riches with which the present-day user of type is confronted; and so I have tried to take a more detached and broad view, and identify what seem to me to have been the most significant changes, and to offer profiles of a number of representative designers.

In writing the earlier edition, my notional readers were the typographers and buyers of print who were more familiar with the appearance on the page of Goudy Old Style, or Perpetua, or Palatino, than with the lives of their creators (I had been asked once if Goudy was the same person as the Catalan architect Antonio Gaudí). Since then, in numbers which must have surprised even the experts, people who are not trained designers have begun to show a curiosity about type, prompted by the spread of what is known loosely as desktop publishing, involving software which can generate acceptable typefaces and arrange the setting in pages, with displayed matter added at the click of a mouse.

Faced with a menu of types on a computer screen, many beginners are perplexed by the range of choice. Many excellent books have been written on design for desktop printing. This is not one of them. On the other hand, many desktop users quickly become interested in the provenance of the types they have at their fingertips, and I hope that what follows will go some way towards satisfying that curiosity.

The literature of the subject, too, has changed dramatically since the mid 1980s. Then I had to rely on a few out-of-print monographs on individual designers which were scarce even on the second-hand market. Many of these were quite valuable, since type design is a specialised field and standards of production are naturally high. These books are acknowledged in the footnotes on the individual designers, though in a few cases I have substituted more up-to-date sources.

Books on type design in general were very few. There were the type-finders and identifiers, such as the *Encyclopaedia of type faces* by W. Pincus Jaspert, W. Turner Berry and A. F. Johnson, London, Blandford Press, 1953 (4th edition, 1970, reprinted 1991, distributed in the USA by Sterling Publishing Inc, New York). But the information given on the origins of the faces was sparse, often self-evident, and sometimes wrong. Lawrence Wallis has now supplemented it, and greatly improved on it, with his extremely useful *Modern encyclopedia of typefaces, 1960–1990* (London, Lund Humphries; New York, Van Nostrand Reinhold, 1990), and last year published his selected essays on the pioneer years of phototypesetting and other subjects, *Typomania* (Lund Humphries, 1993). Other general surveys to have appeared recently are *Rookledge's International handbook of type designers*, by Ron Eason and Sarah Rookledge (Carshalton Beeches, Sarema Press, 1991, distributed in the USA by Moyer Bell, Wakefield, RI), which has brief biographical entries for a wide range of designers, and a book of examples, *Typefaces for books*, by James Sutton and Alan Bartram (London, The British Library; New York, New Amsterdam, 1990). The *FontBook*, by Ed Cleary, Jurgen Siebert and Erik Spiekermann (Berlin, FontShop International, 1993; distributed in Britain by FontWorks, London, and the USA by FontShop, Chicago) is a glorified specimen book with an enormous range and more information than is customary. FontShop also publish *Fuse*, conceived by Neville Brody, each issue of which contains the software for new experimental type designs and broadsides displaying them. The calendar *26 Letters*, published in 1989 and 1990 by Typostudio SchumacherGebler, Munich, contained useful biographies and type samples.

Among recent critical works, Walter Tracy's *Letters of credit* (London, Gordon Fraser, 1986; Boston, David Godine, 1986) appeared too late for me to make use of in the first edition of this book. However, the section on Jan van Krimpen had already been published in *Fine Print*, the San Francisco journal which has been much missed since it closed down in 1990. Some of the articles on type which had appeared in it were collected in *Fine Print on type* (1988, distributed in the UK by Lund Humphries, London). Tracy has been followed by a number of books, notably Alexander Lawson's *Anatomy of a typeface* (Boston, David Godine; London, Hamish Hamilton, 1990) and the handsomely illustrated *Twentieth century type* by Lewis Blackwell (London, Laurence King; New York, Rizzoli, 1992).

Nor have individual designers been neglected. D. J. R. Bruckner's lavishly illustrated *Frederic Goudy* (New York, Abrams, 1990) and the sumptuous *Hermann Zapf and his design philosophy* (Chicago, Society of Typographic Arts, 1987) both in their different ways testify to the growing and widening interest in the subject on the part of the public. Fiona MacCarthy's biography *Eric Gill* (London and Boston, Faber & Faber, 1989), while it received most publicity from its revelations about its subject's sexual voracity, is also a valuable and balanced study of his work.

Type companies continue to have a mixed record so far as publishing information about their designs goes. Unquestionably the best is Adobe Systems of Mountain View, California, whose type staff under the direction of Fred Brady produce well-written and well-designed booklets on their new faces.

Among the new magazines, *Eye*, edited by Rick Poynor, is notable for its serious coverage of type, especially in its two numbers (Nos 7, 1992, and 11, 1993) dedicated to the subject.

In the preparation of the first edition of this book I was greatly helped by Nicolas Barker, Bruce Beck, Will Carter, John Dreyfus, Carolyn Hammer, William Hesterberg, Herbert Johnston, Abe Lerner, Martino Mardersteig, David McKitterick, James Mosley, David Pankow, John Latimer Smith, Walter Tracy, Gerard Unger, Lawrence Wallis, and Hermann Zapf, as well as two designers who are sadly no longer with us, Joseph Blumenthal and Berthold Wolpe. In revising it, I renew my thanks to these, and add the names of Matthew Carter (no relation), Rebecca Carter, Adrian Frutiger, John Lane, Mathieu Lommen, José Mendoza y Almeida, Aldo Novarese, Robert Slimbach, Sumner Stone, and Carol Twombly. My wife Penny Carter has revised her index. Although all these have gone out of their way to protect me from errors, I take full responsibility for those that remain.

For permission to quote material, I am grateful to the following: Brooke Crutchley and Arthur Crook, for Stanley Morison's writings; Huib van Krimpen for his father Jan's; and for Frederic Goudy's, the University of California Press, and the Typophiles, New York.

Sebastian Carter
December 1994

Introduction

The skeleton shapes of the letters of our alphabet change hardly at all. Why then do skilled designers devote so much time, sometimes their whole lives, to drawing different versions of the outlines?

This simplified formulation of a basic question about type design, with which I began the first edition of this book, was criticised by one reviewer, Robert Bringhurst, the Canadian poet and typographer, writing in *Fine Print*. 'Some designers do, of course, draw outlines,' he wrote, 'but those who make substantive contributions to the tradition do something else: they create letters precisely by rethinking their skeleton shapes, by reinventing them, muscle and bone, from the inside out. To ask why they do so is much like asking why, since all trees have branches and leaves, God chose to make more than one species.'

This is eloquently put, but I did not intend my question to be taken quite so literally. In recreating letterforms the type designer inevitably modifies the proportions of the basic shapes, but within very conservative limits. To do more than this offends readers, and to do much more makes letters illegible.

In his *Essay on typography* (1931) Eric Gill illustrated a celebrated, if exaggerated, contrast between acceptable letter forms (the left-hand letters of each row) and what he called 'fancy madness'. He regarded the second D as permissible if extreme condensation is required, but the rest as beyond the pale.

Gill was a muscle and bone man if ever there was one, yet in practice the skeleton shapes of his letters were markedly constant. The characteristic Gill **R** with its curvaceous tail was discernible in its essentials in all his roman types, yet he drew and redrew the profiles in many different ways.

The reasons for this are manifold, and illustrate the responses of most designers to type design. The simplest is that he was asked to: he was approached by a manufacturing company, Monotype, with commissions for a roman type, Perpetua, and a sans-serif, Gill Sans. Subsequently he designed faces for other

Wood engraved illustration by Eric Gill from his 'Essay on typography' (1931).

customers, and one, Joanna, for his own use, though Monotype later took it over. The variety of forms was the result of the different styles he was producing, the dislike creative people feel for repeating themselves, and the desire of customers for something different.

Yet while they are unmistakeably Gill's creations, they are equally unmistakeably in a long tradition of type design. Typefaces in daily use are shaped by a complex blend of historical influences and personal preferences. In the classic romans, even when stored in a PostScript file, there are traces of the manufacturing techniques used to make their ancestors, the punchcutter's file, the scribe's pen, even the stone carver's chisel. These have been transmuted through centuries of slow development in the conventional ideas about the ideal shapes of letters. The changes made by individual designers are limited by the need to respect both these inherited conventions and readers' dislike of change. As Stanley Morison wrote in *First principles of typography* (1930), 'Type design moves at the pace of the most conservative reader. The good type designer therefore realises that, for a new fount to be successful, it has to be so good that only very few recognise its novelty. If readers do not notice the consummate reticence and rare discipline of a new type, it is probably a good letter. But if my friends think that the tail of my lower-case r or the lip of my lower-case e is rather jolly, you may know that the fount would have been better had neither been made.'

Offending readers with distortions of the basic proportions of letters, or even attracting their notice with minor eccentricities of detail, creates a resistance not only to the type but to the message of which the type should be the faithful messenger. This is a negation of its purpose. Many writers on the subject have emphasised the theoretical 'invisibility' of type. The best-known analogy is the one made by Beatrice Warde with a crystal goblet, through which the wine – the text – can be seen without distortion. But goblets, though translucent, are not invisible, and indeed can be studied independently of their contents. Students of type can never again read a text without being conscious of the face in which it is set. It becomes all the more important that the type should be good.

It is always a source of surprise to people fresh to the study of type design that minute differences, which one might think were barely visible to the naked eye, are so important. This is because when you are reading, although you are aware of surrounding lines, all your attention is focused on a short string of words, and the letters are perceived as larger than they actually are. Tiny irritating details are magnified by repetition. In the words of Chauncey Griffith, the typographical spirit behind Mergenthaler Linotype between 1915 and 1950, 'Few people can distinguish what a difference a fraction of a thousandth of an inch can make in [a type's] appearance. But the individual piece of type is like a thread. A single thread might be dyed crimson, scarlet or pink and the human eye would find the difference hard or impossible to detect. But once that thread is woven into cloth, the colour is very apparent. So type must be judged after it is woven into the texture of a paragraph or a page.'

When we contemplate any branch of design history, we tend to waver between conflicting responses. On the one hand we wonder at the amount of effort expended in the sophisticated manipulation of basic shapes, and on the other we welcome the results. We see highly simplified classics of design – a chair by Marcel Breuer, a fork by Arne Jacobsen, or Paul Renner's Futura typeface – and we wonder why anything else is required. But then we experience a natural revulsion, and embrace variety, experiment and amusement, even if it sometimes leads to kitsch. After a while we swing back again to purity. In everyone but a few single-minded zealots there reside both the puritan and the pluralist.

We should welcome typographic variety as the natural consequence of human creativity. Rudolf Koch, the great German calligrapher and type designer, wrote: 'The making of letters in every form is for me the purest and greatest pleasure, and at many stages of my life it was to me what a song is to the singer, a picture to the painter, a shout to the elated, or a sigh to the oppressed – it was and is for me the most happy and perfect expression of my life.' By no means all the designers mentioned in this book operated at this level of creative ecstasy, but all were driven by a love of letters and a burning desire to refine the common stock of printing types.

Much type design has been undertaken by less flamboyant characters, usually working for the drawing offices of type manufacturers. Their task has been to adapt existing designs for the demands of new typesetting methods, to expand master designs into families, or to give the necessary technical guidance to new designs on their way to completion. People such as Sol Hess of the American Lanston Monotype Company, Morris Benton of American Type Founders, Fritz Steltzer of English Monotype, and their staffs, are the largely unsung heroes and heroines of the business. Even with the recent introduction of computer software to aid this kind of work, the work still has to be done. The quality of what they do is intended to be undetected by the untrained eye, and that is its merit.

But side by side with such deliberately subtle technicians, sometimes even among the same people, there is another group of designers. These produce the original faces whose characteristics, even when redrawn by the drawing offices, survive translation, and are even perceptible when distorted by laser printers with the crudest definition. They profoundly change the shapes of the letters we use. It is they who are the main subject of this book.

It is not an encyclopaedia of all the designers of the century, but presents a selection of the best, together with others representative of a particular way of working. It tries to show their methods, their intentions, and how they reacted, or react, to their contemporaries; and it attempts to set them against the background of the changing demands of a rapidly evolving industry. In order to make this background as clear as possible, and to explain some of the technical terms which appear later, the story opens with a brief account of the development of printing and type design up to the turn of the century.

Type casting by hand. From Jost Amman's 'Beschriebung alle Stände' (1568).

Der Schrifftgiesser.

Prologue

As far as we know, the Chinese were the first to print books from moveable type. In the middle of the eleventh century one Pi Cheng apparently worked with re-usable ceramic characters, though no examples of his work survive. Then, early in the fourteenth century, Wang Chen wrote that, since Pi Cheng, types had been cast in tin but had not been successful because Chinese water-based inks did not take readily to metal; he went on to describe his own work with wooden type. Bronze characters cast from wooden masters impressed into sand moulds were later used extensively in Korea, still before the introduction of printing to Europe around the middle of the fifteenth century, but the huge number of characters in the Chinese and Korean languages meant that typographic books never seriously challenged works printed from hand-cut wood-blocks. In Europe, whose alphabetical system of writing required relatively few different symbols, the position was reversed.

We do not know if Johannes Gutenberg of Mainz, generally accepted as the father of the European printing revolution, knew of Chinese printing, though he relied heavily on another Chinese invention, the making of paper. His achievement was in the bringing together of existing techniques, the screw press, oil-based pigments, and above all the metal-working skills of punch-cutting (previously developed for patterning metal) and casting to make possible the manufacture of type, and it was a major achievement. Quite soon after he started experimenting, he produced his first book, the 'Forty-two-line Bible' (circa 1455), which remains one of the most beautiful books ever printed; while the process he developed remained unchanged in its essentials for over four centuries.

In outline, the way the process worked was thus, beginning with the manufacture of the type. A *punch* was cut by hand for each letter of the alphabet needed, in every size and style, and for punctuation. It consisted of the letter cut in relief, and in reverse, on the end of a peg of steel. This punch was then struck

with a mallet, to exactly the same depth as its fellows, into a small bar of copper, the *strike*, which was trimmed into the *matrix* by the techniques of *justification*. For although types (with regional variations) are of equal height-to-paper, and the bodies of any one size are the same from head to foot, the letters vary in width, from the narrow l to the wide m. The *moulds* into which the matrices were fitted to cast the pieces of type were therefore made of two parts which were slotted together and were adjustable to the width of the letter; and the two halves were held apart to the

Chinese compositors. An illustration from a manual on printing from moveable types written by Chin Chien in 1777.

11

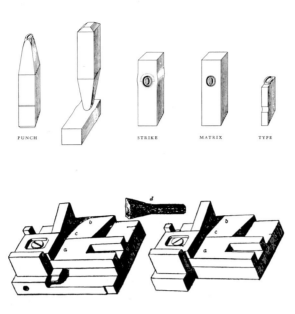

The punch, the strike, the justified matrix, and type; and the type mould.

The early hand moulds, about the size of a cricket ball, were simple mechanisms which most printers could afford. Each mould cast one size only, so a range was needed to make more than one size. To cast type, the craftsman inserted the matrix into the head of the mould and closed it; then with a ladle he poured molten typemetal (an alloy of lead with small amounts of tin, copper and antimony) into the conical opening at the bottom of the mould. He gave the mould a shake to press the metal into all the parts of the letter before hardening, and opened it up to release the cast *sort*, which needed only trimming to remove the excess metal before being ready for printing.

Until the industrial revolution, all type was cast in hand moulds in this way, except for large sizes which were cast in sand moulds, in type metal or brass, or cut in wood; but in the nineteenth century casting machines were developed which mechanised the process without changing it fundamentally.

The type thus cast was put into *cases* divided into compartments, each for a different letter. Traditionally, separate cases held minuscules and capital letters, and when using them the compositor put the pairs of cases on a frame with capitals above the minuscules. This is why the two are often still called 'upper case' and 'lower case', even by people who have never set type by hand.

The compositor stood in front of these cases, with a *composing stick* in his left hand and his setting copy by him. The composing stick was a narrow tray, made or set to the length of line desired. The compositor put the letters in it in the order of his copy, with spaces between the words. Spaces were simply pieces of metal of the same body size as the type, but lower height-to-paper; they were made with varying widths, so that at the end of the line, if the words did not exactly fill out the space available, wider or thinner spaces could be inserted to make the line fit. This process is also called *justification*, but should not be confused with the justification of matrices.

When enough lines had been set in the stick, the compositor carefully lifted them out on to a larger tray called a *galley*. Sometimes, but not always, he inserted strips of type metal or wood cut to the line length, called *leads*, to increase the interlinear space. In this way, a page was gradually built up. In later years, when type was more plentiful and separate proofing presses were used, the type was often proofed in long strips before being divided up into pages, and the

correct width by the body of the matrix. The justification of the matrix was consequently of great importance in the appearance of the type on the paper, because it determined the closeness of the letters to their neighbours, and the evenness of the spacing between them, which are just as important as the shapes of the letters themselves.

Punches were the form in which the master design of a typeface was preserved, and could not be exactly copied. Cutting them was a craft of great skill, and sets of punches were highly prized, not least because they could be used to produce many sets of matrices. Indeed, it is arguable that several early types which were once thought to be different designs were in fact struck from the same punches, with maybe one or two letters substituted; but the matrices were justified with greater or lesser finesse, and the type printed with heavier or lighter impression.

Whereas the early punchcutters were usually independent craftsmen who would produce sets of punches or matrices to order, casting the type was a separate activity which was commonly done by the printer as the type was needed. The growth of foundries which commissioned designs of type and sold cast *founts* to printers was a later development.

A printing shop in the late sixteenth century. An engraving by Philippe Galle after a drawing by Jan van der Straet, from the series Nova Reperta. The representation is comprehensive and lively rather than strictly accurate in all details.

results were known as galley proofs; but originally the pages of type went straight on the press for proofing, and corrections were made on the spot, sometimes, in the less scrupulous houses, after the press run had started.

The first presses were built mainly of wood, with metal parts where necessary. They were slow, and laborious to use, but they had the advantage of cheapness, ease of building and dismantling, and mobility. They were adapted from the wine press, but added to the screw mechanism a sliding track to trundle the type, with the paper laid over it, under the *platen*, which applied the pressure. These wooden presses, pulled by hand, remained in use for a remarkably long time, only being replaced by iron presses early in the nineteenth century.

With these simple tools, printers produced some of the great books of our culture. Without the printing press, the great explosion of learning which took place during the fifteenth and sixteenth centuries would have been a much smaller affair. Texts could be multiplied quickly and cheaply as never before in the West, and moreover, they could be established, corrected and published in a way hitherto impossible, as an edition of acknowledged worth, comprising a number of copies of a book textually identical, even if decorated and bound differently. And in the way these texts were designed, there were new possibilities: lines could be moved or reset at proof stage, permitting second thoughts and improvements, in a way that manuscripts, for all their magnificence, did not allow.

A scribe, before he set to work to produce his one copy of a book, pounced his vellum, sharpened his quill, and had only to decide how big his script would be before ruling his lines and starting work. The script itself flowed from his pen as it was needed, modelled on others, but individual, and always developing: no two **a**'s were the same, and the writing probably changed according to the scribe's mood. Manuscript was always short of perfection, but it was alive. Type was quite different, in that the design of the letters was fixed before they were assembled. In the first typefaces, attempts were made to mimic the informality of manuscripts by cutting ligatures and scribal contractions, but these were slowly reduced in number, on common-sense as well as economic grounds (though never completely: we still sometimes employ the ampersand). Letters were often cut and used in several versions. But gradually the conception

A wooden hand-press. From the
colophon of a book printed by Josse
Bade (1462–1535), a printer
first of Lyon and then Paris, who
used the Latin name Ascensius.

of a fount became more definite, with twenty-four to six lower-case letters (**u** and **j** were introduced subsequently), sets of matching capitals and figures and, later, a related italic for contrast and emphasis, and later still a related bold, small capitals and titling, leading to the modern idea of a type family, typified by Univers, with several varieties of weight and width developed from a basic design.

Nevertheless, although the typeset page was more rigid and less vital than the manuscript, there were compensating advantages. Quite apart from the textual benefits already referred to, there was the realisation that the forms of letters could be perfected, preserved in metal, and repeated endlessly. Thus the idea of a typeface was born.

From the earliest designs, based on contemporary manuscript hands, types quickly established a tradition of their own. Gutenberg and his heirs used only blackletter, or gothic, but with the spread of printing to Italy, especially Venice, a design of roman type was developed based on renaissance humanist script and, shortly after, a sloped and contracted version of handwriting, called italic; later still, the two were used jointly for textual articulation. They were more or less gradually adopted by the French, the Spanish, the Dutch, the English and their colonies, usually side-

by-side with local forms of blackletter, and are loosely called *old face* or, in the Vox classification, *Garaldes*, a merging of the names of the French punchcutter Claude Garamond and the Venetian printer Aldus Manutius.

This family of derivatives from the Venetian originals was dominant up to the middle of the eighteenth century, when a transition began towards what are equally loosely called *modern faces*, or *Didones* (a combination of the names of Didot and Bodoni), characterised by greater contrast between thins and thicks in the modelling of the letters, and vertical stress, so that the thinnest parts of an **O** are at twelve o'clock and six, instead of around eleven o'clock and five, as in old face types.

It was during the transition to modern face types that the first attempt was made to regularise type sizes. Hitherto, sizes had varied between different printers and foundries, and had been given imprecise names, often associated with the kind of work they were commonly used for, such as the French *Saint-Augustin* (14pt) and *Cicéro* (12pt), and the English *Brevier* (8pt) and *Long primer* (10pt). The French typefounder Pierre-Simon Fournier (1712-68) introduced a system of subdivisions of the inch, called

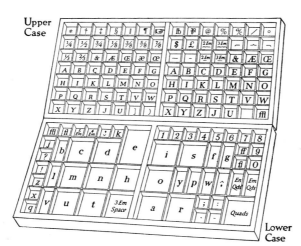

Upper
Case

Lower
Case

A pair of type cases. Although the
arrangement may vary around
the edges, the basic layout is
constant in English-speaking
countries. From Updike,
'Printing types' (1922).

The Vox Classification

The Vox classification was developed in the mid-1950s by the French typographer Maximilien Vox (1894–1974), founder-editor of the journal *Caractère* (with its bumper Christmas number *Caractère Noël*), and founder-president of the typographers' summer school at Lurs-en-Provence. It substituted for the traditional rough-and-ready terms such as old style, modern, transitional, Egyptian, sans-serif and Latin the following categories:

Humanes
Early roman faces such as Jenson's.

Garaldes
Later romans from printers such as Aldus Manutius and his punchcutter Francesco Griffo, and from the punchcutter Claude Garamond.

Réales
Transitional faces. The Réales group was later renamed 'Granvilles', from Philippe Grandjean's Romain du roi and Baskerville. Caslon and Fournier are included in this catch-all category.

Didones
Modern face: Didot and Bodoni.

Mécanes
Slab-seriffed Egyptians.

Linéales
Sans-serifs.

Incises
Types with pointed serifs, however vestigial, based on stone-cut lettering. Latins.

Manuaires
Pen and brush-formed letters, including all blackletter.

Scriptes
Scripts with joining lines.

The Vox classification has been adopted by the Association Typographique Internationale (A.Typ.I.) as well as the British Standards Institution.

In spite of the linguistic elegance of the names and the clarity of the descriptions, the scientific impression is more apparent than real: the classification is as arbitrary as any other.

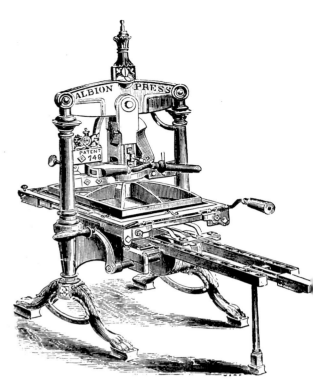

points, and fitted the existing named sizes into his scheme: thus the *Cicéro* was made the equivalent of twelve points. Later in the century the powerful typefounding and printing Didot family revised Fournier's scale, making it slightly larger, and the Didot system remains in use on the mainland of Europe, although it is not metric.

The American point system, which is also used in Britain and the rest of the English-speaking world, was not adopted until the 1880s, and is based on the pica (12pt) em, which is nearly exactly a sixth of an inch, and slightly smaller than the *Cicéro*. When continental metal types were adapted for the American system, they were big on their bodies in the smaller sizes, and in the larger ones cast on the next size of body up. Thus a 12D (Didot) type was commonly cast on 13pt, 30D on 36pt, and so on.

By the end of the first quarter of the nineteenth century the transition to modern face types was complete, and their development from then on was prompted more by utility than beauty; the types of the middle of the century were as bad, if not worse, than any in the four previous centuries. At the same time, the hitherto slow pace of technical development in printing began to accelerate dramatically. Lord Stanhope's introduction of an iron hand press around 1800 was soon followed by the American Columbian designed by George Clymer, and the English Albion, from R. W. Cope. These presses used lever or knuckle mechanisms which considerably increased the power of impression, so that a forme could be printed in one movement instead of the step-and-repeat impressions of wooden presses. Within a few years, moreover, Frederick Koenig and Andreas Bauer, two Germans working in London, had designed presses in which the paper was carried round a cylinder which, as it rolled over the type, applied far greater pressure than the flat platen of a hand-press could do; and Koenig and Bauer's presses were powered by steam. One was installed at *The Times*'s printing house as early as 1814; from newspaper offices, cylinder presses spread to general printers and eventually superseded hand-presses for book work in all workshops save the private presses.

These bigger and faster machines were hungry for type, but the inventions that would fully satisfy them had to wait until the 1880s. For most of the century, armies of hand compositors set books and newspapers as they had always done, but on a much larger scale. Machines were built to cast type more quickly

and reliably than hand moulds, but that type had still to be set manually. Machines were tried, such as the Kastenbein, which mechanised the work of the hand compositor, with the type selection governed by another important nineteenth-century invention, the keyboard; but they were slow, and a companion machine had to be harnessed to redistribute the type back into cases or magazines.

Then, in the 1880s, two American engineers, working independently, brought out machines which applied a new principle: instead of assembling type already cast, they assembled matrices and cast new type from them. Thus the type was always fresh, and laborious distribution after printing was unnecessary since the type went straight back into the melting pot. The Linotype, invented by the German immigrant Ottmar Mergenthaler in Baltimore and first installed at the *New York Tribune* office in 1886, carried a magazine of matrices which were released by the action of the keyboard to fall into a line; the operator then cast the line as a solid slug, a 'line o' type'. These slugs were easy to handle, but less easy to correct, and Linotypes were more commonly used for setting newspapers than books. Tolbert Lanston's Monotype machines, developed in Washington at the same time, had two parts, keyboards and casters, which could be separated geographically and multiplied according to need. The keyboard operator punched a paper spool with coded messages to the caster in the form of pairs of co-ordinates. The caster was equipped with a matrix case, a grid of separate matrices making up several alphabets, figures and punctuation; it read the spool, using compressed air to depress plungers, and the co-ordinates determined the position of the matrix case over a casting point, and therefore the letter to be cast. The Monotype, as its name implies, cast separate sorts, and so it could be used for both text setting and for filling cases for hand-setting; and corrections were simpler than with Linotype slugs.

Both machines, but particularly the Linotype, needed a great number of matrices. Before they appeared, the traditional hand-cut punches had kept up with the demand; but, though strong, they were not indestructible and, as we have seen, they could not be precisely duplicated. Coincidentally and fortunately, the necessary invention was made at the same time as Lanston's and Mergenthaler's. In 1884 the Milwaukee type founder Linn Boyd Benton (1844–1932) patented a punchcutting machine which worked from a large pattern: by means of a pantograph, the minute engraving drill was moved around the outline of the letter on the end of the punch.

The Benton machine had far-reaching implications for the design of type. The first was the relative ease of the new technique. There had been cases already of designers who were not punch-cutters conveying their ideas to craftsmen by means of words or drawings: Baskerville and Bulmer spring to mind, and there was the well documented case of the pioneering design of the French *Romain du roi*, conceived at the turn of the seventeenth and eighteenth centuries by the Académie des Sciences according to precise mathematical rules, the drawings meticulously engraved on a grid, and the punches cut by Philippe Grandjean. But in general, the scarcity of skilled interpretative punchcutters severely limited these endeavours. Now it was possible for anyone who could draw letters, and even people who could not, to design typefaces which could be licked into practical shape by the foundry drawing office.

The second implication was less beneficial, and concerned the question of scale. The hand punch-cutter necessarily worked at actual scale, and made minute adjustments to the shapes of letters accord-

Dawson's 'Wharfedale' cylinder press of 1879. The paper was carried by the cylinder and rolled over the type, greatly increasing the power and precision of impression.

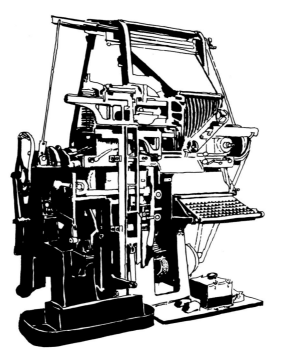

design type. This sometimes fostered talent previously debarred from the field by lack of technical expertise, and gave opportunities to the amateur designer. An example is the Cheltenham face, which was designed in 1896 by an American architect, Bertram Goodhue, for the private use of the Cheltenham Press of New York. It was cut for them by American Type Founders, for hand setting. Although it has found few friends among typographical critics, it proved so popular that ATF and Linotype in partnership issued it to the printing trade, and between 1904 and 1911 ATF's immensely skilled and prolific designer Morris Fuller Benton (1872–1948), the son of the inventor of the pantographic machine, drew eighteen different weights and other variants.

A handsomer portent of things to come was the appearance of Century in 1895, the year before Cheltenham. It was a strengthened modern face produced by Linn Boyd Benton for Theodore L. DeVinne (1828–1914), the distinguished American master-printer, for *The Century*, a magazine which was produced at his works; and again it was cut by ATF, who afterwards marketed it. Morris Benton produced eighteen variants between 1900 and 1928, including the ever popular Century Schoolbook.

The Linotype composing machine: a 'square base' model introduced in 1890. The keyboard on the right governed the admission of matrices from the large wedge-shaped magazine above it into the line; the slug was cast in the hot-metal section at the left; and the matrices were then carried to the top of the machine and distributed back into the magazine.

ingly, for the sake of legibility: the bowls of the lower case **e** and **a**, for example, were customarily enlarged in smaller sizes to lessen the chance of their clogging with ink. The pantographic machine, however, could cut many sizes from one set of drawings, and the instinctive modifications of the craftsmen were endangered. The more scrupulous manufacturers cut fewer sizes from any one set of drawings, and made more sets of drawings with the adaptations that were needed, but their example was not always followed. With the introduction of filmsetting, described in a later chapter, type sizes were altered with interchangeable lenses, and many types conceived for filmsetting had to be designed with the knowledge that one set of drawings would have to work properly in all composition sizes. Before the introduction of the Benton machine, types had been preserved as sets of punches, one set for each size, each slightly different. Now one set of master drawings served the same purpose.

Thus at the beginning of the twentieth century, type designers faced great challenges. Because punches could be cut by machine from drawings, and did not necessarily need the interpretative skills of a hand punchcutter, it was easier for a non-specialist to

An early Monotype keyboard and caster, of 1897. The paper spool at the top of the keyboard was punched with letters in coded form, and then put on the caster, where it can be seen on top at the right. The coded letters controlled the position of the diecase over the casting point, and the individual letters were ejected into lines in the galley on the left.

ABCDEFGHIJKLMNOPQRSTUVWXYZ&.,-:;!?''""[]()
abcdefghijklmnopqrstuvwxyz$1234567890fifffflffifflstct
ABCDEFGHIJKLMNOPQRSTUVWXYZ&

ABCDEFGHIJKLMNOPQRSTUVWXYZ&.,-:;!?'
abcdefghijklmnopqrstuvwxyz$1234567890fifffflffifflstct

ABCDEFGHIJKLMNOPQRSTUVWXYZ
abcdefghijklmnopqrstuvwxyz
1234567890

ABCDEFGHIJKLMNOPQRSUVWYZ
abcdefghijklnopqrstuvwxyz
1234567890

Two new typefaces of the 1890s. Benton and DeVinne's Century (1895), and Bertram Goodhue's Cheltenham (1896).

The manufacturers of the new typesetting machines, Monotype and Linotype, took several decades to start commissioning new designs, and at first remained content to adapt existing faces for their systems. But before the old century was out they took the step of licensing the rights to manufacture their machinery in other countries; Linotype formed a British company in 1895, and Monotype in 1897. These companies were autonomous, and their typographical programmes quite separate from the American parents'. As we shall see, the team of engineers at English Monotype's Salfords works, and the typographical guidance of Stanley Morison, led the Corporation to play a significant role in fostering the revival of printing between the two world wars, from which it also benefited greatly, but all the companies appointed advisers and encouraged their own designers.

Also in the 1890s, there took place in Britain an experiment in printing which, although rooted in the past in almost all respects, had a powerful if indirect influence on the designers of the next century. The pioneer industrial designer and socialist William Morris (1834-96), in the last years of his life, returned to one of his earliest ambitions, and set up a private press, called the Kelmscott Press. Books were printed there using hand presses, on dampened hand-made paper, in hand-set type designed by Morris himself and cut by a hand punchcutter, with wood-engraved ornament. The typographic style was backward looking, and recalled Morris's much loved incunabula, those books printed before 1500. His greatest book, the Kelmscott *Chaucer*, is a singular and unrivalled achievement. Yet despite this, Morris's search for excellent materials, for harmony between type and illustrations on the printed page, and in particular his discriminating investigation of early printed books for models for his own types, all commended themselves to the next generation, and many typographers, while in no way copying Morris's style, were profoundly stimulated by his ideas and his books.

Morris designed two types for his Press. The second, cut in two sizes called Troy and Chaucer, was a round blackletter of the kind known as rotunda. The first, Golden (1891), was more influential, because based on the magnificent roman types produced by Nicolas Jenson of Venice in the early 1470s (though the immediate model, which Morris followed by inking in letters on photographic enlargements, was

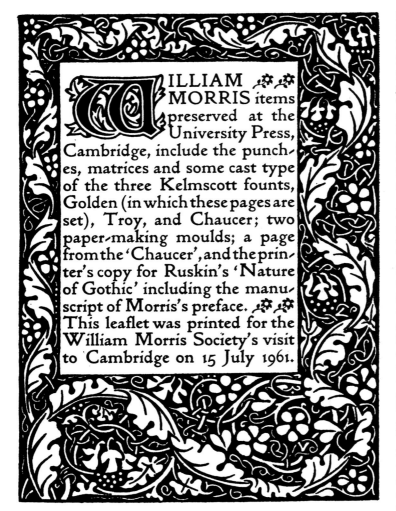

WILLIAM MORRIS items preserved at the University Press, Cambridge, include the punches, matrices and some cast type of the three Kelmscott founts, Golden (in which these pages are set), Troy, and Chaucer; two paper-making moulds; a page from the 'Chaucer', and the printer's copy for Ruskin's 'Nature of Gothic' including the manuscript of Morris's preface. This leaflet was printed for the William Morris Society's visit to Cambridge on 15 July 1961.

William Morris's Golden type (1891). Morris also designed the border.

printed from Jenson types by Jacobus Rubeus in 1476). In drawing over the letters, Morris made them much heavier. It is usual to say that he made them more 'gothic', but just as accurate to point out that he also made them more Victorian, strengthening the serifs to look like the slab serifs of nineteenth-century 'Egyptian' display faces.

Morris's choice of the Jenson model was widely imitated, and led to a flood of 'Venetians' and 'Jensons'. Its immediate successor was a far more elegant version for the Doves Press, begun in 1900 by the barrister-turned-bookbinder-turned-printer Thomas J. Cobden-Sanderson (1840-1922). The Doves Bindery had bound books for the Kelmscott Press, but the Doves Press, though it shared with Kelmscott the Jenson model for its one and only type, its hand-press technology, and its adviser in the person of Emery Walker (1851-1933), the *éminence grise* of the English private press movement, produced very different books. They were spare and undecorated, and in keeping with this the type was made lean and austere. The Doves *Bible* is another of the great achievements of the private presses, and it is hard to believe that only nine years separate it from the *Chaucer*. Whereas the Kelmscott book looked medieval, the Doves one belongs to the new age.

In the subsequent bitter arguments between Emery Walker and Cobden-Sanderson over the management of the Press, which culminated in 1916 when Cobden-Sanderson threw the type into the Thames off Hammersmith Bridge to prevent its use by anyone else, both parties claimed authorship of the type; but it seems clear that though Cobden-Sanderson's ideals may have influenced the way it was refined, Walker's technical knowledge and the skill of his draughtsman Percy Tiffin were essential to its success. Walker closely supervised the punch-cutter Edward Prince, who had previously engraved the Kelmscott types, similarly supervised, and went on to produce the types of several of the other English private presses, as well as those of the Cranach Press, begun in 1913 by the German diplomat and art patron Count Harry Kessler (1868-1938) at Weimar. The Ashendene, Eragny and Vale Presses all commissioned types which were at best individual, and at the worst a hideous reversion to nineteenth-century archaism, but the Cranach Press returned to the classical discipline of Doves. Kessler was a cosmopolitan who had been to school in England, and came to London for the advice he needed for his Press. A roman very similar to the Doves type was produced by Walker, Tiffin and Prince, but the same team ran into difficulties with a companion italic lower case, which neither the Doves type nor Jenson had.

The problems they encountered, which have been well chronicled by John Dreyfus,* were met with again and again in one form or another whenever

John Dreyfus, *Italic quartet, a record of the collaboration between Harry Kessler, Edward Johnston, Emery Walker and Edward Prince in making the Cranach Press italic,* Cambridge University Press (privately printed), 1966.

Unlimited in capability   Cleon
For joy, as this is in desire for joy,
To seek which, the joy-hunger forces us.
That, stung by straitness of our life, made strait
On purpose to make sweet the life at large—
Freed by the throbbing impulse we call death
We burst there as the worm into the fly,
Who, while a worm still, wants his wings. But, no!
Zeus has not yet revealed it; and, alas!
He must have done so—were it possible!

⟨ Live long and happy, and in that thought die,
Glad for what was. Farewell. And for the rest,
I cannot tell thy messenger aright
Where to deliver what he bears of thine
To one called Paulus—we have heard his fame
Indeed, if Christus be not one with him—
I know not, nor am troubled much to know.
Thou canst not think a mere barbarian Jew,
As Paulus proves to be, one circumcised,
Hath access to a secret shut from us?
Thou wrongest our philosophy, O king,
In stooping to inquire of such an one,
As if his answer could impose at all.

1   153

The Doves roman (1900),
designed by Cobden-Sanderson
and Emery Walker.

Beim SATZ wurde die vollkommene einheit des werkes als prinzip zugrundegelegt. Satz und satzspiegel sind als eine einzige fortlaufende architektur gedacht. Hierbei schuf die gegenüberstellung des lateinischen und deutschen textes auf jeder seite neue probleme, gestattete aber auch immer neue lösungen. In engster anlehnung an diesen satz hat sodann ARISTIDE MAILLOL SEINE HOLZSCHNITTE geschaffen: d. h. er hat bei diesen sich immer vom prinzip leiten lassen, daß ihr ton und linienspiel mit der architektur, dem linienspiel und dem ton des satzbildes

The Cranach Press roman (1913), designed by Emery Walker.

manufacturers tried to reconstruct historic faces, and so are worth summarising here.

The italic model chosen by Walker was a quirky and irregular type designed by the Venetian scribe Tagliente about fifty years after Jenson. The page of Tagliente's 1525 writing manual which Walker enlarged was badly printed, which made it difficult for Tiffin, who did not know very much about type, to deduce their shape successfully when inking in the letters. In all such cases, when an original type no longer exists in metal but only in the form of printed pages, the draftsman must try to perceive the outline of the characters as if they had been cleanly inked and well printed on smooth paper, eliminating all the splodges produced in the originals by ink spread and impression on rough paper. He must then bear in mind that the first punchcutter deliberately engraved

his letters on the fine side, knowing that they would be made bolder in the printing. Only then can he decide how far to restore the accidentals to prevent the type from looking too deodorised when printed with modern presses on smooth papers. All kinds of ethical considerations about the nature and purpose of workmanship arise, which were argued over in the decades that followed.

Prince cut a set of punches from Tiffin's drawings and made smoke-proofs, which were trial impressions made by coating the punches with soot from a candle flame and pressing them on paper. Kessler saw how the type had been misinterpreted and, aware that he was engaged in recutting the first chancery italic in modern times, asked the calligrapher Edward Johnston (1872-1944) to supply Prince with new drawings. Johnston, who held firm Art and Crafts principles, felt that he should only do 'character sketches' to guide Prince, who was the craftsman and therefore in control. Prince, however, was a craftsman of a different school, who was used to working with more precise instructions (and in this, although he was a hand punchcutter, he was reacting as any drawing office would). It took all Kessler's diplomacy to persuade Johnston to provide finished drawings, and even then the type was only half successful. Johnston's character comes through too forcefully for the type to be considered a true historical recutting, and yet the constraints of following Tagliente's type clearly made him unhappy. Some designers resolved this conflict, as we shall see in later chapters, and created new types from old models, but Johnston's calligraphic genius was hampered by it. It is ironical that his best-known type, designed two years later in 1915, was a sans-serif, commissioned by Frank Pick of London Transport for use in the Underground.

The work of the Cranach Press was interrupted by World War I, and then by Kessler's political career, and it was not until 1931 that an edition of Rilke was printed in the Johnston italic. In 1933, with Hitler's rise to power, Kessler left Germany and the Press closed down.

DIE FÜNFTE ELEGIE

Frau Hertha Koenig zugeeignet

er aber sind sie, sag mir, die fahrenden, diese ein wenig

Flüchtigern noch als wir selbst, die dringend von früh an

Wringt ein wem — wem zuliebe

Niemals zufriedener wille? sondern er wringt sie,

Biegt sie, schlingt sie und schwingt sie,

Wirft sie und fängt sie zurück; wie aus geölter,

Glatterer luft kommen sie nieder

Auf dem verzehrten, von ihrem ewigen

Aufsprung dünneren teppich, diesem verlorenen

Teppich im weltall.

Aufgelegt wie ein pflaster, als hätte der vorstadt-

Himmel der erde dort wehegetan.

                Und kaum dort,

Aufrecht, da und gezeigt: des dastehns

Grosser anfangsbuchstab . . ., schon auch, die stärksten

Männer, rollt sie wieder, zum scherz, der immer

Kommende griff, wie August der Starke bei tisch

Einen zinnenen teller.

The Cranach Press italic (1913),
designed by Edward Johnston.
From the Cranach edition of
Rilke's 'Duineser Elegien'
(1931), with wood-engraved
initials by Eric Gill.

55

Old types for new machines

The introduction of mechanical typesetting at the end of the nineteenth century seemed to many to signal the end of the established foundries, who supplied the printing trade with cast type for hand setting. In the event, the new machines took longer to be completely accepted, and many foundries survived longer than anyone could have predicted.

They did so in a variety of ways. Firstly, because among the mechanical systems only the Monotype could, using the Supercaster (introduced in 1928), cast type in display sizes for hand setting up to 72 pt (that is a body height of six pica ems, or one inch, the largest size in which metal type is normally cast). For their display sizes the users of slug casters such as the Linotype had to use either a display slug casting machine such as the Ludlow, which had a different repertoire of designs, or hand-set type from a Monotype machine or from a foundry.

Also, some of the more astute foundries rapidly adapted themselves to the new conditions by amalgamating with other foundries, their former rivals, the better to resist the new threat to their livelihoods, and by diversification into printing machine manufacture. Some also formed links with the opposition. The great German foundry of D. Stempel* in Frankfurt, founded in 1895, absorbed a number of smaller firms over the years, sometimes in partnership with their closest rivals in Germany, the Bauer and Berthold foundries, and in 1918 acquired a controlling interest in the small but enterprising Klingspor foundry in Offenbach. But Stempel also, as early as 1900, signed an agreement with the Berlin branch of Linotype to manufacture their matrices, and the close collaboration over many years between Stempel and Linotype in the development of new typefaces remains a model of productive harmony.

On the other side of the Atlantic, the United States, as the cradle of the new machines, naturally felt their impact even earlier.

Up to the last decade of the nineteenth century, most of the type foundries there had depended for the bulk of their sales on supplying newspapers with small sizes of type for text setting by hand, and had found this market killed almost overnight by the Linotype machine. The newspapers, while they were still using foundry type, had always wanted it quickly to keep production going, and in this had encouraged small foundries in almost every city that had a newspaper, dependent on it and so extremely vulnerable. In 1892, of the twenty-nine foundries which were to form American Type Founders, only a handful were in a strong position. In that year twenty-five of the foundries decided to join together to form ATF, and the other four joined later. Thirteen of the weakest quickly closed down, and the federation that remained lacked cohesion and a sense of direction until the appointment in 1894 of Robert Nelson* (1851-1926) as general manager, and in 1901 as president. Nelson realised that the various constituent foundries were run by talented men who were under-employed because of the group's policy of keeping each foundry separate. Joseph W. Phinney of the Dickinson Foundry in Boston had tried to issue Morris's Golden type commercially and, on Morris's refusal, had produced his own version, Jenson Old Style, in 1893. He was a man of considerable perception, and in 1896 issued the first type sent to him from Chicago by a young aspiring designer called Frederic Goudy, with results which will be described later. Linn Boyd Benton had invented the pantographic punchcutting machine which had been so helpful to the composing machine manufacturers who were now threatening

Chronik der Schriftgiesserei D. Stempel AG, Frankfurt a.M., sechzig Jahre im Dienst der Lettern, 1895–1955, Frankfurt, Stempel, 1954.

H. L. Bullen, 'Robert Wickham Nelson, an intimate history', *The inland printer*, September 1926.

the foundries, but he also developed the similar machine for engraving matrices, which was ATF's standard practice; and his son Morris Benton was ATF's house designer. Morris Benton drew many competent versions of classic types, notably Cloister and Garamond; he skilfully expanded many faces into families; and he produced a variant of Goudy Old Style, called Goudy Catalogue, which is arguably better than the original.

Nelson managed to insist that these independently minded men work for ATF rather than for themselves. He had the foresight to see that while from then on text would almost always be set by machine, displayed matter needed foundry type, and with the growth of advertising and the emergence of the advertising designer there would be an increasing hunger for new designs. Nelson was always a type man, even when ATF diversified into printing machinery; he developed the idea of the type family, in which a design could be produced in bold, semi-bold, extra bold, and expanded and condensed forms without losing its character, and unity could be given to a typographic design when employing different weights of type. He also backed, in spite of the reluctance of his colleagues, ATF's first great suc-cess, the cutting of the Cheltenham family, in association with Mergenthaler Linotype.

Nelson was assisted at ATF by his advertising manager Henry Lewis Bullen (1857-1938), who was a far more influential figure than his position might suggest. He had been with the company from the start, but it was after he rejoined it in 1908 after a period elsewhere that he began to build up the great typographical reference library for which he is best known, and from whose resources he and Morris Benton drew in devising their variations on the Jenson model sanctified by William Morris, Venetian (1911) and the highly popular Cloister (1913).

In 1914, Bullen, taking his lead from the French foundry Deberny & Peignot, suggested a new his-torical model for recutting, the 'Garamond' types used by the Imprimerie Nationale in Paris, and though production of the ATF version was held up until 1917 as the foundries had been requisitioned for war work, it was to prove widely influential.

By comparison with the more adventurous of the European foundries, who pursued an energetic programme of persuading outside designers to create innovative typefaces, ATF's more cautious policy, with one or two exceptions such as Goudy Old Style,

THE POPE

&

THE WAR

Stanley Morison, *A tally of types, with additions by several hands*, edited by Brooke Crutchley, Cambridge University Press, 1973. (An enlarged edition of the privately printed Cambridge Christmas book which appeared in 1953.)

Caslon, hand-set. Maxwell wanted to change to Monotype composition for reasons of cost, but Monotype had not issued Caslon. However, they agreed to cut a trial version, and Maxwell presented Shaw with two specimen pages, one set on the Monotype and one by hand, without telling him which was which. Shaw preferred the machine set page, and the day was carried.

The English Monotype Corporation* at this time, although its typographical achievement, with three exceptions, had been unspectacular, was technically proficient and well managed. The two chief officers were both American. The managing director, Harold Duncan, was a man of education and vision, and the works manager, Frank Pierpont, was a highly skilled engineer, who ruled the works at Salfords, just south of London, like a separate empire. He was assisted in the drawing office by Fritz Steltzer, whom he had brought from Germany. Steltzer was responsible for the redrawing and adaptation of most of the great

Cloister (1913), designed by Morris Benton. Here used in a pamphlet published by the Guild of the Pope's Peace, printed at the Pelican Press (1917). The two Ts are variants, so neither is a wrong fount.

was to rely on the skills of its own design department under Benton to adapt well established type styles for a clearly perceived market. Their conservatism was equalled, even exceeded, by that of the manufacturers of the new typesetting machines, whose engineering innovations were not matched by any corresponding audacity in design for many years. We must remember that Monotype and Linotype were not selling type design, or even type, but composing machines, and the temptation was understandably to equip them with faces that looked as like the foundry type they were replacing as possible. The first English Monotype faces were simply recuttings of the old styles and moderns then familiar to printers, publishers and readers, and the Corporation considered adding to the repertoire only if a customer made it a condition of buying a new machine, or otherwise brought influence to bear.

In 1915, for instance, William Maxwell of the Edinburgh printers R. & R. Clark, who printed the plays of George Bernard Shaw, came to Monotype with a problem. Shaw was type-conscious, and insisted on his writings being set in Caslon, the perennial English favourite old face dating from the early eighteenth century; and moreover on foundry

Monotype Caslon (1915).

ABCDEFGH
abcdefghijklmn
opqrstuvwxyz

ABCDEFGH
abcdefghijklmnop
stuvwxyz

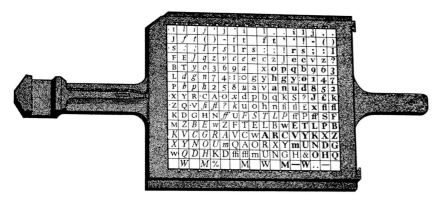

with too much use of rulers, compasses, and French curves. The subtle concave waisting of uprights, the organic growth of serifs from stems, and the flow of freehand drawing, were often lost in rigid mechanical redrawing.

Nevertheless, objections such as these were minor criticisms of Monotype's success: in the first decades of the century there was less to criticise because less was being done. There were, however, three types which were a foretaste of things to come. These were Imprint, Plantin and Bodoni.

The Imprint was a printing trade journal which appeared in 1913. It was a crusading venture, which attempted to raise printers' consciousness of design. Not altogether surprisingly for the time, it did not last a year, but its contents were remarkably informative and wide-ranging, dealing with aesthetics as well as such more practical matters as printing processes, trade education and costing. The editorial board reflected the range of interest, including as it did the calligrapher Edward Johnston as well as Gerard Meynell, manager of the Westminster Press, who printed the journal.

Not the least interesting thing about *The Imprint* was its type, cut by Monotype. When preparing

historical recuttings to the demands of the Monotype machine, as well as the designs of letterers such as Eric Gill, who were not specialists in type design.

The work of the drawing office in all type manufacture using pantographic engraving consisted of preparing large patterns for the pantograph to follow, and in the case of mechanical composition each machine had constraints which the draftsmen had to bear in mind. The particular limits of the Monotype machine lay in the make-up of its diecase. The matrices were arranged in grid formation in the case, with all the letters of a given width in a row. The letters in any one row had to be of equal width. Inevitably, the drawing office had to do some expanding and contracting of letters to make them fit, and their skill lay in making such distortion as unnoticeable as possible. Double and single f-ligatures were particularly useful sorts for this purpose, since the space between the letters could be altered without changing the letters themselves.

Such skilful adaptations of letter forms to fit the diecase were accepted by most designers, with the vocal exception of the Dutchman Jan van Krimpen. But others, notably Eric Gill, pointed out the tendency of the drawing office to regularise letters

Monotype Imprint (1912).

ABCDEF
abcdefghij

ABCDEFGHIJK

abcdefghijklmnopqrs

ABCDEFGHIJKLMNOP
abcdefghijklmnopqrstuvwx
ABCDEFGHIJKLMNOP
abcdefghijklmnopqrstuvwxyz

Monotype Plantin (1913).

layouts for the magazine, J. H. Mason (1875-1951), who as a former helper at the Doves Press and present adviser to Kessler's Cranach Press at Weimar represented the private press interest on the editorial board, had wanted Caslon. Caslon was then available only as foundry type for hand composition, as we have seen. Meynell wanted to use his Monotype equipment, both as a practical measure and as a point of editorial policy, but was unable to produce a typeface from the hundred series so far cut by the English company that satisfied his colleagues. At the beginning of November 1912, with only three months to go before the first number, the editors approached Harold Duncan, the managing director of Monotype, and asked for a new type to be made to their specification, which, broadly speaking, was for a composition size of Caslon redrawn with the vigour of some of the display sizes. The Monotype drawing office produced the design, trials were made and criticised, and the type was ready by the last day of the year. Imprint Old Face, Series 101, was the first Monotype face of any distinction, and their twelfth most commercially successful; and it is still in common use today. From the first *The Imprint's* editors made it clear that their type was for general

sale, as part of their declared ambition to raise standards in the trade. This is often cited as evidence of their altruism, although they undoubtedly took the practical view that widespread sales would help the magazine's parlous finances, by defraying the costs of development and cutting.

Monotype's other early success has proved even more enduring. Plantin, Series 110, was proposed by Pierpont and Steltzer at Salfords, and cut in 1913, only eight months after Imprint. It was designed with the specific intent of building the effect of ink-spread into a typeface intended for printing on smooth and coated papers, which in effect meant that it was a bolder type than its model. As we have seen, the early punchcutters reduced the weight of their letters, knowing that the printing process would make them bolder. The model for Plantin was a type used in an *Index characterum* printed in 1905, listing the types used by the Plantin-Moretus Press in Antwerp, and compiled by Max Rooses, the first director of the Plantin-Moretus Museum, the fine collection of early printing presses and equipment still housed in the original buildings. The complete fount, the work of Robert Granjon, Garamond's approximate contemporary, was never used by the great Christophe

Plantin (1514-89), although he used some letters from it to augment a Garamond fount he had; but it was bought by the Moretus family, his heirs, later in the seventeenth century. Over the years, some wrong fount letters were introduced by the Moretuses, retained in the *Index*, and reproduced in Monotype Plantin.

The choice of the Plantin model was adventurous in that it was not a fifteenth-century Venetian type, but a sixteenth-century French one. In this, Pierpont was making a very similar choice to Bullen's when he selected 'Garamond' for recutting at much the same time. But Pierpont simply wanted a type that was large on its body and economical of space, selected the Moretus Granjon for that practical reason, and had it much redrawn. ATF Garamond, which began to appear at the end of World War I and was bought eagerly on both sides of the Atlantic, stayed much closer to its original, which was chosen more for its aesthetic merits.

This original was a collection of types at the Imprimerie Nationale in Paris, called the *caractères de l'université*. They became widely known by being used to set the introduction of Anatole Claudin's *Histoire de l'imprimerie en France au XVe et au XVIe siècle*, published between 1900 and 1914 in four magnificent volumes, and were ascribed by Claudin and Arthur Christian, director of the Imprimerie Nationale, to Garamond. The authority of these men made the attribution generally accepted, and though Bullen had doubts that the type actually was by Garamond, he did not broadcast them. It was not until 1926 that Bullen's former assistant Beatrice Warde, writing under her pen-name Paul Beaujon in *The Fleuron* 5, revealed that the *caractères de l'université* were copies of Garamond's types cut in the early seventeenth century by the little known Jean Jannon of Sedan.

The success of ATF Garamond, however, was untroubled by such questions, and the type quickly began to attract imitators. Shortly after his appointment as 'art adviser' to the American Lanston Monotype Company in 1920, Frederic Goudy suggested to its president J. Maury Dove 'that there seemed to be a movement on the part of foundries to revive some of the old book types and "why should not the Monotype present its products first instead of following the others?"' Though this rather brash approach did less than justice to ATF, Dove was persuaded to try the idea out. Goudy took his copy of Claudin, and drew his own version, which was

considerably closer to its original than most of his types tended to be to their declared models, though it was, by comparison with the earlier ATF version and the slightly later English Monotype one, somewhat gauche in its details. Goudy had a certain amount of trouble with the Philadelphia drawing office, who tried to regularise the irregularities of his drawings, and he had to appeal to Dove to have them followed exactly. The type appeared in 1921 to much acclaim, and was only overshadowed by the English Monotype version. Goudy, writing in 1946 in *A half-century of type design*, appeared unaware that Garamond's authorship of the face had been disproved, and only noted that his spelling Garamont had been questioned on many occasions.

The relationship between the two Monotype versions puzzled many people, including Daniel Berkeley Updike, the great Boston printer, although his curiosity was academic: he was a slow and reluctant convert to mechanical composition and did not allow it at his Merrymount Press until 1932. He wrote* to Stanley Morison of English Monotype in 1923 asking for enlightenment, and observing that a trade magazine in the United States had referred to the English cutting as 'a version of the Goudy type'. Morison replied with some heat, objecting to Goudy's (or his press agent's) tacking his own name on to Garamond's, and making it clear that the types were separately conceived. He defended the English cutting, particularly its better background research, and concluded, 'I am sure that the English Monotype version is not in every respect to be commended. At least however it is known as Monotype-Garamond. I shudder to think of the terrible things that Mr Goudy now threatens to do. I suppose he too will do a Blado italic – and call it Goudy – I must get ahead first.' Morison did. He and Updike often reviled Goudy in their correspondence, though Morison was polite enough about him in print.

Goudy himself said of his version:

'Most of the favourable criticism regarding my own version of the type is misleading. Its final form as drawn by me was not the result of inspiration or of genius on my part, but was

Stanley Morison and D. B. Updike, selected correspondence, edited by David McKitterick, New York, Moretus Press, 1979. (Published in Britain by Scolar Press, 1980.)

abcdefghijklmnopqrstuvxyz&

abcdefghijklmnopqrstuvwxyz&

ABCDEFGHIJKL *ABCDEFGHIJK*

caecitate cordis liberari. Summum igitur studium nostrum sit, in vita Jesu Christi meditari.

*caecitate cordis liberari. Summum igitur stud-
ium nostrum sit, in vita Jesu Christi meditari.*

vitam ejus & mores imitemur, si velimus veraciter illumi-
nari, & ab omni cæcitate cordis liberari. *Summum igitur
studium nostrum sit, in vita Jesu Christi meditari.*

Qui sequitur me non
ambulat in tenebris:
by which we are taught

Qui sequitur me, non ambulat in tenebris:
dicit Dominus. Haec sunt verba Christi, qui-

Qui sequitur me, non ambulat in tenebris: dicit
Dominus. Haec sunt verba Christi, quibus ad-
monemur, quatenus vitam ejus & mores imite-

A gathering of Garamonds. The top three rows show the early seventeenth-century Imprimerie Nationale 'caractères de l'université', cut by Jean Jannon; the next four are ATF Garamond (1917–); the next three Lanston Monotype Garamont (1921), designed by Goudy; the next three English Monotype Garamond (1922); the next two Stempel Garamond (1924); and the bottom three are Linotype Granjon.

ABCDEFGHIJKLMNO
abcdefghijklmnopqrstuvw
£1234567890.,:;!?""
ABCDEFGHIJKLMNOPQ
abcdefghijklmnopqrstuvwxyz

Monotype Baskerville (1923).

merely the result of an attempt to *reproduce* as nearly as possible the form and spirit of the "Garamond" letter. I made no attempt to eliminate the mannerisms or deficiencies of his famous type, realizing that they came not by intention, but rather through the punch-cutters's handling, to his lack of tools of prevision and his crude materials; for he worked "by eye" and not by rule.

'I did find it impossible to eliminate, in my own rendition of the letter, that subtle something we call "personality", that something made up of items so intangible as practically to be imperceptible when individual types are compared, yet clearly manifest when the page they form is viewed as a whole. The subtleties of "Garamond's" drawing I couldn't neglect, yet I did not *consciously* include them in my own drawings, and these are the touches that mark my face as belonging to the present and not to the sixteenth century.'

Meanwhile, in England, Harold Duncan at Monotype was under pressure to cut a Garamond, in particular from the firm of Lund Humphries, who wanted it for the 1922 edition of their printing trade publication *The Penrose annual*. In the January-February 1922 issue of *The Monotype recorder*, the handsome house journal of the English company, the type was announced, and work was begun. Series

156 was issued towards the end of the year, and was to prove Monotype's eighth most successful face.

One of the figures behind the English Monotype Garamond was a young typographer and printing historian called Stanley Morison, then aged thirty-three. Although Morison's work as a designer is described in a later section, as an adviser his work is inextricably linked with Monotype. Almost entirely self-taught, he had made himself an expert on typographical history, but he had a practical turn of mind which saw in the past a wealth of material useful for the present, and a persuasive pen when it came to convincing his employers that they should back his judgement (although he always maintained that they did not employ him, but he them).

The issue of *The Monotype recorder* announcing Garamond was printed at the Cloister Press, where Morison was then working, and the announcement was set in ATF Garamond, bought at his insistence. It also had two articles he had written. Moreover, he had been asked by Eric Humphries to design *The Penrose annual*, and probably helped by that route to influence Monotype to undertake the cutting. And he began his direct association with Monotype by supplementing Claudin's book with extra material from the Imprimerie Nationale for the drawing office to work from. Early in 1923 his position as typographical adviser was made more formal, and though he had a long struggle with Pierpont, who understandably felt that his hegemony was threatened by an amateur, his influence over the Corporation's policy was incalculable.

Even after Monotype Garamond was cut and issued, Morison did not lose interest in its origins. Beatrice Warde had moved to London, and later became an imaginative publicity manager at Monotype. Morison encouraged her to investigate Bullen's doubts about Garamond's authorship of the type, which resulted in her 1926 article on Jean Jannon already mentioned. In a postscript, she noted two other recuttings which used as models not the *caractères de l'université*, but the genuine Garamond types shown in a 1592 specimen sheet from the Egenolff-Berner foundry in Frankfurt, who had obtained matrices after Garamond's death. The first was the Granjon type cut in 1924 by English Linotype to the designs of George W. Jones, which was, in spite of its name, 'immeasurably the best of the modern revivals of this letter'. The other 'Egenolff' Garamond was cut by the Stempel foundry in 1924, and was

copied by Mergenthaler Linotype in what Beatrice Warde called 'a poor variant'. This is the version currently available from Linotype in digital form.

Warde pursued her altruism in summing up the qualities of the Jannon type which was the model for Monotype Garamond as having 'a certain "prickle" to cut the eye, the italic a certain erratic twist, that justify our calling it a somewhat precious design, one which should have been left in the romantic privacy of the Imprimerie Nationale.' In this, she was harsher than Morison, who defended the type, and preferred to call the prickle 'crispness'.

The next type cut by Monotype was Baskerville, begun in January 1923, again following the lead of ATF. Interest in the work of the great eighteenth-century English type designer had been rekindled by Straus and Dent's biography of 1907, and Stephenson Blake, the Sheffield foundry, had revived their version of the Baskerville copies produced by the Fry foundry after Baskerville's death. It was these copies that ATF used in their 1917 cutting, working from strikes provided by Stephenson Blake. Monotype, at Morison's suggestion, decided to return to the original, and used as a model an edition of Terence's comedies printed by Baskerville in 1772. Although

THE THIRD ROMAN USED BY ALDUS MANUTIUS AND FIRST SHOWN IN THE HYPNEROTOMACHIA POLIPHILI VENICE 1499. FIRST RECUT IN 1923 BY THE MONOTYPE CORPORATION

To which is added a recutting of the fourth italic of Ludovico Arrighi, originally used for the 'Apologia of Petro Collenucio', Rome 1526.

LATIN was not the abiding love of Teobaldo Manucci, better known as Aldo Manuzio or Aldus Manutius. He early became a devotee of Greek, talked Greek in his household, staffed his office with Greeks and printed his first book in Greek. Latin letters came next and the tract (see pp. 46 ff.)

IERRE SIMON FOURNIER is not appreciated as he deserves in his native country, because the French bibliophile is less interested in what is old than in what is new; his interest in a prospective addition to his library is governed principally by the novelty of its pictorial illustrations. Unillustrated books make little appeal in Paris.

In spite of the hard and fast rules elaborated during and since the renaissance for the construction of Roman capitals, the fact remains that however reverently the designer keeps in mind the epigraphic tradition he is still far less bound by convention here than in the less ancient lower-case. In fact, the more learned he is in the forms of inscriptional letters, the better he realizes that there is not one "classic" M but five or six at least, and that

Monotype Fournier and (below) Barbou (both 1924).

the original was considerably cleaned up by the drawing office to make the somewhat odourless type we know, Series 169 was Monotype's third most successful type. (A similar cleaning up had been given to Monotype Bodoni, cut in 1921 before Morison's arrival, from the far more flavoured original types of Giambattista Bodoni (1740-1813) the Italian father of modern face. Once again, Bodoni had already been recut by ATF in 1907 from drawings by Morris Benton.)

Almost at the same time as Baskerville, Monotype produced a far more precise facsimile. It was called Poliphilus after its model, the type cut by Francesco Griffo for Aldus Manutius of Venice for the *Hypnerotomachia Poliphili* (1499), one of the most famous of illustrated incunabula. The Medici Society of London were planning a translation of the book with reproductions of the woodcuts, and wanted an exact copy of the type to set it in. The Monotype works duly obliged. Morison, in writing about the type in the *Tally* in 1953, expressed dissatisfaction with the result only because he had been too busy elsewhere to search out the clearest impressions of the original for them to work from. He did not appear to regret, as he might well have done, the illogicality of reproducing

in a type the furry outlines of the original which were due to the accidentals of ink-spread in one particular case, although he later qualified his position in a letter to Van Krimpen, crediting Pierpont with the decision. He was involved in the type chiefly in finding a companion italic, which the 1499 Aldine edition did not have. This he found in the chancery italics based on the designs of the scribe Lodovico degli Arrighi and used by the Papal printer Antonio Blado of Rome early in the sixteenth century; and as if to emphasise the different backgrounds of the two types, the italic was confusingly given a separate name, Blado. In a later case where a roman based on a Venetian original was yoked to a chancery italic, the same practice was followed, and Centaur roman has an italic called Arrighi.

The first of Morison's folio historical works, *Four centuries of fine printing*, was published by Ernest Benn in 1924, set in Poliphilus-and-Blado, and printed at the Cambridge University Press. The new University Printer, Walter Lewis, had been works manager at the Cloister Press when Morison was designer there, and had formed a high opinion of him, which was not universally shared at first by other master printers. He was able to persuade the Syndics, the governing body of the University Press, to appoint Morison as typographic adviser to the Press and, from 1925 on, Morison was able to create a demand for Monotype faces which greatly helped his plans at the Corporation.

In 1924, Monotype began the cutting of their next major revival, and the first in which Morison can be said to have been fully responsible for both the roman and italic, in that no other foundry had anticipated him, and no outside customer had asked for the type to be cut. This type, Fournier, Series 185, grew out of his admiration for the types of the French designer Pierre-Simon Fournier, an enthusiasm that was shared by his friend and mentor Updike (whom he was to meet the same year after a voluminous correspondence) and expressed in the latter's influential two-volume study, *Printing types, their history, forms and use*, which had appeared in 1922.

By the autumn of 1924 the Monotype works had cut two trial weights in 14pt of the Fournier model, and needed a decision on which one to proceed with. But Morison was away in the United States, and in October Harold Duncan died, being replaced by his second-in-command, William Burch. Monotype chose to cut the lighter weight of letter. Morison bitterly regretted this decision and always preferred the heavier version; he managed to rescue this in the one size that was cut, called it Barbou, and installed it at Cambridge University Press; he used it for the last three numbers of his journal *The Fleuron*. In the 1950s some smaller sizes were cut, but too late for the type to achieve the popularity it deserved. Morison's disappointment over this mistaken cutting coloured his relations with Monotype for some years, while on the other side Burch took a little time to show the same support for his advice that Duncan had done. As part of his historical studies, but also in order to gain enough technical knowledge to out-manoeuvre the often obstructive Monotype works, Morison began to work with some hand punchcutters, a fast disappearing species of craftsman. He first became interested in the cutting by Charles Plumet of the foundry version of the Arrighi italic designed by Frederic Warde, Beatrice's husband, and then pursued his interest with the trials of Eric Gill's Perpetua.

In January 1926 Morison began a spirited correspondence* with the great Dutch type designer Jan

van Krimpen, whose first type, Lutetia, had appeared in its foundry version the year before. Van Krimpen's review of *The Fleuron* in the Dutch journal *Het Boek* set it going, but the exchange of letters soon branched out into other subjects, and continued until Van Krimpen's death in 1958, interrupted only by World War II. Both men held pronounced opinions, and their correspondence is a curious blend of the crusty and the affectionate. Very early on, Van Krimpen taxed Morison and Monotype with being too concerned with recuttings of types of the past, and neglecting new designers. It was a theme he returned to repeatedly, although Monotype cut three of his four major book faces. Morison wrote to him in 1926, within a few months of his first letter:

'You are quite right to object to the copying of old types which is a current characteristic of English typography. It is found at present impossible to secure a new design of any interest. On the other hand, it seems a pity that a number of fine classical types are out of reach of printers of today because they have been destroyed by careless printers of the past. I think, however, that in two or three years it will be possible that the printing community in England will have been educated to the point of preferring a new work of art rather than a reproduction, and it may then be possible to persuade type founders to employ the services of an artist.'

His acquiescent tone was undoubtedly prompted by his having already begun to persuade Eric Gill to design Perpetua. Although Perpetua and the enormously successful Gill Sans were plainly Gill's designs, without Morison's activity as both impresario and stage manager they would never have appeared, and they, together with his work in promoting the designs of Van Krimpen, and the production of Times New Roman, answer the criticism that Morison was concerned only with old types.

In January 1928, however, he returned to the practical championship of the romans cut for Aldus Manutius, and instigated his most successful revival, cut by Monotype as Series 270 and called Bembo, after the writer of the model used; Cardinal Bembo's short treatise *De Aetna* (1495). Morison always defended the Aldine romans as distinct from the earlier Venetian faces of Jenson and his followers, in reaction to the preferences of Morris and Emery Walker, and we must bear in mind that his was the pioneering work. In the *Tally* he wrote:

'In the pages of *De Aetna* the type, then new, looks almost fresh as if it had come off a present-day type caster.

'Stanley Morison and Jan van Krimpen: a survey of their correspondence', ed. Sebastian Carter, in four parts, *Matrix*, 8–11, 1988–91.

ABCDEFGHIJKLMNOPQRSTUVW
abcdefghijklmnopqrstuvwxyzfiflffffiffflæœ

ABCDEFGHIJKLMNOPQRSTUVWX
abcdefghijklmnopqrstuvwxyzfiflfffffifflæœ

The first endeavour was to create a new chancery cursive based upon the hand of the most accomplished living English scribe available for the purpose, Alfred Fairbank. This italic was duly commissioned and cut. It appears before the reader in the present paragraph.

Monotype Bembo (1929) and Alfred Fairbank's Narrow Bembo italic.

Manifestly it did come from the hand of a uniquely competent engraver who, perhaps because Aldus had access to some hardening element, encouraged the cutting of serifs finer than had been the custom. The lower case is more brilliant than any of its predecessors, and the design as a whole ranks with the roman of Louis XIV (which brought to a close the two-hundred-year reign of the Aetna type) as one of the major typographical "watersheds".'

The roman was cut to everyone's satisfaction by the end of 1928, but once again there was the problem of a companion italic which did not exist in the Aldine original. Morison had taken the unusual step of commissioning a modern calligrapher, Alfred Fairbank, to design an italic based loosely on an Arrighi original. Morison always preferred this type, which was later called Fairbank or Narrow Bembo, but at Monotype there was opposition to it as being too condensed and jittery, and it was dropped in favour of a blander and more harmonious italic derived from a design by the Venetian scribe, Tagliente, contemporary with Arrighi. Bembo was issued early in 1929, and has been highly regarded ever since, ranking eleventh out of all the Monotype faces.

The production of Bembo was almost exactly concurrent with the Monotype adaptation of Bruce Rogers's Centaur, which was initiated and supervised by Rogers himself with no detectable help from Morison. Indeed, in the *Tally* he wrote, 'its recutting for Monotype composition necessarily, as it was private property, lay outside the programme adopted by the Corporation in 1922.'

The programme referred to was one 'of typographical design, rational, systematic and corresponding effectively with the foreseeable needs of printing', which Morison wrote that he had laid before Harold Duncan in 1922, which was accepted by Duncan and ratified by his successor Burch. Doubts have been cast on this claim by James Moran.* Nevertheless, there is evidence that from early on Morison had ambitions for Monotype that were wide in scope if unclear in all the details, though he probably had the sense to reveal them to the Corporation gradually, as both his prestige and the perceptible needs of the trade developed.

In 1929 Morison began his association with *The Times*, whose history he wrote, whose *Literary Supplement* he edited, and whose appearance he trans-

James Moran, *Stanley Morison, his typographic achievement*, London, Lund Humphries, 1971.

ABCDEFGHIJK
MNOPQRSTU
abcdefghijklmnopq

ABCDEFGHIJKLM

OPQRSTUVWXY

abcdefghijklmnopqrst

Monotype Bell (1931).

formed. But in spite of the prodigious labour involved in the design and cutting of *The Times* type, he found time to push through a project very close to his heart, the reinstatement of the fame of the newspaper owner, publisher and type founder John Bell (1745-1831), whose types he had admired for many years.

At the Bibliothèque Nationale, at the beginning of 1925, he had come across a prospectus issued by Bell's British Library in 1788, set in a type which he recognised as the same as one used by Updike at the Merrymount Press, called Mountjoye, and by Bruce Rogers at the Riverside Press in Boston, where it was called Brimmer. Brimmer had been bought as type in 1864 by Henry O. Houghton, of the publishers Houghton Mifflin, who owned the Riverside Press. Updike in 1903 bought strikes from Houghton's suppliers, Stephenson Blake of Sheffield, who could not, however, tell him where the type came from. Morison's discovery at the Bibliothèque Nationale led to his researches into Bell's career which resulted in a book, *John Bell*, printed and published by the Cambridge University Press in 1930, where it was hand-set in type newly cast by Stephenson Blake from the original matrices.

The book's success, and an exhibition of Bell's

publications put on to celebrate the centenary of his death the following year, persuaded Burch to recut Bell for Monotype composition, and Stephenson Blake gave their permission. With the pressure of work on Times, nothing more was done until the end of November 1931, when the Monotype works was told to go ahead.

Morison considered Bell's type the first modern face and, while influenced by French types of the period, patriotically and deliberately British. Bell's punchcutter Richard Austin cut a sharper letter than any hitherto attained, and twenty years later cut the so-called Scotch romans for the Wilson and Miller foundries in Scotland, which had such an influence on type design in the nineteenth century. Morison was unusually satisfied with the Monotype cutting of Bell, calling it 'an admirable reproduction'.

There was a gap of five years before the last major type revival Morison undertook, Ehrhardt, Series 453, which was one of the most useful. Ehrhardt came out in 1937, a few months after the death of Frank Pierpont, to whom, in spite of their differences, Morison's programme owed so much. Work on *The Times* kept Morison busy in the early 1930s, but by 1936, with the first volume of his *History* out, he was in a position to give more time to a fifteen-year-old enthusiasm. This was for a seventeenth-century type, thought to have been of Dutch origin, and resembling the Oxford University Press's Fell types (another of his passions); it was cast by the Stempel foundry of Frankfurt from materials formerly belonging to Drugulin of Leipzig, and known as Janson. In one of his earliest letters to Updike, in 1921, Morison asked if he knew of the type, and Updike revealed that he had had some at Merrymount since 1903, having bought it from Drugulin. Morison continued to worry away at the type's history, and through the printing historian Gustav Mori (1872–1950) located an early eighteenth-century specimen of the type from the Ehrhardt foundry in Frankfurt. (It was not until the 1950s that the typographical scholars Harry Carter and George Buday revealed that it was originally the work of the Hungarian punchcutter Nicolas Kis.)

In 1936, when both Mergenthaler Linotype (1933) and Lanston Monotype (1935) had issued recuttings of Janson, English Monotype were under pressure to do the same, and had cut a trial size. Morison found it too heavy and rotund, and issued new instructions for the drawing office in January 1937 for a type made larger on its body and more condensed. As a result,

Kreditbank Offenbach am Main *Stadtrundfahrten durch Heidelberg*

Garçon de comptoir *Bathing-establishment*

ABCDEFGHIJKLMNOPQRSTUVWXYZ

abcdefghijklmnopqrstuvwxyzfiflffffifflæœ

ABCDEFGHIJKLMNOPQRSTUVWXYZ

abcdefghijklmnopqrstuvwxyzfiflffffifflæœ

Ehrhardt is an economical face, legible, and irregular enough to keep it alive. This book is set in it.

It was the last of Morison's significant revivals, although he continued to advise the Corporation for many years, keeping his office at Monotype even after his place was taken by John Dreyfus in 1955. The list given here is by no means complete: there were several other revivals done at the same time, notably Walbaum (1933), Van Dijck (1937), and Bulmer, first cut for the Limited Editions Club in 1937, though not issued to the trade until 1967. The comprehensiveness of the range does, I hope, justify concentrating on the story of the Monotype programme at the expense of its competitors, for it illustrates the way a major manufacturer faced the challenge of equipping its machines with a wide variety of classic designs. As we have seen, other manufacturers did the same, sometimes before Monotype; and, as later chapters will show, new designs were cut as well as old.

Although the general policy of historical recuttings was pursued largely in response to the demands of the printing trade, Morison's role being primarily in recommending the best types to be followed, grumbles were occasionally heard, especially from Jan van Krimpen, that not enough new designs were cut.

In 1956 Van Krimpen issued a memorandum in which he put in an extremely purist form the case against the Monotype programme of revivals, seizing for his text on the account of them that Morison had written in *A tally of types*. Van Krimpen wrote (and he wrote in English):

'I need hardly say here once more that I am no friend of copying or even adapting historical type faces . . . for no other reason than that they are neither flesh nor fish: they are not, nor can they be, the thing they pretend to be; they only have a mock flavour of antiquity because of the many violations of the nature of the machine – the punch-cutting machine, that is, in this instance – and the many concessions made to the limitations of the Monotype composing machine; all of these violations and concessions being unavoidable in the process of making them fit for modern use. And, on the other hand, they are not actually products of our time because of the mock flavour of antiquity that has to be aimed at and retained or they could not be spoken of as copies or adaptations; nor could they be named, as it is done, after their models.'

He went on to quote Morison's justification of the early Monotype recuttings as taking a step backwards in order to go forward, and commented acidly, 'Particularly in Great Britain, so many steps backward had already been made, by William Morris and his disciples, that I take the liberty to doubt whether any more of such steps were really necessary.'

Van Krimpen singled out for particular obloquy the cutting of Poliphilus, which was a careful reproduction of Aldus's original. Of such reproductions he complained,

'Not only that they pretend to be, or are hoped to look, old while in fact they are new; but over and above this ambiguity they are given a look of being handiwork, inasmuch as they follow painstakingly the engraver's and even the typefounder's irregularities . . . while in fact they are made by machine. And this I do not hesitate to call – but may it be well understood: philosophically speaking – dishonesty.'

The other type Van Krimpen specifically objected to was Monotype Centaur, of which a foundry version had already existed. The recutting had been supervised by Rogers in person, and Van Krimpen's objection was that he had instructed the Monotype works to keep the irregularities of the hand-cut type (although the 'hand cutting' was in fact done pantographically by Robert Wiebking of Chicago, to whom Rogers presumably gave the same instructions). Van Krimpen wrote, 'This should, I think, be taken for an objectionably arbitrary piece of conduct [given] the size of the drawings and the great flexibility of the punchcutting machine; a cheap proceeding of arbitrarily determining one's own chosen "imperfections" while, when punches are being cut by hand, one has to wait and see how the punchcutter's genuine imperfections will look.'

Neither of the two faces he particularly disliked was Morison's concern. Poliphilus was, as we have seen, cut for the Medici Society's facsimile, so that the 'dishonest' finish was part of the design brief; and Centaur was Rogers's type from first to last. Morison's reply to Van Krimpen was good-humoured and mostly beside the point. However, he dissociated himself from Pierpont's rapture over Poliphilus, and said firmly that there was nothing mock-antique about Bembo.

There was really no answer he could make. The issue which divided the two men is at the root of the argument about revivals. Each of them had a profound sense of the history of letterforms; but Van Krimpen felt that the types of the past should be preserved only in the medium for which they were designed, and each new step in technology required new designs, while Morison on the other hand believed that some types represented ideal forms which could survive the translation to new machines and be as valid as they ever were.

Another familiar criticism of revivals came from Updike in a letter of 1924:

'I am certain that after the uproar has ceased over decoration and historical styles, and we have begun to take them more as matters of course, we shall ultimately find that they are only fitted for work of a limited nature, and shall have to invent new types of a more modern feeling, or else use more colourless types which, since they do not reflect any particular period of their own, will be less "in the way" of the mind when we print works by modern authors.'

Time has proved Updike only partly correct. The best Monotype revivals, Baskerville, Bembo, Ehrhardt and Garamond, and to a lesser extent Bell and Fournier, have survived without any historical allusiveness standing 'in the way', just as Imprint and Plantin, less historically correct, have done. This is because in a sense their history has become 'colourless'. At the same time, most modern designers, as we shall see, have found it hard to blot out the past completely, and even when preparing fresh faces have, unwittingly or not, kept history in the corner of their eyes. As Goudy said, 'The old fellows stole most of our best ideas.'

The designers – 1

If some difficulties of approach arose in the adaptation of historical types for modern printing methods, there were others when new designs came to be cut. Almost every way of translating the idea of a letter into metal type was followed by one or other of the designers who appear in this chapter. Koch cut his own punches for some of his types, believed by some to be the ideal way of proceeding; Van Krimpen closely supervised a skilled punchcutter, P. H. Rädisch, in the production of all his faces in their first foundry versions; Goudy engraved the matrices of his later types himself on a pantographic machine; Dwiggins drew accurate full-scale patterns for the pantograph to follow; Morison employed a draftsman, Victor Lardent, to draw Times New Roman; and Gill, by trade a letter carver rather than a type designer, drew mostly freehand alphabets for the drawing offices of Monotype and the Caslon foundry to convert into type.

However, designers of very different kinds seem to be united in disliking the mechanical look of letters given too much finish by drawing offices left to their own devices, and many have struggled hard to prevent its happening to their types. The ethical question they faced, and still face, is whether, if machines can produce theoretically 'perfect' letters, they ought to be allowed to. It is a problem stated explicitly by Gill, writing about Joanna, and, as we have seen, by Van Krimpen; and it was answered tacitly by many more designers, largely in the negative. Goudy, Rogers, Dwiggins, and many more all carefully supervised the inclusion of deliberate irregularities in their types to counteract the sanitising tendency of the mechanical engraver. Van Krimpen, who disapproved of such artificial imperfection, observed a progress towards lifelessness in the developing stages of his own drawings, and suggested* that the vigorous pencil outlines should be followed by the pantograph operator rather than the later, more polished ink drawing. By this means he believed that vivacity could be retained with no sacrifice of honesty: the kind of irregularity which the hand punchcutter introduced naturally would be there in the drawing, and not added artificially. But this argument really only moves the problem one step back, since a deliberate selection of a preferred 'imperfection' is still being made. The question remains one about the difficulties of wider choice introduced by new machines, which exist in many fields beside type design.

The designers who follow, in the order they were born, had their different answers to the difficulties, some conscious and some intuitive. It is fitting that the story should begin in the United States, where the new machines were invented which transformed the type designer's craft.

Jan van Krimpen, *A letter to Philip Hofer on certain problems connected with the mechanical cutting of punches,* with an introduction and commentary by John Dreyfus, Cambridge, Harvard College Library/Boston, Godine, 1972.

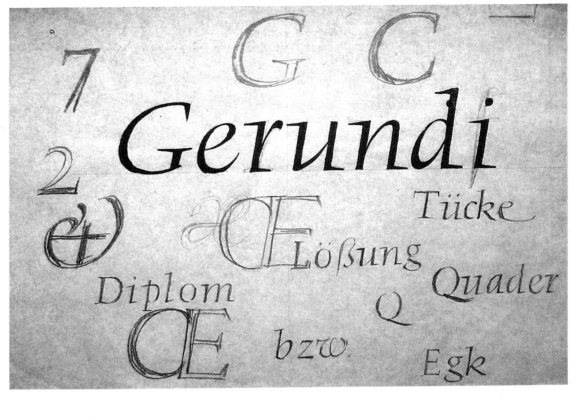

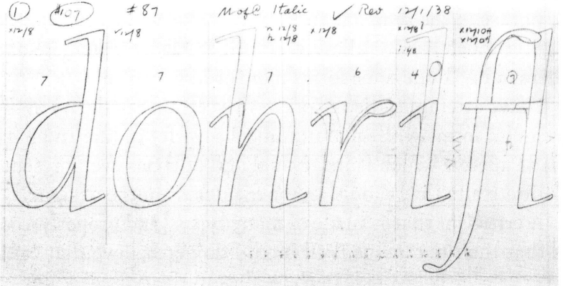

Working drawings by Frederic W. Goudy for University of California Old Style (1938). From 'Typologia' (1940).

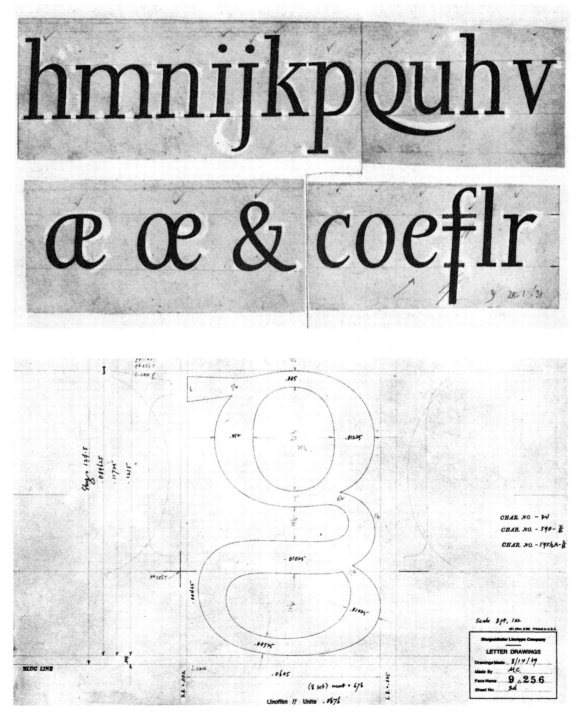

Working drawings by Eric Gill for Joanna italic (1931). By courtesy of the Monotype Corporation.

Finished drawing by Matthew Carter for Olympian (1969).

Frederic W. Goudy

Goudy was the oldest, one of the most prolific, and possibly the most dedicated of the great innovative type designers of this century. After a slow and uncertain start, and apart from his writings on the alphabet and lettering, and a small amount of printing conceived chiefly as a vehicle for his own creations, he gave himself single-mindedly to the drawing and manufacture of type. He occupied a pivotal position between the passing world of the craftsmen who cut punches by hand, and the new breed of type draftsmen. In this he worked to some extent against the grain of the century, for he began as a freelance designer sending his drawings to foundries for a fee, and only later became increasingly involved in the manufacture of his types. He then supervised the engraving of matrices by a craftsman, Robert Wiebking of Chicago, commissioned the casting, and marketed the founts himself; and shortly before Wiebking's death in 1927, he took up his own matrix engraving and casting. On a celebrated day, Thanksgiving, 1933, he showed the advantages of his method. Bruce Rogers had come to lunch, and was complaining that he could find no capitals exactly the right size and style for a title page he had in hand. His host suggested one of his own faces, Goudy Antique, went out to his workshop, engraved the necessary matrices in the intermediate size wanted, cast the type, and handed the sorts to Rogers as he left the house. 'Some service', he commented drily.

He was extraordinarily productive. In his own list of designs, set down at the end of his life in the Typophile Chap Book* devoted to his work, he included well over a hundred entries, and though he counted roman and italic as two designs, it remains a formidable achievement. Many of the types are

similar in conception, several are not very good, and some are so terrible that even their author, inclined to view his own work with a favourable eye, did not reproduce them in *A half-century*; but the ones that remain are enough to place Goudy among the handful of designers who have changed the look of the types we read. His faces are completely individual and, with the exception of his one historical recreation, Garamont, could not be by anyone else.

Goudy did not shrink from self-promotion, and attracted critics, one of whom sourly commented, 'It's all Goudy thin and Goudy fat, Goudy this and Goudy that.' But we should remember that he was marketing his types, and needed to sell them to eat. The name became a selling point, and so naturally he used it.

Goudy was born on 8 March 1865 in Bloomington, Illinois, the first of three designers to be born in the mid-west within fifteen years of each other, all of whom went east and between them changed the face of American book design: the other two were Bruce Rogers and Dwiggins. His father was an inspector of schools, and his childhood was spent in various small towns around the state. While quite young he showed an aptitude for lettering, and was also much impressed by the sight of a pantograph, which an itinerant artist was demonstrating as a drawing aid. At the age of twenty-four he went to Chicago, and began a series of clerking jobs, one of which was for a bookshop; it led him to the rare book department of A. C. McClurg, where over the years he could look at the new publications of the English private presses, Kelmscott, Doves, Eragny and Vale, as they appeared.

He proved better at losing his clerking jobs than keeping them, and at the end of one he and a friend began a small printing business, the Booklet, later renamed the Camelot Press. 'This, mind you,' Goudy wrote later, 'at a time when I hardly knew which end of a type was the printing end.' In spite of his protested innocence, the design of the Press's work was noticed by the publishers Stone and Kimball,

Frederic W. Goudy, *A half-century of type design and typography, 1895–1945*, New York, The Typophiles, 1946. (Two volumes. Reprinted in one volume, New York, Myriade Press, 1978.)

Frederic W. Goudy (1865–1947). By courtesy of the Cary Collection, Rochester Institute of Technology, New York.

who asked it to set some issues of their magazine, *The chap book*. Soon, however, Goudy sold his share and in 1896, while waiting for his next job, drew a set of capital letters one evening in his room. Not quite knowing what to do with them, he sent them to the Dickinson Type Foundry in Boston, part of the recently formed American Type Founders group, from whom he had bought type. The foundry accepted the design, called Camelot, and the next one he sent them. Neither showed conspicuous promise, and both were distinctly of the 1890s. Nevertheless, the very fact they were cut is significant, for as Goudy wrote, 'We must remember that original type designs were not at that time regular items of purchase by type foundries; most of their designs were produced by their own punchcutters, and were usually mere variations only of the types of other foundries.'

After a short spell in Detroit working as a cashier for a weekly magazine, *The Michigan farmer*, Goudy finally decided that such work was not for him, and set up as a freelance lettering artist in Chicago, working for a number of department stores as well as for Herbert S. Stone, whose partnership with Kimball had ended amicably; Kimball had gone to New York to set up the Cheltenham Press, which commissioned the type of the same name. Goudy also joined the teaching staff of the new Frank Holme school of illustration as a lettering tutor.

During this time, Goudy designed a few proprietary faces for local businesses. In 1903 one of them, commissioned by a department store but found by them to be too expensive to cut and cast, became the house type of his second printing venture, the Village Press, which he set up with the collaboration of Will

43

ABCDEFGHIJKLMNOPQ
RSTUVWXYZ&.,';:!?-
$1234567890

ABCDEFGHIJKLM
NOPQRSTUVWX
YZabcdefghijklmnoprst
uvwxyz *The and & of* ÆŒ
£$ft(]-?.::,.!'1234567890

Early Goudy faces: Camelot (1896), his first design, and Pabst (1902).

Goudy now turned almost exclusively to the design of type. He was commissioned to produce a roman for the American Lanston Monotype Company, his initiation into working with the limitations of the Monotype diecase; the type was briefly called Goudy Old Style against his wishes, a name which was given to another face before attaching itself to the type we know by it today. This first face was later given the unromantic title of 38-E. Next, Goudy was given the opportunity of designing his first major typeface. In 1911 the New York publisher Mitchell Kennerley invited him to design an edition of H. G. Wells's story *The door in the wall.* They had specimen pages set in 18pt Caslon, but Goudy was dissatisfied with them, and suggested to Kennerley that he should design a new type for the book, which they could market later to help with the costs. Kennerley agreed, and Goudy, inspired at first by the Oxford University Press Fell types, but later shedding the influence as he began to draw, produced Kennerley Old Style, engraved and cast by Wiebking, and sold in founts by Goudy at his Village Type Foundry. In 1920 it was bought by the Lanston Monotype Company for mechanical setting, and by the Caslon foundry for sale in Britain and the rest of Europe. Together with Forum titling, de-

Ransom at Park Ridge, outside Chicago. The matrices of the type were engraved pantographically by Robert Wiebking. In spite of its debt to the English private press types, in particular to Charles Ricketts's Vale type ('What an ancestry for an advertising face!' commented Goudy while it was still intended for the Kuppenheimer store), and the consequent quaintness of appearance in our eyes, Goudy considered Village as the first of his types to show maturity.

Within a year, Goudy read about a crafts society at Hingham, a small town outside Boston, Massachusetts; he was himself becoming increasingly fired by craft ideals, and although he had built up a regular clientele in Chicago, he moved to Hingham in 1904. He was joined shortly by Dwiggins, whom he had taught at the Frank Holme school, but whereas Dwiggins stayed on for the rest of his life, Goudy found it difficult to break down Bostonian social barriers and to establish himself professionally, and moved to New York in 1906. Here, on 10 January 1908, his workshop and the Village Press's equipment were destroyed in the first of two disastrous fires he suffered in his lifetime. Paradoxically, however, the destruction of the Village Press, which had been a drain on his pocket, left him financially better off.

Village (1903) and Copperplate Gothic (1905), a design which had many imitators.

IT WAS THE TERRACE OF
God's house
That she was standing on,—
By God built over the sheer depth
In which Space is begun;
So high, that looking downward

ABCDEFGHIJKLMN
OPQRSTUVWXYZ&
$1234567890.,';:!?-
FWG SAYS: THE OLD
FELLOWS STOLE ALL
OF OUR BEST IDEAS.

ABCDEFGHIJKLMNOP
QRSTUVWXYZ&ÆŒ℅]
abcdefghijklmnopqrstuvwxyz
æœfifffffiflfflctst.,';:!?-$1234567890

Speaking of earlier types,
Goudy says: The old fellows
stole all of our best ideas.

ABCDEFGHIJKLMN
OPQRSTUVWXYZ&
1234567890˙.,

FWG SAYS · THE OLD FELLOWS
STOLE ALL OF OUR BEST IDEAS

*Kennerley and Forum titling
(both 1911).*

signed at the same time, it established Goudy's reputation both abroad and at home, though he always deplored the fact that his worth was recognised in England before his native land. Both Kennerley and Forum were in use at Francis Meynell's Pelican Press in 1921, and much admired.

The year after Kennerley, another commissioned type was abandoned, this time because of the death of the sponsor, and so Goudy marketed it himself. Although this type was first called Goudy Old Style, it should be confused neither with Monotype 38-E already mentioned, nor with the face we now call by the same name, which was designed two years later. On the appearance of the later type, it was renamed Goudy Antique (another name which was used again later), and then, when cut by American Monotype, Goudy Lanston; and as if confusion had not already made its masterpiece, Caslon in England issued a version and called it Ratdolt.

Goudy was unhappy with Caslon's cutting and their name, but nevertheless he went to England in 1914, intending to visit them and interest them in cutting his next type. Although Caslon could not undertake the work, because of the approaching war and the likely requisitioning of their factory for

*Goudy Lanston (1912) and
Goudytype (1916).*

munitions work, they were interested in buying Goudy's designs, and their enthusiasm so impressed Clarence Marder of ATF, who was with Goudy, that on their return to the United States he persuaded Robert Nelson, the president of ATF, to commission a new Goudy type. Thus at last the face now known as Goudy Old Style was designed and cut.

Goudy was at pains to restrain the desire of the ATF drawing office to modify his design, and Nelson backed him, although in the end he was persuaded to allow shorter descenders than his judgement suggested, to the detriment of the type. With a characteristic mixture of braggadocio and modesty he wrote, 'The face, as finally produced, was almost as great an innovation as my Kennerley . . . I am almost satisfied that the design is a good one.' It was certainly the most successful of his types, though one of its best variants, Goudy Catalogue, was actually drawn by Morris Benton. It still shows the rather fluid outlines of his early letters, but there is enough tautness to give it strength.

Over the next few years Goudy continued to show his curious ability to design good types side by side with bad ones; indeed, it is improbable that any distinguished designer has produced more awful

ABCDEFGHIJKLMNOP
QRSTUVWXYZ&.,';:!?-
abcdefghijklmnopqrstuvwx
yzfifffffiflfflctæœ$1234567890
Speaking of earlier types,
Goudy says: The old fellows
stole all of our best ideas.

ABCDEFGHIJKL
MNOPQRSTUVW
XYZabcdefghijklm
nopqrstuvwxyz$&

DEFGHIJKLMNOPQRSTUVWX

abcdefghijklmnopqrstuvwxyz 1234567

abcdefghijklmnopqrstuvwxyz 123456789

ABCDEFGHIJKLMNOPQRSTUV

Goudy Old Style (1915).

types. Two faces drawn for ATF to fulfil a contractual arrangement, Booklet Old Style and the unattractively named Goudytype, were competent, and the latter rather better than its author seemed to think it; but National Old Style for the National Biscuit Company has little to recommend it.

Two display types followed, both in 1918: the handsome, classically inspired Hadriano, and the refined Goudy Open. The second was an inline type based on lettering engraved on a French print, and had the unusual result of prompting an unadorned version, Goudy Modern. Decorated faces normally follow the plain parent design, not the other way about. Goudy Modern is a crisp and distinguished letter, and one of his best; when cut by English Monotype in 1928, it was well used by Francis Meynell at the Nonesuch Press.

In 1920 Goudy was asked by J. Maury Dove, president of the Lanston Monotype Company of Philadelphia, to advise them on design, thus anticipating by about three years the similar decision of the English company to appoint Stanley Morison. The first fruit of the partnership was the Garamont already described; the second was Italian Old Style. Monotype had a customer who was prepared to buy their machinery, but wanted to be able to set in Morris Benton's Cloister, designed for ATF. Dove wanted to adapt ATF's design for the Monotype. Goudy argued that this was unethical, and Dove that it was common practice; but he eventually yielded to Goudy's suggestion of a new face based freely on the same Venetian models. The result was Italian Old Style (a different face from English Monotype's own earlier type of the same name, Series 108), which is one of Goudy's best book faces.

On his own behalf he designed Goudy Newstyle (1921), suggested originally by the writings on phonetics of the English Poet Laureate Robert Bridges. The type was equipped with twenty alternative sorts intended to clarify the notoriously illogical spelling of the English language; but, like most such experiments, it did not catch on, and the unaugmented type, handsome though it is, was used only by a few private presses, most magnificently by the Grabhorn Press of San Francisco in their edition of Whitman's *Leaves of grass* (1930).

Newstyle was the last major face engraved for Goudy by Robert Wiebking, who died in 1927. In 1923 the Goudy family moved from New York to a watermill up the Hudson river at Marlboro, and with the enlarged workshop space here Goudy could make the Village Foundry a foundry in fact as well as in name. He first looked round for a matrix engraving machine. Because foundries in the United States usually had machine shops which could build the equipment they needed, he could not find one for sale at home, and so he went to Europe and through the agency of Stempel he was able to buy one in Frankfurt. With the help of Dove at Monotype, he put in a Monotype caster with adaptations to the mould to take Wiebking's and his own matrices. He was thus set up to cut his own patterns and supervise every stage of the production of his types. As he wrote in *Typologia*:* 'I feel that an artist is unjust both to himself and to his public when he is content to present merely good mechanical reproductions of his work – reproductions which may not convey the vitality and personality of his own handling of them – and it is to make sure that my matrices are carried out in the spirit in which the letters themselves were designed, and to retain in them those infinitesimal

Hadriano titling (1918), Goudy Modern (1918), Goudy Newstyle (1921), here used in the Grabhorn Press, 'Leaves of grass' (1930), and Italian Old Style (1924).

Frederic W. Goudy, *Typologia, studies in type design and type making*, Berkeley, University of California Press, 1940. (Paperback edition, 1977.)

qualities of feeling which only the designer may give, that I engrave them personally.'

Goudy had a native American immunity to the austere European view of typography as outlined by Stanley Morison in 'First principles of typography', and quoted in the introduction to this book.

'Type design moves at the pace of the most conservative reader', Morison wrote. 'The good type-designer therefore realises that, for a new fount to be successful, it has to be so good that only a few recognise its novelty. If readers do not notice the consummate reticence and rare discipline of a new type, it is probably a good letter. But if my friends think that the tail of my lower-case r or the lip of my lower-case e is rather jolly, you may know that the fount would have been better had neither been made. A type which is to have anything like a present, let alone a future, will neither be very "different" nor very "jolly".'

Goudy drily observed in *Typologia*, 'I am not sure that I accept his dictum completely'. In fact he did not accept it at all: Goudy's types are individual, always recognisable, with characteristics which can sometimes become irritating. But his drawings were extremely beautiful and full of subtle curves, and when the types were being cut by ATF or Monotype,

ABCDEFGHIJKLMN
OPQRSTUVWXYZ.
1 2 3 4 5 6 7 8 9 0 &

FWG SAYS: THE OLD
FELLOWS STOLE ALL

GOUDY MODERN
ROMAN & ITALIC

FIRST CUT
FOR HAND COMPOSITION
1918

Come, said my Soul,
Such verses for my Body let us write, (for we are one,)
That should I after death invisibly return,
Or, long, long hence, in other spheres,
There to some group of mates the chants resuming,
(Tallying Earth's soil, trees, winds, tumultuous waves,)

Speaking of earlier types, Goudy says: The old fellows stole all of our best ideas.

47

he resisted every attempt by their drawing offices to tame the letters. When working with Wiebking, or engraving his own matrices, he could get exactly what he wanted.

The first type for which he cut matrices was intended for the private press run by Spencer Kellogg. He began in 1925, and his efforts to master the new technique took so long that Kellogg tired of printing and cancelled the order. This design, originally called Aries, was later reworked and recut and called Franciscan, the private type of the Grabhorn Press (1932). It was the first of a line of blackletter and semi-blackletter faces which Goudy worked on intermittently for the rest of his life, and which he often confessed to preferring to his romans. The best known of these is Goudy Text (1928), inspired by the type of Gutenberg's 'Forty-two-line Bible', of which he had bought a single leaf, and perfected in various hand-drawn versions in earlier publications. Originally called Goudy Black when issued by the Village Foundry, it was seen by Harvey Best, who had succeeded J. Maury Dove at Lanston Monotype in Philadelphia, and when cut for the Monotype was renamed Text. It was followed by Medieval (1930), which he thought one of his most original designs, and the *bâtarde* Tory Text (1935),

Goudy Text (1928) and Franciscan (1932).

'one of my favourite types and I enjoyed every minute of its making'. There was also Friar (1937), influenced by the uncials of Victor Hammer, and the series culminated in the curious and original 'posthumous' type, Goudy 'Thirty', (1942), when Harvey Best asked for a design that would be cut after Goudy's death (it was finally issued in 1953). Goudy was aggrieved to find it described as his last type, but it is hardly surprising.

While he was enjoying himself with blackletter, Goudy was also designing more romans. In 1927 he cut Deepdene, having first offered it to Monotype, who were not then interested in a new book face. William Edwin Rudge, the great printer and publisher of Mount Vernon, New York, saw and liked the type, and wanted it for his own use; but he would need to be able to set the text sizes by machine. As he was a consultant to the Mergenthaler Linotype Company he was naturally anxious for them to cut the type for their machines, but Goudy pointed out that he was under contract to Monotype, who must be approached for permission. When Rudge did so, Harvey Best misunderstood the situation and thought that Goudy was deserting to Linotype. Eventually an agreement was reached whereby Deepdene was cut by Monotype, although Goudy was annoyed that the drawing

often to be working, and both should be gentlemen, in the best sense. As it is, we make both ungentle, the one envying, the other despising his brother; and society is made up of morbid thinkers and miserable workers.

138. LEAVES OF GRASS | COMPRISING ALL THE POEMS WRITTEN | BY WALT WHITMAN | FOLLOWING THE ARRANGEMENT | OF THE EDITION OF | 1891/'2 | [wood/cut] | RANDOM HOUSE, INC., NEW YORK | 1930
14½ x 9¾. Six blank leaves; pp. (i/x); pp. 1/424; five blank leaves: consisting of title p. (i), page of limitation p. (ii), table of contents pp. (iii/viii), half title p. (ix), verso blank, text pp. 1/423, p. 424 blank.

The stars are a bitter seasoning
over ice. Look to a difficult time,
little moments like snapped pipes
that will break you, and unnoticed
heroics: waking, walking, kindness.
This is the month the Romans gave two
faces. Look to water and snow
to explain this. Bundle. Buffer.
Tell winter stories: A man
walks into a tavern, orders bitter,
cold soup and slaps his coin down.
——Face up, though. That's my advice.

Goudy 'Thirty' (1942).
By courtesy of the Bieler Press.

Deepdene (1927).

'It is hardly possible to create a good type face that will differ radically from the established forms of the past: nevertheless it is still possible to secure new expressions of life and vigor. The types in daily use, almost without exception, betray too fully the evidences of their origin, and do not always follow the best traditions. It requires the skilled hand, the appreciation and taste of the artist, and the trained mind of the student to select suitable models which may be adapted to our use and to which we may give new graces suited to our times. I have made designs that reverted for their inspiration to the lapidary characters of the early Romans; others that were based on the classic types of Jenson, Ratdolt, Aldus; still others that were suggested by the scribes' hands which were also the source of the types of those masters; and now, in the autumn of my labors, I draw with practically no reference to any of the sources mentioned; relying largely on the broad impressions of early forms stored up by years of study and practice, and governed by a technical knowledge of the requirements of type founding and typography, I attempt to create those impressions into new designs of beauty and utility.'

In his Typophile Chap Book *A half-century of type designs*, Goudy wrote, 'University of California Old Style is one face for which I have no regrets.' He

office adapted the type for the diecase without consulting him. He admitted that the design was influenced by 'a Dutch type which had just been introduced into this country', and it certainly shows the characteristics of Lutetia, only slightly 'Goudy-fied'.

After two more romans, Village No.2 and Saks for the famous department store, both of which pleased their author more than on the whole they have pleased posterity, Goudy designed one more major type. This was originally commissioned as a proprietary face by the University of California Press at the end of 1937, though mooted earlier. Goudy cut patterns for punchcutting by Monotype in the composition sizes, planning to engrave matrices for the display sizes himself and supply finished type to the Press. Fortunately he had sent the master patterns to Monotype when on 26 January 1939 his workshop was burned to the ground in a second disastrous fire. He overcame this setback with remarkable fortitude. Monotype cut all the type sizes, and it was first used for Goudy's own account of its creation in *Typologia*. This book is one of the best and most thorough accounts of type design ever written. Describing his type, Goudy wrote,

A B C D E F G H I J K L M N O P
Q R S T U V W X Y Z & . , ' ; : ! ? -
A B C D E F G H I J K L M N O P Q R S T U V W X Y Z &
a b c d e f g h i j k l m n o p q r s t u v
w x y z fi ff ffi fl ffl [ ] 1 2 3 4 5 6 7 8 9 0
Speaking of earlier types, Goudy says:
The old fellows stole all of our best ideas.

A B C D E F G H I J K L M N O P Q R S
T U V W X Y Z & a b c d e f g h i j k l m
n o p q r s t u v w x y z fi ff ffi fl ffl & . , ' ; : ! ? -
A B C D E G M P R T k z g gg gg gy
Speaking of earlier types, Goudy says:
The old fellows stole all of our best ideas.

ABCDEFGHIJKLMNOP
QRSTUVWXYZÆŒ
ABCDEFGHIJKLMNOPQRS
TUVWXYZÆŒ
abcdefghijklmnopqrstuvwx
yzfffffiffllfiflæœɛtſt
&1234567890''!?.-;:,$

ABCDEFGHIJKLMNOPQRSTUVWXYZ ÆŒ ABCDEGMRT
abcdefghijklmnopqrstuvwxyzfffffiffllfiflæœɛtſt ''!?.-;:,&gvw

University of California Old Style (1938).

should not have done, for it is a beautiful, crisp type, with no trace of the flaccidity which afflicts many of his earlier designs, and was well used at the University Press, notably in his book *The alphabet* (1942), the second edition of a book published a quarter of a century earlier by the patron of his first mature type, Mitchell Kennerley. In 1959, Lanston Monotype issued it to the trade as Californian, and in 1983 the International Typeface Corporation brought out a version called Berkeley Old Style which has given the face a new lease of life in advertising.

The California type was a fitting climax to an astonishing career. Goudy died on 11 May 1947,

heaped with honours, and has kept his place as one of the first and most original of the new kind of type designer who emerged with the new century. His faces are not widely used for the setting of books: they do not fulfil the customary demands of reticence for such purposes. But for displayed work and advertising design they have always been deservedly popular. The old fellows may have stolen all his best ideas, as he used to maintain, but he certainly stole them back again.

D. J. R. Bruckner, *Frederic Goudy*, New York, Abrams, 1990.

Bruce Rogers

Bruce Rogers (1870–1957)
in his studio at October House,
New Fairfield, Connecticut.
Photograph by courtesy of
Mrs Fanny Duschnes.

Born five years after Goudy, Rogers nevertheless went east before him, and unlike him had a sucess as a young man which made his later life seem to him an anticlimax. Whereas Goudy was a type designer who occasionally produced books, Rogers was the other way about: a book designer whose attention to the minutiae of his work led him occasionally to the design of type. Updike called him 'the most distinguished designer of books of our time', and Meynell went further: 'the greatest artificer of the book who ever lived'. Frederic Warde, the designer of the Arrighi italic which accompanies Rogers's Centaur in its Monotype cutting, dubbed him 'prematurely an old master'. Working always in close contact with a number of well-known printing houses in the United States and England, and benefiting from what Warde called their 'leisurely idealism', Rogers designed his books meticulously and supervised every detail of their production with painstaking care, even in some cases down to the smell of the ink. He was a perfectionist who out of a total of some seven hundred books chose only thirty that he was pleased with. But that list included several which are classics of design, and chief among them was the Oxford Lectern Bible (1935), one of the great books of the century.

His quest for perfection as a designer led him to mix types from different founts to get the effects he wanted, and to design special characters. In one case he produced a modified Caslon by rubbing down both the face and the sides of an existing fount, to darken the face and fit the letters closer together; new matrices were then made electrolytically and founts of 'Riverside Caslon' (1909) cast from them.

It was inevitable that such attention to detail would lead Rogers to design type, and his major achievement in this field, Centaur, has been described by Professor Herbert Johnson as 'perhaps the finest of the five or six great typefaces designed by Americans'.

Bruce Rogers was born in Lafayette, Indiana, on 14 May 1870.* His family came of English Yorkshire stock, and he maintained a lasting affection for England, where he did much of his best work, though it was not unmixed with dislike of the discomfort of actually living there. At the age of sixteen he went to Purdue University in Lafayette, studied art, and after graduation became a newspaper artist, in the days before journalistic photography, and then for a short period a landscape painter. Already at university he had shown a flair for lettering; now his feeling for the design of books was stimulated, as so many others had been and were to be, by the sight of the Kelmscott Press books which were just beginning to appear. They were bought direct from Morris by Rogers's friend J. M. Bowles, who worked in an Indianapolis art shop and produced a magazine, *Modern art*, as a sideline. Rogers, who had begun drawing lettering for publishers, also contributed work to the magazine, and when in 1895 Bowles and *Modern art* were taken to Boston by the Prang chromolithography firm, and needed a designer, Rogers joined him. The work was leisurely, which suited Rogers. 'He was guaranteed at least $10 a week, which he made occasionally', Bowles remembered. 'He can live on peanuts and popcorn for as long as necessary; not only can he live the simple life but he actually enjoys it.'

A year after his arrival in Boston, Rogers was invited by George H. Mifflin to join Houghton Mifflin at their Riverside Press as designer, and in 1900 he persuaded Mifflin to set up within the Press a department for the production of fine books for the collector. A number of Rogers's finest books appeared as Riverside Press editions, and he was doubtless influenced by the example of Updike at the Merrymount Press close by, who had been producing handsome books since 1893, some of them in an historically eclectic style which, Warde remarked, had been found in the nursery and left in the drawing room. Rogers paid close attention to each title, foreshadowing in the variety and subtle allusiveness of his books the work of Meynell at the Nonesuch Press twenty years later. Within a few years, for the three volume folio edition of *The essays of Montaigne* (1902-4), Rogers designed his first type, called Montaigne. It was a refinement of the much-copied Jenson letter, which Rogers was not entirely pleased with. 'In a way', wrote Warde, 'the punchcutter had done his work too well; Mr Rogers decided that there had been too much "improvement" over the original, and he resolved to return to Jenson at some later time for a more direct inspiration.' He did, a decade later, and the result was Centaur.

In 1912, after sixteen years at the Riverside Press, Rogers decided to leave and become his own master again; and although he sometimes regretted the insecurity, he remained a freelance for the rest of his life. He spent the summer of 1912 in England, the

Joseph Blumenthal, *Bruce Rogers, a life in letters*, Austin, W. Thomas Taylor, 1989.

THIS IS THE MONTAIGNE TYPE cut only in sixteen-point size for the use of the publishers, Houghton Mifflin Company at The Riverside Press in Cambridge, Mass.

THIS SHOWS THE CENTAUR TYPE which follows the proportions of Jenson's roman. It is cast only for The Metropolitan Museum of Art, New York, and for private use by its designer.

ABCDEFGHIJKLMNO PQRSTUVWXYZ

abcdefghijklmnopqrstuvwxyz

Printing is fundamentally a selection of materials already in existence and an assembling of these different

Montaigne (1902), foundry Centaur (1914) and Monotype Centaur (1929), with the Arrighi italic designed by Frederic Warde.

first of many visits, but did not find work that would keep him in the comfort Mifflin had done; so he returned to four difficult years in the United States.

It was at this time that he designed Centaur, originally commissioned as a private type by Henry Watson Kent, secretary of the Metropolitan Museum of Art in New York, for use by the Museum Press for ephemeral printing. The designer was allowed use of it, and the first appearance in a book was in *The Centaur* by Maurice de Guérin, printed in 1915 at Carl P. Rollins's Montague Press.

For Centaur, Rogers took as his model Jenson's edition of Eusebius, *De evangelica praeparatione*, 1470, an earlier work than the 1476 Pliny followed by Walker for the Doves type, and more lightly printed. Because it was so much copied, Jenson's type was unnecessarily denigrated by campaigners for a change in taste such as Stanley Morison; but its beauty is undeniable, and is all the more remarkable for its being so early, nearer in date to Gutenberg's 'Forty-two-line Bible' than to Aldus's *De Aetna*. It is usually said that Rogers refined the Jenson letter, but that is only by comparison with Morris's Golden or Benton's Cloister. Even the Doves type, fine though it is, seems mechanical in its detail next to Centaur.

Centaur is lighter than the Eusebius type on the page, but that is probably due only to differences in impression, and truer of the Monotype version than it is of Robert Wiebking's original foundry version.

Centaur is therefore not a 'new' design, but an imaginative recreation. Its merit is in the way an artist guided a superlative craftsman to recapture the spirit of an early type by paring away the accidentals of impression.

The type was cut for mechanical composition in 1929. Rogers was approached by Harvey Best of Lanston Monotype, but preferred to entrust English Monotype with the work. He travelled to England in 1928, accompanied by Frederic Warde, and closely supervised the recutting. In view of Van Krimpen's strictures over this type, it is amusing that when Beatrice Warde was lecturing about the recutting of Centaur, she remarked that Rogers was the most difficult designer Monotype ever had to deal with; then, catching sight of Van Krimpen in the audience, she added, 'until Mr Van Krimpen'.

The Arrighi italic cut to accompany Centaur was thoroughly redrawn by Beatrice's husband Frederic Warde (1894-1939) from a foundry type made under his supervision by the punchcutter Charles Plumet of

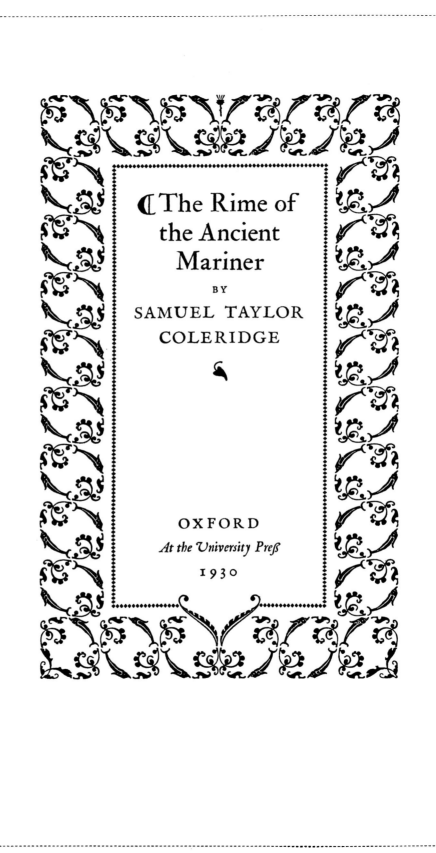

CThe Rime of
the Ancient
Mariner

BY

SAMUEL TAYLOR
COLERIDGE

OXFORD
At the University Preß
1930

A Rogers title page, using the seventeenth-century Fell types in the Oxford University Press collection, and showing Rogers's mastery of type ornament.

54

Paris in 1925, from Arrighi's first italic shown in *Coryciana* (1524). Warde's type was a rarity, used to best effect by Giovanni Mardersteig at the Officina Bodoni, but Rogers had harnessed it with the foundry Centaur, which had no italic, for an edition of John Drinkwater's *Persephone* (1926), printed and published by Rudge. They went so well together that Rogers asked Warde to revise Arrighi for the Monotype recutting, which he did so extensively that the new italic bears very little relationship to the old.*

An earlier visit Rogers made to England, shortly after the first cutting of foundry Centaur, was in 1916. It was the middle of World War I, and the journey was made at the invitation of Emery Walker, with the aim of printing fine editions in the tradition of Kelmscott and Doves. He took with him a commission from the Grolier Club of New York for an edition of Dürer's *On the just shaping of letters*, which was the first and only book printed by the Mall Press. Most of Walker's press workers had been called up, so that the actual printing was largely done by Rogers himself, learning as he went, in a cold Hammersmith basement in the early months of 1917.

The association with Walker ended, Rogers was invited at the suggestion of Sydney Cockerell, formerly Morris's secretary at the Kelmscott Press and now director of the Fitzwilliam Museum at Cambridge, to come to advise the Cambridge University Press on its typography. Rogers's report has become a well-known analysis, and was extremely unflattering. The reforms he proposed had to wait until after the aftermath of the war and its attendant shortages, but led to the appointment of Stanley Morison as typographical adviser to the Press under the next University Printer, Walter Lewis. While in Cambridge, Rogers designed a poster type for Meynell's Pelican Press, which was cut in wood,

somewhat unskilfully because of the shortage of craftsmen. Warde wrote, 'it is hoped by those who have seen the original drawings that one day all the letters will be recut competently'.

Rogers returned to the United States in 1919, and spent the next decade on book design, notably for William E. Rudge at Mount Vernon, outside New York. But the three books which are by general consent his greatest were still to come, and dated from the same stay in England which began with the supervision of Monotype Centaur, in which all three were set. T. E. Lawrence (of Arabia) had made a translation of Homer's *Odyssey* at Rogers's suggestion, which was printed at Emery Walker's works under Rogers's eyes; then there was another commission from the Grolier Club to design Stanley Morison's essay on Fra Luca de Pacioli, the Italian writing master; and there was his masterpiece, the Oxford Lectern Bible. It was set in 22pt Centaur with slightly shortened extenders, after trials with Bembo and Goudy Newstyle. (The latter type was used later, in a version modified by Rogers in collaboration with Sol Hess of Lanston Monotype and called Goudy Bible, for the World Bible of 1949.)

The Lectern Bible has been criticised for not being monumental enough, but this was Rogers's declared intention: he wanted it to look as if he 'was accustomed to knocking off large folios daily, or at least weekly, as mere routine work'.* While it is too grand really to give that impression, it has an agreeable lack of pomposity together with that grandeur, and though he designed many more books, he was never to reach such heights again.

Bruce Rogers died at his house in New Fairfield, Connecticut, in 1957, a few days after his eighty-seventh birthday.

Herbert Johnson, 'Some notes on Frederic Warde and the story of his Arrighi type', *Fine print*, 12, 3, 1986.

Bruce Rogers, *Paragraphs on printing, elicited from Bruce Rogers in talks with James Hendrickson on the functions of the book designer*, New York, Rudge, 1943. (Paperback edition, New York, Dover Books.)

Rudolf Koch

Rudolf Koch (1876–1934),
photographed in 1931.

The new generation of type designers in Germany, like their counterparts in the United States, saw their faces appear first as foundry type for hand setting; but here it took longer for the designs to be adapted for mechanical composition, sometimes until the arrival of filmsetting: many of them were blackletter founts, since blackletter was the standard script used in German printing up to the early 1940s, and so the costly adaptation for Monotype or Linotype machines could not be supported by large overseas sales. Some of the new faces were experimental hybrids between blackletter and roman, and a few were romans, though most of these were idiosyncratic renderings of the classic letter as seen through the eyes of designers who were not altogether at home with it.

Another difference between Germany and the English-speaking countries was that the German traditional foundries were far more energetic in soliciting new designs from artists who were not specialist typographers. Typical was the well-established Bauer foundry of Frankfurt, which confronted the challenge of mechanical composition directly in the area where the new manufacturers were most laggard. The foundry commissioned many faces from teachers and artists, notably Lucian Bernhard's family of types bearing his name (1912 on), Paul Renner's Futura (1928 on), Imre Reiner's Corvinus (1934) and the odd, but still popular Weiss Antiqua designed in 1926 by the distinguished graphic artist Emil Rudolf Weiss (1875-1942), who also contributed a Fraktur blackletter and some attractive type ornaments. On the whole Bauer deliberately concentrated on roman faces, issuing alongside these types new cuttings of older classics such as Bodoni (1926) and the Egyptian Beton (1936), and they competed hard in the foreign market, opening a New York office in 1927.

The professors and industrial designers from whom the big firms commissioned their flagship faces relied on the foundry craftsmen to turn their drawings into type. A conspicuous exception to this pattern was the career of Rudolf Koch, who spent most of his working life as a staff designer at the small Klingspor foundry in Offenbach.

This business,* since 1841 called the Rudhard foundry, had been bought in 1892 by a wealthy manufacturer for his two sons, Karl, then aged twenty-four, and Wilhelm Klingspor; they changed its name in 1906. Wilhelm Klingspor died in 1924, and it was Karl who was the driving force in the imaginative type design programme the foundry undertook, who set up a fine printing office to advertise their types, and established the 'Klingspor style'. He died in 1950.

The first fruits of Klingspor's new policy appeared in 1900: designs by Otto Eckmann, who died two years later aged thirty-seven, and Peter Behrens, the distinguished architect and industrial designer. Both faces were Jugendstil curiosities, and caused a considerable stir at the time; they represented a conscious effort to escape from the domination of blackletter. They can still sometimes be found in the catalogues of dry-transfer lettering, and Eckmann is available on Linotype digital machines. The punch-cutter of the original type was Louis Hoell, who afterwards moved to the Bauer foundry, where he cut the Bremer Press type, the designs of E. R. Weiss, and Joseph Blumenthal's Spiral/Emerson. Behrens went on to produce a roman and italic (1907-8) which show clearly the difficulties German designers found in tackling Renaissance scripts. Klingspor also used the heraldic artist Otto Hupp, who produced a handsome condensed blackletter Liturgisch (1906),

ABCDEFGHIJKL
abcdefghijklmnopq

ABCDEFGHIJKLM
abcdefghijklmnopqrstuv

UCELLINI

Grammophon-Matinée
von Emanuel Strasser

Weiss Antiqua (1924), designed by E. R. Weiss, and Imre Reiner's Corvinus (1934).

Julius Rodenberg, 'The work of Karl Klingspor', *The Fleuron* 5, 1926.

ABCDEFGHIJKLMNOPQR
ZÆŒGSCHSZabcdefghijklmno

ABCDEFGHIJKLMNOPQRST
abcdefghijklmnopqrsstuvwxy

ABCDEFGHIKLMNOPQ
XYZÆŒ abcdefghijklmnopq

*ABCDEFGHIJKLMNOPQuR
ZÆŒ abcdefghijklmnopqrsstuv*

ABCDEFGHIJKLMNOPQRSTUVW
mnopqrsstuvwxyzchckschffififlftffistht

Eckmannschrift (1900), designed by Otto Eckmann; Behrensschrift (1901), Behrens Antiqua and its italic (1907–8), by Peter Behrens; and Liturgisch (1906), by Otto Hupp.

which is very similar to the later Goudy Text (perhaps because they were both based on Gutenberg), a good Fraktur, and a roman equally as awful as Behrens Antiqua.

During Koch's years at the foundry, Klingspor's chief outside designer was Walter Tiemann (1876-1951), a co-founder of Germany's first private press, the Janus Press (1907), with the distinguished printer Carl Ernst Poeschel. Tiemann was a painter and a teacher: he was the director of the Leipzig academy of graphic art and book crafts when Jan Tschichold studied there. His types were nowhere near as original as Koch's, and suffer from comparison with them. Tiemann's Mediäval (1909) is scarcely more convincing than Behrens's, though the italic (1912) shows interesting parallels with the Cranach Press italic which Edward Johnston was designing at the same time. Narziss (1921) had a considerable success in advertising display work, and Tiemann Antiqua (1923), a Didone which shows an inclination towards French refinement without the necessary knowledge of the letter forms, has recently been adapted by Adrian Frutiger for Linotype. Tiemann's later faces, Orpheus (1928), Daphnis (1931) and Offizin (1952), did not maintain even this standard.

Designs by Walter Tiemann. Tiemann Gotisch (1924), Peter Schlemihl (1914), Narziss (1921), Tiemann Antiqua (1923) and its italic (1926).

In the first decades of the century, there was a strong English influence in German fine printing, encouraged by men like Harry Kessler, both at his Cranach Press, which in many ways was an English private press which happened to be in Weimar, and earlier in his use of Edward Johnston and Eric Gill to draw lettering for books published by the Insel-Verlag of Leipzig. Willy Wiegand's Bremer Press, which ran from 1911 to 1939, used the designer Anna Simons, who had been a pupil of Johnston's, and her 1910 German translation of Johnston's *Writing and illuminating and lettering* (first published in 1906), was widely influential. But already in 1903, Rudolf Koch, then a struggling young designer in Leipzig, had begun experimenting with a broad pen, which set him on the way to mastery of many calligraphic styles.

Koch was born on 20 November 1876 in Nuremberg, which had been one of the first great centres of printing, and the home of Albrecht Dürer. His father, a sculptor and inspector of museums, had died when Koch was only ten, and the reduced family circumstances which resulted meant that the boy had to leave school early and take up an apprenticeship as a metal worker in Hanau, near Offenbach and Frankfurt, while studying at the art school in his spare time. His

ABCDEFGHIJKLMN
VWXYZÆ abcdefghijklmno

ABCDEFGHIJKLMNO
VWXYZ abcdefghijklmnoprsss

ABCDEFGHIJKLMN
VWXYZ abcdefghijkl

ABCDEFGHIJKLMNOPQ
YZÆŒ abcdefghijklmnopqr

*ABCDEFGHIJKLMNOPQ
YZ abcdefghijklmnopqrsstuvwx*

𝕬lte 𝕭urgen und 𝕾tädte am 𝕽hein

𝕿he 𝕷ife & 𝕯eath of 𝕸r. 𝕭adman

Koch's Fette Deutsche Schrift (1906–10), and Deutsche Zierschrift (1921).

ambition to be an artist grew, and before his four year apprenticeship was completed, he returned to Nuremberg to study to be an art teacher at the arts and crafts school, of which he later wrote that it was 'rather a refuge for aged but deserving professors than an institution for the education of young people'. He moved to Munich, but shortly before he was to take his examinations he found that his apprenticeship, being outside Bavaria, could not count towards his qualification; so, in 1898, he went to Leipzig to work as a designer with various printers and binders, and from 1902 on as a freelance. His style at that time was the Jugendstil then in fashion, which he quickly left behind. 'May God forgive me for the things I produced in those years', he commented afterwards.

In the autumn of 1905, Koch saw an advertisement in the magazine *Kunst und Dekoration* for a post at the Rudhard foundry, shortly to be renamed Klingspor. He joined them in 1906, and stayed there until his death in 1934. He began in a relatively humble capacity, but Karl Klingspor soon recognised his talents as a penman, and he began to design types. At the same time he was appointed as a teacher of lettering at the Offenbach technical institute, where later, in 1921, he set up an important workshop for students.

All Koch's types were designed for Klingspor, with the exception of the Deutsche Anzeigenschrift family done between 1923 and 1934 directly for Stempel, who had a controlling interest in Klingspor from 1918 onwards. In 1929, when he was being wooed by an American foundry, Koch paid this tribute to Karl Klingspor: 'If I have produced a useful type design, it is in large measure due to the proprietor of the Klingspor foundry, whose advisory rôle in each task I have undertaken for the firm has amounted to a collaboration. My relationship with Klingspor goes far beyond a question of business, and I will never seek another.'

More than half of Koch's types were blackletter faces, to which he brought a rough calligraphic strength rarely seen before in type. Almost all of them grew from his own styles of writing, practised for long periods of preparation before the type itself was designed, frequently in quotations from the Bible, since Koch was a deeply religious man who, like Eric Gill, tried to unite life and work in an harmonious whole. His first type, called simply Deutsche Schrift, was a bold blackletter which occupied him until 1910, and its narrow version until 1913. A medium weight appeared in 1918, and the attractive decorated form

Die
zeitgemäße Schrift

Nʀ· 24

An example of Koch's calligraphy.
A magazine cover from 1933.

Deutsche Zierschrift, well used in England by Francis Meynell at the Nonesuch Press, in 1921. It showed from the start the powerful graphic imagiation of its creator. In 1914 a light-weight Fraktur, Frühling, appeared, of which Koch wrote, 'everything in this letter is conventional, so it looks new', and in the same year he began the design of Maximilian, which entailed a long series of type trials which ended when he was called up for war service in 1915. Maximilian was the first blackletter for which Koch drew matching roman capitals. Although no designer knew, or exploited, better than he the graphic potential of blackletter capitals, he also realised their illegibility when used together, and his later experiments with combining blackletter lowercase with romanised capitals greatly helped the non-German reader to read texts set in his types. At this stage, however, the decorative inline Maximilian Antiqua capitals were intended for display, not for word combinations with the lower-case; but they showed the way his mind was working, and were the first of his types to be widely used abroad.

Koch's army service as a grenadier was a painful time for him. He saw action on the French and Russian fronts as a private soldier, spent seven months in an army hospital in Offenbach during 1916 before being sent back to the front, and finally was discharged because of ill health in October 1917. The war years saw the design, and the next few years the cutting, of a new and original development in his work, the delicate roman and italic called Koch Antiqua and Kursiv. (Outside Germany, where it is his best known type, it is called Locarno, after the optimistic treaty signed there in 1925, which guaranteed Germany's western frontiers.) One of the most successful advertising faces of the inter-war period, still often used to suggest the vanishing luxury of ocean liners, it nevertheless grew directly from Koch's calligraphy, which he used in texts celebrating the joys of domesticity. As well as the roman and italic, there was also a Grobe, or heavy weight.

After the war, Koch's most productive period began. He started work on a newspaper Fraktur type for the Ullstein publishing group, which was intended for foreign as well as native readers and, although the type was not put into production, it must have given more food for his thoughts on the legibility of blackletter. Next, basing the design on his boldly hand-written text of the Beatitudes, he produced the magnificent Wilhelm Klingspor Schrift (1924-6),

Aus reiner Anschauungslust und Köpfen das Zustandekommen eines das weckt mehr Gemeinschaftsgefühl als aller

Buch, ja irgend eine Drucksache anzusehen. PETER JESSEN

DIE DEUTSCHE BUCHKUNST

the summit of his achievement in a purely Germanic blackletter tradition, which confined him largely to local audiences, and Klingspor to local sales.

But this blackletter tradition was being challenged within Germany from a powerful new quarter: not the humanist roman designs of the Italian Renaissance, but the modernists of the Bauhaus, who advocated the universal acceptance of sans-serif types. The kind of geometrical design proposed, which found its complete expression in Futura, was on the face of it antithetical to Koch's intuitive approach, and he refused on principle to draw one. For his own reasons, however, he relented, and designed the interesting and elegant Kabel (1926-7), with an inline companion called Zeppelin (1929) and, most remarkable of all, the striated version called Prisma (1931), which looks as fresh today as when it first appeared. As Georg Haupt wrote in his study of Koch's work, 'So it happened that the master of vernacular script also created the clearest, most logical, and at the same time the most vital, constructed alphabet'.*

Georg Haupt, *Rudolf Koch der Schreiber*, Leipzig, Insel Verlag, 1936.

ABCDEFGHIJKLMN
OPQRSTUVWXYZ
abcdefghijklmnopqrſstuvwxyz
chckſchffffiflſtſſliſtß a tz &

ABCDEFGHIJKLM
NOPQRSTUVWX
abcdefghijklmnopqrſstuvwxyz

Die Kunst ist ein ernsthaftes
Geschäft, am ernsthaftesten,

Die Klugheit ist zwar sehr geeignet, zu erhalten was man besitzt, aber allein die Kühnheit läßt gewinnen. Die Reden Friedrichs des Großen

Wir wollen jedem Menschen und jedem Ding die schuldige Ehre erweisen, aber nichts fürchten, als das Tun des Bösen.   Ralph Waldo Trine

DAS TALENT ARBEITET, DAS GENIE SCHAFFT. SCHUMANN

NEUES THEATER IN FRANKFURT

Kabel (1926–9), with two decorated versions, Zeppelin (1929) and Prisma (1931).

Koch felt the need to reach beyond the blackletter tradition in other directions, and also to try his hand at cutting his own punches. As a first attempt which would not stretch his punchcutting skills too far, he produced Neuland (1923), a brutal sans-serif again based on his rough pen-drawn lettering, again a popular advertising type (imitated by Monotype and called Othello), and again used with imagination by Francis Meynell, in the Nonesuch Press *Genesis* (1924), where it goes well with Paul Nash's powerful woodcuts.

In the Peter Jessen Schrift, called after the director of the Berlin museum of arts and crafts whose lectures had influenced many German graphic designers, Koch returned to a simplified blackletter, with romanised capitals for use with the gothic lower-case for the first time. The initial impetus for the type was a great edition of the four Gospels printed at the Klingspor Press in 1926. It remained a popular face in the Koch circle, and was bought by the Grabhorn Press of San Francisco, who called it Koch Bibel Gotisch, and first used it for their handsome edition of Mandeville's *Travels* for Random House in 1928. Koch himself cut the punches of two sizes, except for the 12pt capitals, which were cut by his son Paul; the

other sizes were cut by Gustav Eichenauer.

Koch's experiments with capitals continued with Wallau (1930), called after a Mainz printer who in 1885 had anticipated William Morris in suggesting the revival of the round blackletter script known as Rotunda, common among the printing types of the first centuries after the invention of printing, and including those of Anton Koberger, the great printer of Koch's native Nuremberg. This kind of design had prompted Morris's Troy and Chaucer types, and later influenced Eric Gill's Jubilee (1935), but none of those can match the calligraphic verve of Koch's drawing. For Wallau he made two sets of capitals, blackletter and romanised, and the latter were used more often. They and the lighter Offenbach roman capitals (1930), designed to accompany a blackletter lower case, were of a pen-formed sans-serif design which strongly influenced the capitals of pupils and admirers. Although their lower-case characters were quite distinct, ATF Lydian (1938-46) by the American Warren Chappell, who had studied with Koch in the early 1930s, and Monotype Klang (1955) by Will Carter, who had spent some months at Paul Koch's workshop in 1938, both show Koch's clear influence. Hans Kühne's Stahl, produced for Klingspor in

Die Wallau=Schriften von Gebr. Klingspor, Offenbach erwerben sich immer mehr Freunde

✠

Evangelium Johannes   15. Kapitel

Ich sage hinfort nicht, daß ihr Knechte seid; denn 15 ein Knecht weiß nicht, was sein Herr tut. Euch aber habe ich gesagt, daß ihr Freunde seid; denn alles, was ich habe von meinem Vater gehört, habe ich euch kundgetan. Ihr habt mich nicht er= 16 wählt; sondern ich habe euch erwählt und gesetzt, daß ihr hingehet und Frucht bringet und eure Frucht bleibe, auf daß, so ihr den Vater bittet in meinem Namen, er's euch gebe. Das gebiete ich 17 euch, daß ihr euch untereinander liebet.

Wallau (1930) and Peter Jessen Schrift (1924–30).

Writings of Honey & Alers
EXCURSION IN WINTER

Die Klugheit ist zwar sehr geeignet, zu erhalten was man besitzt,
aber allein die Kühnheit läßt gewinnen.　　Friedrich der Große

Marathon (1930–8) and Claudius (1931–7).

1939, is a different case, in that it took the Offenbach capitals virtually without change, and added a new stressed sans-serif lower case.

Koch designed two script types, an uninspired brush-formed latin script called Holla (1932), and a complicated face derived from German handwriting, Koch Kurrent, which because of the difficulties of its cutting was not finished until 1935, after his death.

The last type cut by Koch, in one size only, was a curious gawky roman called Marathon (begun 1930; other sizes finished 1938) which cannot be called a success; but from his designs his son Paul cut the beautiful dancing blackletter Claudius (1931-7), drawn with great dash, which is a more fitting end to the career of this inspired and inspiring designer. Koch died on 9 April 1934, but his work was carried on by Paul Koch, who ran a workshop in the old quarter of Frankfurt, called the Haus zum Fürsteneck, where the young Hermann Zapf, among others, came to study. Paul Koch disappeared, and was presumed killed, on the Russian front in 1943.

Rudolf Koch was driven by a religious sense of purpose, and, combining as he did the talents of calligrapher and punchcutter, ought theoretically to have produced perfect types. That he did not do so is due partly to his calligraphy being too free, and his punchcutting too rough, and partly to his belonging to a graphic tradition outside the European mainstream. Nonetheless, we can recognise his anachronistic, personal and undeniably magnificent achievement, which should be kept in mind by type designers whenever they find their work becoming anaemic: for that is something Koch's types never were.

William Addison Dwiggins

*William A. Dwiggins
(1880–1956) at work at
Hingham, Massachusetts, around
1939. Photograph by Randall W.
Abbott. By courtesy of the Trustees
of Boston Public Library.*

Ten years younger than Rogers, and fifteen younger than Goudy, Dwiggins also came late to the design of books and type. He was an original and exuberant graphic artist with an instantly recognisable style, who nevertheless, when he came to type design, produced a handful of faces which are remarkable for their comparative sobriety.*

Dwiggins was born in Martinsville, Ohio, on 19 June 1880, the son of a doctor. His interest in art took him at the age of nineteen to Chicago, where he went to Frank Holme's school and studied lettering with Goudy. After a brief, unsuccessful spell as a jobbing printer in rural Ohio, he followed Goudy to Hingham, Massachusetts; and when Goudy moved on to New York, he stayed on at Hingham for the rest of his life, though for many years he also had a studio in Boston. A prolific worker, he was, according to his wife, 'a man who loved his work so much, that no day was long enough'; indeed he often maintained that his aim was to campaign for a forty-eight hour day. In addition to his lettering and illustration, he ran an ambitious marionette theatre, for which he made stage, sets and cast, and wrote the plays.

Dwiggins's early graphic work was for advertising, but he came increasingly to prefer designing books. In 1923 he met the publisher Alfred Knopf, for whom he was to design close on three hundred books over the years, and established the Borzoi visual style indelibly. But it was for another publisher, Random House, that he designed his most celebrated edition, H. G. Wells's *The time machine* (1931), full of his characteristic vignettes, which were built up by the skilled application of stencilled elements. Many of his books and jackets were decorated with his very individual calligraphy, which was an eclectic amalgam of late eighteenth and early nineteenth century scripts and romans freely redrawn with a flexible nib and a lot of dash. In view of his interest in lettering and also in repetitive stencilling techniques, it is surprising that he took so long to take up type design, but he was in his late forties before a chance observation in his manual *Layout in advertising* (1928) led to an invitation from Harry L. Gage of the Mergenthaler Linotype Company. In the book, Dwiggins criticised contemporary sans-serifs, especially the capitals, and wrote, 'the type founders will do a service if they will provide

Postscripts on Dwiggins, essays and recollections, edited by Paul A. Bennett, New York, The Typophiles, 1960. (Two volumes.)

ABCDEFGHIJKLMNOPQRSTUV
WXYZ&ÆŒæœ
1234567890
abcdefghijklmnopqrstuvwxyz
[($£,.:;'-'?!*†‡§¶)]

ABCDEFGHIJKLMNOPQRSTUV
WXYZ&ÆŒæœ
1234567890
abcdefghijklmnopqrstuvwxyz
[($£,.:;'-'?!*†‡§¶)]

Alternative Characters

AGJMNVWWaegvw,;'
AGJMNVWWaegvw,;'

a Gothic of good design.' Gage challenged Dwiggins to do better, and he responded with trial drawings for a sans-serif which was accepted, cut, and called Metro (1929-30), with the various weights of the family called Metrolite, Metroblack, and so on. It is an interesting rather than a successful type, with a lower case which is too idiosyncratic for the generation of constructed sans-serifs to which it belonged, and not convincing enough to establish its own tradition.

The association with Linotype lasted twenty-seven years until Dwiggins's death, and his contact was chiefly with C. H. Griffith, the vice-president in charge of typographical development, with whom he kept up a busy and lively correspondence. His first book type, Electra, appeared in 1935. It was equipped with both a sloped roman and a slightly cursive italic, and is a kind of calligraphic modern face. In a characteristic and amusingly schizophrenic essay introducing the type (in *Emblems and Electra*, 1935), Dwiggins argued with an *alter ego*, not for once Dr Hermann Püterschein, his regular fictional *doppelgänger*, but a Japanese sage Kobodaishi, who insisted that the type reflect the modern age of speed and steel, while Dwiggins replied, 'if you don't get your

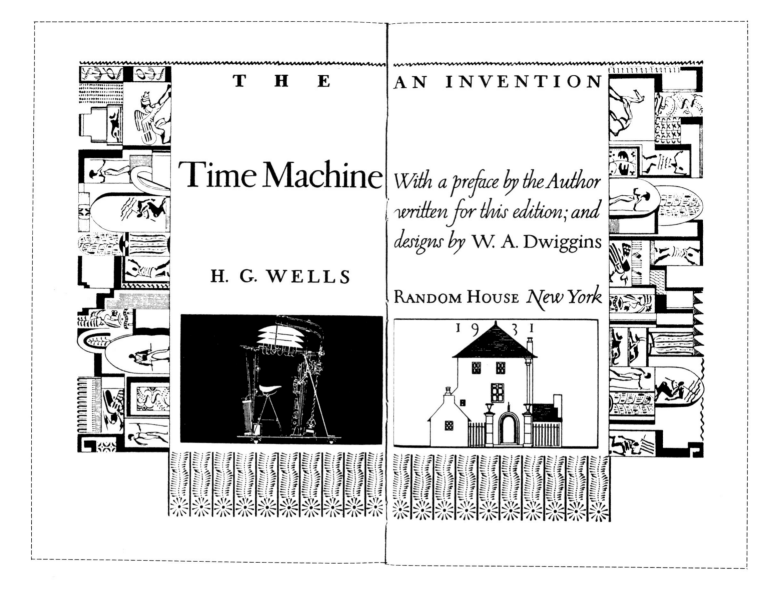

THE
AN INVENTION

Time Machine
With a preface by the Author written for this edition; and designs by W. A. Dwiggins

H. G. WELLS
RANDOM HOUSE New York

1931

An example of Dwiggins's book design. Title spread from 'The time machine' (1931), with his calligraphy and stencilled decorations.

Electra (1935).

type *warm* it will be just a smooth, commonplace, third-rate piece of good machine technique – no use at all for setting down warm human ideas – just a box full of rivets . . . By jickity, I'd like to make a type that fitted 1935 all right enough, but I'd like to make it *warm* – so full of blood and personality that it would jump at you.'

Dwiggins himself seemed to have thought that he had succeeded too well, and that the type showed less of 'the metal shavings part' than originally intended. Nonetheless, it still looks extremely crisp and fresh and, in its author's words, 'moves along the line nicely'.

In 1939, Dwiggins produced Caledonia, his best and most successful type. The design process, as described by Dwiggins in his introduction to the first specimen, began with a liking for the Scotch romans cut by the Wilson foundry of Glasgow in the late eighteenth century, and developed as a cocktail of styles with the addition of elements of the slightly later Bulmer types cut by William Martin. In the end, Dwiggins transcended his models. 'The face as it emerges', he wrote, 'is not at all like Bulmer's Martin nor like Wilson's Scotch, but it has touches of both of them in spots. Also it has something of that simple, hard-working, feet-on-the-ground quality that has kept Scotch Modern in service for so many years. About the "liveliness of action" that one sees in the Martin letters, and to a less degree (one modestly says) in Caledonia: that quality is in the curves – the way they get away from the straight stems with a calligraphic flick, and in the nervous angle on the under side of the arches as they descend to the right. The finishing strokes at the bottoms of the letters, cut straight across without "brackets", making sharp angles with the upright stems, add "snap" to many of the old "modern face" designs – and why not to Caledonia?'

Dwiggins took great care with his working drawings, and drew Caledonia at full ten-inch working size. The type designer Rudolph Ruzicka (1883–1978), the recipient of Dwiggins's essay on type design, *WAD to RR*,* wrote 'I have not the least doubt that Dwiggins could have achieved whatever results he wanted by means of any one of the many techniques he commanded, yet in Caledonia, roman and

William A. Dwiggins, *WAD to RR, a letter about designing type,* Cambridge, Harvard College Library, 1940.

THE

ALPHABET

A B C D E F G H I J K L M N O P Q R S T
U V W X Y Z & Æ Œ
a b c d e f g h i j k l m n o p q r s t u v w x y z
fi fl ff ffi ffl æ œ 1 2 3 4 5 6 7 8 9 0
A B C D E F G H I J K L M N O P Q R S T U V W X
Y Z & Æ Œ
A B C D E F G H I J K L M N O P Q R S T
U V W X Y Z & Æ Œ
a b c d e f g h i j k l m n o p q r s t u v w x y z
fi fl ff ffi ffl æ œ 1 2 3 4 5 6 7 8 9 0
( ) [ ] $ £ , . : ; '-' ? ! *
† ‡ § ‖ (( ) $ £ , : ; '' ? !

❂

g j p q y Q J 3 4 5 7 9   *g j p q y Q J 3 4 5 7 9*
§ (( ) ( ) [ ] ‖

Oh for the coast of Maine, a cove, a cot

Disposed in that salubrious situation,—

The rocks, the hills, the pines! And yet it's not

A circumstance to linear decoration.

a theory that the proponent thinks may have sense in it: Fine type letters were, in the first place, copies of fine written letters. Fine *written letters* were fine because they were produced in the most direct and simple way by a tool in the hands of a person expert in its use, by a person, moreover, who was an artist, *i.e.*, a person equipped to make sound judgments about lines, curves, proportions, etc. The artist of

through 1942 to 1953, the Eldorado shown here, is in no direct way a copy of the de Sancha face (which, be it noted, is more French than Spanish) *but it has called on the Madrid specimen for help in the anatomy of its arches, curves, junctions, etc.* In the matter of "color": with the kind of presswork we have now in books, an inking which adds about one-thousandth of an inch

italic, there is apparent no pen or any other ancestral "mark of the tool", and what there is of his individual hand is felt rather than seen. Caledonia has the ease of good clear speech, with just a hint of a pleasant Scotch accent.'

Dwiggins designed several types for Linotype which were not taken beyond the experimental stage, though in a few cases limited editions were printed from them. Stuyvesant, Winchester, Arcadia, Tippecanoe and Hingham all showed interesting features, but only Eldorado (1953) was released in Dwiggins's

lifetime. (Falcon appeared in 1962.) He died on Christmas Day, 1956.

Dwiggins's easy writing style, and the *joie de vivre* of his graphic work, partly serve to hide his professionalism; but it is precisely that combination of freedom and discipline that makes his types as good as they are. Although he did not cut his types, he made careful pattern drawings and left the cutting to other professionals; he managed to keep the controlled informality of his drawings intact in the final type, and he made it look easy.

WAD to RR
A letter about designing
Type

Title label for 'WAD to RR' (1940), and an illustration showing a stencil for a basic letter form.

6/18/37
221 #2 lighter stem

01175

Eric Gill

Eric Gill described himself on his own gravestone as a stone carver, which embraced the two activities for which he was most famous, sculpture and the cutting of inscriptional lettering. He might have added: wood engraver, for he was a versatile and original artist in that medium, and his engravings for the Cranach Press *Canticum Canticorum* and the Golden Cockerel Press *Four Gospels* (both 1931) are magnificent achievements of book illustration. He might also have added: essayist, since he was an indefatigable writer on a great variety of subjects from sex, politics, religion and the nature of workmanship to art, clothes and typography. And he might also have added: type designer, since in Gill Sans and Perpetua he designed two of the most popular faces of the century.

Gill's emphatic assertion of the holiness of sex frequently offended the Catholic hierarchy, who nevertheless remained oddly tolerant of his reputation as a sexual predator. Fiona MacCarthy's recent biography* has shown that the *droit de Seigneur* he exercised over virtually every female member of his entourage extended to his sisters and daughters.

Eric Gill was born on 22 February 1882 in Brighton, the second child of a large family. He showed an early talent for drawing, and was sent to art school at Chichester, where the family had moved. At the age of seventeen his obvious interest in lettering and architecture led to his being apprenticed to W. H. Caroë, architect to the Ecclesiastical Commissioners in Westminster. At the same time he began to carve lettering, encouraged by W. R. Lethaby, the principal of the Central School of Arts and Crafts, and very rapidly began to get commissions. At the Central School he attended lettering classes given by Edward Johnston, ten years his senior, and was profoundly influenced by Johnston's integrity and approach to his work. In 1902 the two men shared rooms in Lincoln's

Inn, until Johnston's marriage the next year, closely followed by Gill's the year after.

In 1903 he left Caroë's office, where he had never been content, and began his life-long career as a self-employed craftsman. He was immediately successful, and soon, besides carved work, he was commissioned by W. H. Smith to paint the sign on their bookshop in Paris, and several other branches thereafter, and by Count Harry Kessler to draw and engrave lettering for the title pages of books published by the Insel Verlag in Leipzig. The early lettering was drawn and reproduced by line blocks, but Gill was so dissatisfied with the result that for *Die Odyssee* (1910-11) he had the drawn lettering photographed on boxwood blocks, and cut the lettering by hand.

Gill's workshop in Hammersmith was proving too small, and with a young family to think of he moved in 1907 to the Sussex village of Ditchling. Here he began to carve sculpture, the medium in which some of his best work was done. His large public commissions, such as the work for the BBC on Broadcasting House in Portland Place, London, made him nationally famous. Quite early on plans were made for him to work with Maillol and Epstein; both came to nothing, for Gill was very much his own man, but they indicate the esteem in which he was held early in his career. At the same time, his spiritual progress led him towards the Roman Catholic church, and he and his wife were received in 1913. Shortly after this he was given the task of carving the Stations of the Cross in Westminster Cathedral, completed in 1918, his first major sculptural commission, because of which he was excused army service during World War I.

Meanwhile the community at Ditchling began to grow. Edward Johnston went to live there in 1912, and in 1916 an acquaintance of Gill's from Hammersmith, Hilary (Douglas) Pepler moved in and set up the St Dominic's Press, a small hand-press workshop for which much of Gill's early engraving was done. But after a few years Gill quarrelled with Pepler,

Fiona MacCarthy, *Eric Gill*, London, Faber and Faber, 1989.

mostly over money: Pepler was a comparatively wealthy man and casual about business, whereas Gill had to support himself and his family, and was almost fanatically methodical about keeping time-sheets and accounts. In 1924, Gill moved his growing entourage to a remote abandoned monastery in the Welsh mountains at Capel-y-ffin.

Shortly before he went, he had been asked by Stanley Morison to write about typography for *The Fleuron*, but had declined, saying that typography was 'not his country'. Morison and he had met about ten years before when Morison was working with Francis Meynell at the Meynell family publishing firm of Burns and Oates, and had commissioned Gill to engrave some initials for them. By November 1925, Gill had given in to Morison, and was drawing alphabets for him, alphabets which were, in the course of time, to become Perpetua.

Early in 1924, Morison had announced his hope that Monotype users would soon be able to add to their repertoire of classic revivals 'at least one original design'. Much later he described in *A tally of types* (1953) the way he came to ask Gill to make that design. He had found that the private press types were mostly too quaint. 'What was wanted was a design that, while being new, was of general utility and in no respect unusual.' The calligraphers like Edward Johnston were trained to write letters that were formed freshly by the pen, with not enough of the modifications made by centuries of expertise in cutting punches. 'The fine serif is not in origin calligraphic but epigraphic; not written but sculptured. It follows that a set of drawings of a finely serifed face by a contemporary practitioner of lettering could best be made by one who was either an engraver on metal or wood; or, preferably, a sculptor

The Heroic Age is well typified for us in Achilles, in the
early doom that hangs over him, and the great renown

of generations it would last. The richest hoped it
might last for ten. Our traditions say, in the
second generation after Agamemnon the deluge
came.
It came, the ancients said, in the form of the
avenging Heraclids, come back to regain the heri-

ABCDEFGHIJKLMNOPQRSTUVWXYZ
Æ Œ Ç Qu
abcdefghijklmnopqrstuvwxyz

*Charles Malin's pilot cutting of
Perpetua. In the first paragraph
he used Gill's capitals, while in
the second, clearly thinking them
too small, he substituted some
larger old-style capitals from
another fount.*

on stone or slate. On this analysis the problem
became soluble, and Gill was the obvious man to solve
it.'

In 1925 Morison, somewhat disenchanted with
Monotype because of the mistake over Fournier, and
also with a growing interest in the technique of hand
punchcutting, was becoming interested in the cutting
of Frederic Warde's Arrighi italic by Charles
Plumet. He had also been introduced by François
Thibaudeau of Deberny & Peignot to Charles Malin
(1883-1955), a younger man than Plumet, who was to
complete the cutting of Arrighi after Plumet's retirement. It was to Malin that Morison turned for his plan
of turning Gill's drawings into type in the traditional
way. This was partly also as a concession to Gill's
initial reluctance to have anything to do with machine
production, and his condemnation of industrial
design, in the generally accepted sense of the process
whereby an 'artist' makes drawings for 'workmen' to
carry out. Within a few years, as we shall see, Gill
changed his mind completely, not without a good deal
of self-justifying sophistry, and designed Gill Sans.

Years later, Morison wrote in *A tally*:

Long before the cutting of Perpetua, the Corporation had
cut punches from new drawings made for the purpose by
draughtsmen capable of making clear outlines. But as to a
book-type of the highest ambition, no reproduction direct
from the drawing-board had been as satisfactory as those
made from type already existing, e.g. Bell's roman and italic.
The difference between the drawn pattern and the engraved
letter was crucial. Virtue went out with the hand-cutter
when the mechanic came in with his pantograph and the rest
of the gear. The new engineers were not what the old
engravers were. They could mass-produce, or reproduce,
punches; they could not create, or recreate, the engraved
quality that had belonged to typography in the roman letter
since 1465.'

This is a curious passage in the context of
Perpetua, since Bell was cut several years after it was
begun. It is even more curious in the context of
Morison's relations with Monotype, since some of the
most successful faces he supervised there were
recreations of types which certainly had existed but
did so no longer. Moreover in the same book he had
condemned Monotype Caslon, of which the foundry
types *had* been available as models, as 'a complete
failure as a facsimile'. Morison's whole work at

Monotype was dedicated to proving that the engineers could produce good letters, given the right models in graphic form, an endeavour which culminated in his own Times New Roman, which was drawn by a non-specialist draftsman and had never seen a hand punchcutter. The last part of the passage is the most curious because in 1953 he did not believe it: certainly when Van Krimpen made a similar point a few years later, Morison replied, 'I do not really believe that you mean that Monotype and foundry type are two essentially different things. I do not believe these differences are essential. I believe they are different but I question whether the difference is so great.'

Yet there is no doubt that in 1926 Morison thought that Malin's work was a necessary preliminary to any cutting by Monotype. He did not doubt Monotype's ability to cut the type, but he did question their skill in transforming the drawings of a self-confessed amateur type designer into a coherent fount. He was confirmed in this opinion by Van Krimpen, whose Lutetia had been cut as a foundry type shortly before, and was recut by Monotype some years later. Yet whereas Van Krimpen and his punchcutter Rädisch were expert partners in close daily contact at Enschedé, Gill, who had little knowledge of type design, was dealing with Malin at a distance and with Morison as an intermediary.

In the event, Malin's contribution to Perpetua was almost forgotten. Beatrice Warde did not mention him by name in her article introducing the type in *The Fleuron* 7, and Gill ignored him completely in his note on the type, giving all the credit to Monotype: 'These drawings were not made with special reference to typography – they were simply letters, drawn with brush and ink. For the typographical quality of the fount, as also for the remarkably fine and precise cutting of the punches, the Monotype Corporation is to be praised. In my opinion "Perpetua" is commendable in that, in spite of many distinctive characters, it retains that commonplaceness and normality which is essential to a good book-type.'

The Paris foundry of Ribadeau Dumas cast a fount from Malin's punches, which was passed to Monotype in January 1927 for what became a long series of trials, since the sight of the cast and printed letters began to disturb Gill, who had up to then seen only smoke proofs. He objected to the blob on the tail of the **y** which Malin had introduced, found the **g** and the **r** too heavy, and agreed with Morison that the

Monotype Perpetua (1929).

ABCDEFGHIJKLMN OPQRSTUVWXYZ

abcdefghijklmnopqrstuvwxyz

1234567890

Lettering is a precise art and strictly subject to tradition. The 'New Art' notion that you can make letters whatever shapes you like, is as foolish as the notion, if anyone has such a notion, that you can make houses any shapes you like. You can't, unless you live all by yourself on a desert island . . .

Gill's drawing of a 'constructed' capital I, and a natural one, with comments, in a letter to Stanley Morison, November 1926. By permission of the Syndics of Cambridge University Library.

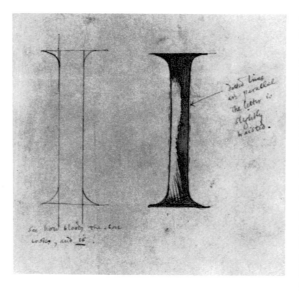

different characters and terminal flicks rather than serifs.) Morison's belief was that as italics were originally intended for independent use, they should not be used for articulation in prose set in roman, a belief which was set out in his essay 'Towards an ideal italic' (*The Fleuron* 5, 1926). Felicity italic finally made its appearance in Beatrice Warde's article in *The Fleuron* 7 in 1930, which introduced the type; it looked rather like the later Joanna italic and was hardly ever seen again. A year later Gill made drawings of what became standard Perpetua italic, with a greater angle of slope and a few more cursive characters. As Morison confessed to Van Krimpen, 'The sloped roman idea does not go down so well in this office [Monotype] as it does outside. The reason for this is that when the doctrine was applied to Perpetua, we did not give enough slope to it. When we added more slope, it seemed the fount required a little more cursive in it. The result was rather a compromise.'

Perpetua, Series 239, was finally issued to the trade in 1932.* For the specimen which appeared in the

James Mosley, 'Eric Gill's Perpetua type', *Fine Print*, 8, 3, 1982.

capitals were too short; and the comments were passed on to the Monotype works to make the changes required. In spite of this, Perpetua exhibits in an extreme form the tendency of the Monotype works to draw letters with ruler and compasses. In a letter to Morison in November 1926 Gill drew two diagrams which illustrated his contention that the uprights of roman letters should be imperceptibly 'waisted', and that the serifs should grow from them as though organically. Under his parody of the drawing office version with its parallel-sided uprights and mathematically circular brackets to the serif, Gill wrote, 'See how bloody the above looks, and *is*.' If Morison passed this on to the works, they took no notice, as they hardly ever did, and as a result in the larger sizes of the Perpetua titlings, as in many Monotype faces, the point where the compasses take over from the ruler is quite perceptible.

The type was delayed both by attention to the details of the roman, and by the italic. Gill was persuaded by Morison, as Van Krimpen was with Romulus a few years later, to substitute a sloped roman for the more usual cursive italic. (Sloped romans keep the roman letter forms and incline them, more or less mechanically, while italics have a few

Drawings of decorated letters (1928), which later became Gill Floriated. By courtesy of the Monotype Corporation.

76

Edward Johnston's London Transport alphabet (1916), and Monotype Gill Sans (1929).

JOHNSTON

This broadsheet is set in Johnston type. Edward Johnston (1872-1944) was one of the followers of William Morris (1834-1896) who took a leading part in reviving an interest in good lettering after the decadence of the late-Victorian fashions. In 1916 Johnston was commissioned by Frank Pick (1878-1941) to design a special fount for the exclusive use of London's Underground and its associated companies. The resulting Johnston sans-serif type was the forerunner of many sans-serif founts both in England and abroad, including that of Eric Gill (1882-1940) who was Johnston's friend and pupil in this specialised field of design. Johnston is the standard type used for all official signs and notices throughout the London Transport system, and it is also used, where appropriate, for much of London Transport's general typographical publicity.

1930 *Fleuron*, Gill also drew a delightful decorated capital **N**. Morison asked him to design the complete alphabet for Monotype, but he declined: Robert Harling* suggested he thought the design too free-hand for the mechanical process of Monotype reproduction. In 1936 he changed his mind, and these Floriated Initials were cut as Series 431. For while Perpetua was making slow progress through the works, Gill was beginning to make typography very much his country. As early as 1925, he had designed some block letters for the Army and Navy Stores, and used similar forms for signs at Capel-y-ffin to warn off uninvited visitors. Then in October 1926 he was asked by a young bookseller in Bristol called Douglas Cleverdon (who later published several books of his) to paint his bookshop name in these same capitals. While in Bristol he developed 'flu, and to pass the time in bed he drew some alphabets for Cleverdon to use as models for lettering in his shop, including the sans-serif capitals. A few weeks later, Morison was staying with Cleverdon, and was interested in the alphabets. Earlier in the year he had tried to interest

Robert Harling, *The letter forms and type designs of Eric Gill*, Westerham, Eva Svensson, 1976.

ABCDEFGHIJKLMNOPQRST
abcdefghijklmnopqrstuvwxyz
ABCDEFGHIJKLMNOPQRSTUV
abcdefghijklmnopqrstuvwxyz
£1234567890.,;:!?''

The first public showing of Gill Sans.

Solus (1929).

increasingly fascinated by the processes involved. From 1928 he was paid a retainer by Monotype to act as an adviser. He even made drawings and annotated trial proofs of some of the more outlandish variants of the Sans family, including the Kayo, or Ultra Bold, which he nicknamed Gill Sans Double-Elefans.* He was a professional; and he also had a way of constructing elaborate arguments in favour of an expedient solution. Thus he convinced himself that if the trade demanded types for such ugly purposes as advertising, it ought to have ugly types.

The titling, Series 231, was ready for the British Federation of Master Printers conference in May 1928, which Morison addressed; and the assembled dignitaries were duly horrified by the new type. The upper and lower case, Series 262, appeared in 1930, and the type became a phenomenal success.

In view of the warm relationship which Gill had developed with Monotype, and always had with Morison, it is surprising that the only other issued type he designed for them was Solus. It was based on a skeletal Egyptian alphabet in the Cleverdon alphabet book which Morison, by a quirk of typeface nomenclature described as 'blonde' in colour, by contrast with darker Egyptians. Gill immediately dubbed it 'Gents' preference' after Anita Loos's

the Stephenson Blake foundry in cutting a version of the Army and Navy capitals without success, and the Cleverdon alphabet book convinced him that Gill could produce for Monotype the kind of sans-serif family that overseas foundries were beginning to produce with such success.

Both Gill and he were aware that while sans-serif capitals are not difficult to draw, it is the detailing of the lower-case which presents the problems. Gill admitted that his design was modelled on Edward Johnston's London Transport alphabet, with which he had given considerable assistance; but he improved upon it in detail. He kept, and strengthened, the classical proportions, and the eye-glass **g**, and introduced his own favourite curved-tailed **R**. The early drawings differ considerably from the type as cut, and Monotype were responsible for many of the improvements. Indeed, when the drawings of the capitals were first sent to the works in July 1927, Pierpont wrote to Burch, 'I can see nothing in this design to recommend it and much that is objectionable.' He also complained about the descending tails on the **J** and **Q** of a titling fount, but was told to fit them in. Morison left most of the work on the type to be done between Gill and the works, and Gill became

David Saunders, 'The type drawing office' in *Eric Gill: the continuing tradition*, *Monotype Recorder*, New Series 8, 1990.

The Solus type, Series No. 276 was designed by Eric Gill for The Monotype Corporation in 1929.

The type is available in 48-pt display, in the 18-pt and 14-pt, and in this 12-point text size. No italic fount was designed to accompany the roman.

O Lord, how manifold are thy works? in wisdom hast thou made them all: the earth is full of thy riches. So is the great & wide sea also, wherein are things creeping innumerable, both small & great beasts. There go the ships and there is that Leviathan, whom thou hast made to take his pastime therein. These wait all upon thee, that thou

PAGES FROM THE
FOUR GOSPELS

Golden Cockerel Roman (1930).

Gentlemen prefer blondes. Solus was designed and cut in 1929, and was intended for the publications of the Empire Marketing Board, but never used.

It is also surprising that in 1928 he entered into an agreement with Robert Gibbings by which he was to design types exclusively for the Golden Cockerel Press, although the agreement was a friendly one and not rigorously enforced.

Caslon was the standard type face of those private presses that did not design their own, and Gibbings had inherited it when he bought Golden Cockerel in 1924. He soon became unhappy with the italic, and asked Gill to design one to replace it. Very quickly, however, the plan grew to design a completely new face, strong enough in weight to accompany the wood engravings, by Gibbings, Gill himself, Eric Ravilious and others, which were Golden Cockerel's primary interest in the Gibbings years. Although Gill first suggested that Monotype might give Golden Cockerel exclusive rights to Perpetua for five years, and then consulted Morison on the details of the new type, Golden Cockerel Roman was cut by the Caslon foundry under the supervision of Tom Collinge. The drawings were complete in April 1929 and the type finally delivered in January 1930, in two sizes, 14pt

with an italic, and 18pt without. There were also two titlings, a 24pt which was enlarged from the 18pt capitals, and a 36pt for which Gill made new drawings: these latter are the most beautiful capitals he produced.

The Golden Cockerel Roman* is clearly related to Perpetua, but is in many ways a more conventional old face: the angle of stress is greater, and some details, such as the lower case **d**, less idiosyncratic. In its 18pt size it was used for *The four Gospels* (1931), the Golden Cockerel. masterpiece and one of the most magnificent books of the century.

In 1928, the remoteness and difficulty of life at Capel-y-ffin, added to the increasing amount of time Gill had to spend in London, led to his last move, to Pigotts, a farm-house near High Wycombe. In 1930 his youngest daughter Joan married René Hague, who wanted to set up as a printer, and as a result the firm of Hague & Gill was established at Pigotts. For it Gill designed Joanna, begun in March 1930 and first used in his own *Essay on typography*, which came

James Mosley, 'Eric Gill and the Golden Cockerel type', *Matrix* 2, 1982.

For if the sinewy thread my brain lets fall

    Through every part,

Can tie those parts, and make me one of all;

These hairs which upward grew, and strength and art

    Have from a better brain,

Can better do 't; except she meant that I

    By this should know my pain,

As prisoners then are manacled, when they're condemn'd to die.

Nevertheless, as in the first days of printing the printing types were as close imitations as possible to the handwriting which preceded them (for letters are letters and A is A whether you write it by hand or dent it in by metal type), so in the first years of factory production every attempt was made to produce things which looked the same as the things made before. And this was by no means a matter of commercial deceit even if, as some hold, commercial deceit had been the motive of the first printers. A is A whether written or printed, and tables and chairs and all other things are like letters in this respect. They are an accepted convention. A chair for the parlour is recognised as being a certain kind of chair, different from a kitchen chair, different from an office stool. It is not only different in architectural shape, it is different in the kind of decoration which is applied to it. Decoration is what is decorous. The trappings of the drawing-room are indecorous in the kitchen. So a factory-made chair had to conform to the conventions. If it differed in workmanship it

Monotype Joanna (cut 1938, issued 1958).

out the following June.* Although Joanna owes a clear debt to Solus, and although Gill wrote of it as a type without frills, intended to echo the nature of machine production, it was cut and cast by the Caslon foundry, and always hand set at Hague & Gill. However, the business was badly hit by the Depression; the publishers J. M. Dent bought the rights to Joanna in 1938 and commissioned Monotype to cut it for machine composition for their exclusive use. Gill made some changes to the italic for the Monotype cutting, and also introduced italic capitals which had not existed in the foundry version. Joanna was finally issued to the trade in 1958.

In form Joanna has most of the expected Gill features, given a crisp, slab-serifed finish. The italic, extremely condensed and upright, is to all intents and purposes the sloped roman Morison originally wanted for Perpetua. But in general Gill seems in Joanna to have left behind the quirks of Perpetua, and the result is his best type.

In 1932 Gill designed Aries, a privately commissioned type for Fairfax Hall's Stourton Press. Cast at the Caslon foundry, Aries is a condensed roman, which because of its private press usage has been little seen. Then in 1934, for Stephenson Blake, Gill designed his only type consciously intended to fill a perceived gap in the market for advertising types: first called Cunard, but when issued in 1935, twenty-five years after the accession of George V, rechristened Jubilee, it is a rotunda in the tradition of Morris's Troy, with more of the feel of penmanship, but without the verve of Koch's Wallau.

Gill's last roman type, Bunyan, dates from 1934. It was designed for an edition of Sterne's *A sentimental journey* which Hague & Gill printed for George Macy's Limited Editions Club of New York, and is a cross between Joanna and Golden Cockerel Roman. It was cut once again by Caslon, and remained a private type until 1953, when Linotype introduced an adaptation called Pilgrim, first used in a posthumous edition of Gill's *Jerusalem diary*, with an italic based on one which Gill had prepared for Bunyan but never cut. Pilgrim was an extremely successful text face, more comfortable than Perpetua, and deliberately promoted by Linotype as a rival.

To accompany Pilgrim, Linotype commissioned a

Eric Gill, *An essay on typography*, London, Sheed & Ward, 1931. Reissued by Lund Humphries, London and David Godine, Boston, 1988.

¶ The type from which this edition of 'A Sentimental Journey' will be printed is a new 14-pt Roman designed by Eric Gill and cut by H. W. Caslon and Co. Ltd. ¶ The paper has been made by hand by J. Barcham Green and Son, Hayle Mill, Maidstone. ¶ The 8 Illustrations are etched in copper by Denis Tegetmeier. ¶ The size of the book is Demy 4to, about 150 pages. ¶ The binding will be in full linen with gilt top. ¶ The printers are Hague and Gill, High Wycombe, England.

ABCDEFGHIJKLMNOPQRSTUVWXYZ
abcdefghijklmnopqrstuvwxyz
1234567890   1234567890
ABCDEFGHIJKLMNOPQRSTUVWXYZ
abcdefghijklmnopqrstuvwxyz

Bunyan (1934), and Reynolds Stone's Minerva (1954), designed to accompany Linotype's version of Bunyan, called Pilgrim (1953).

display face from the distinguished wood engraver Reynolds Stone (1909–79), which was called Minerva (1954). As a young man, Stone had spent a fortnight working at Pigotts under Gill's instruction, but Gill had said there was nothing he could teach him, and sent him away; certainly, Stone's lettering in wood is unsurpassed, by Gill or anyone else. Nevertheless, Minerva lacks the vigour of Gill's types.

In September 1935 Gill drew for Monotype a stressed sans-serif type with many prophetic qualities: it looked forward to Hermann Zapf's 'serifless roman' Optima of nearly a quarter of a century later. Although it was given a series number (430), and a few trial sorts were cut, it was never issued to the trade.

This completes the catalogue of Gill's types, designed by a man whose principal activities lay elsewhere. He was extraordinarily active, and any one of his occupations could easily have filled an ordinary life. In his writing, and possibly in his engraving, he may have spread himself too thin, though his best works excuse the more routine ones; but his type designs are clear, distinct, and necessary, and among the few which have been appreciated by not just the specialists, but also the general public.

Eric Gill died on 17 November 1940 at Harefield Hospital in Middlesex.

ABCDEFGHIJK
LMNOPQRSTU
VWXYZ & abcdefg
hijklmnopqrstuvwxyz

Alphabets cut in stone by David Kindersley (top) and Will Carter (bottom).

David Kindersley and Will Carter

Only one of Gill's assistants became a type designer. David Kindersley (b. 11 June 1915) worked at Pigotts between 1934 and 1936, at the beginning of his career as a leading stone carver and lettering designer. In the late 1940s he in turn taught letter carving in Cambridge to the printer Will Carter (b.24 September 1912), already mentioned as the designer of the popular jobbing face Monotype Klang. Their discussions about letter forms led in 1955 to an approach to Monotype for the cutting of a private type, which they were designing jointly, for use at Carter's Rampant Lions Press. Stanley Morison had then retired from Monotype, but he had been hoping that the Corporation would commission a type for use in a folio Bible planned by the Cambridge University Press, and offered to cut the Carter/Kindersley design, Octavian, Series 603, for it. The design work, complicated by the usual problems of collaboration, took several years to complete, and the type was issued, in 14pt only, in 1961. The folio Bible project came to nothing, while the cutting of Univers and the switch to filmsetting at Monotype prevented further sizes being cut, but the face was adapted for the Monophoto in 1978.

In Jan van Krimpen's 1955 memorandum to Monotype already referred to, a suggestion was made which bore fruit in Octavian. Van Krimpen criticised the way the Monotype drawing office adjusted the width of letters to fit the Monotype diecase, and suggested that in future scrupulous designers should draw their alphabets from the start according to the various unit widths available, rather than making adjustments later. Carter and Kindersley, in discussion with John Dreyfus at Monotype, followed this suggestion, and much detailed work was done in establishing the framework of the design before a letter was drawn.

Octavian roman is a condensed face; the lower case has a family resemblance to Gill's Aries, but the capitals are more inscriptional, as befits the creation of two stone carvers rather than one. The italic is an independent and handsome face.

Carter's dry transfer alphabet, Dartmouth (1963) for Letraset, had a family resemblance to Octavian, but was much less condensed.

David Kindersley's main interest since Octavian was in the automatic spacing of capital letters. This difficult job was always done optically, if at all, in the metal type era, to standards which varied from one compositor to the next. Kindersley's work in establishing a method for discovering the optical centre of letters, first by photo-electric means and more recently by computer, and taking in lower-case as well as capitals, attempted to do away with rules of thumb.

David Kindersley died on 2 February 1995 and Will Carter on 17 March 2001.

This is the first full showing of 'Monotype' Octavian, Series 603–14, a new roman and italic designed by Will Carter and David Kindersley at Cambridge.

The designers, both letter-carvers and one a printer, have set out to give the established pattern a fresh appraisal, with an eye to close fitting, even colour and a generous x-height. The name Octavian is intended to stress the roman-ness of the design.

Begun in 1955 as a roman, with no general purpose in mind beyond that of creating a type satisfying to the designers, it soon became clear to some others that it had certain desirable characteristics; so the italic and small caps were added. The latter, after the example of Dr Giovanni Mardersteig, are slightly above the x-height.

100 advance copies of this specimen have been printed by Will Carter at the Rampant Lions Press, Cambridge on the occasion of the 165th meeting of the Double Crown Club

Octavian (1961).

Victor Hammer

Victor Hammer (1882–1967) at his work bench. Photograph by Martin Jessee.

Hammer was born on 9 December 1882 in Vienna. At the age of fifteen he was apprenticed to an architect and town planner, and a year later went to study at the Vienna academy of fine arts. His early career was in portraiture, both in oils and tempera, and also in mezzotint, a nowadays little-used intaglio medium he made his own. He continued throughout his life to make portraits in a formal realistic style close to that of the early Renaissance in Germany, as well as painting biblical and allegorical subjects.

Around 1910 he began experimenting with a quill pen and this, together with a developing interest in bookbinding, aroused a passion for the arts of the book which consumed the rest of his life. He soon modelled his own handwritten script on uncials, the form of writing prevalent in Europe between the end of the Roman empire and the time of Charlemagne, in which capital letters began to show signs of change, before the development of the true Carolingian minuscule. He justified this choice on personal and instinctive grounds rather than historical necessity, partly because he felt that the roman and blackletter alphabets had been taken as far as they could go.

After World War I, which he spent first in the army and then as a war artist, Hammer lived in a small house at St Martin im Innkreis in upper Austria, and there in the winter of 1921, a punchcutter called A. Schuricht from Vienna cut the first of his types, Hammer Unziale, which was issued by Klingspor in 1923. Hammer was never satisfied with this type; it uses a high proportion of capital forms, which he was in his later faces progressively to reduce, adding founts of capitals to help the legibility of his last two types. Hammer Unziale is jumpy and unrhythmical, and has not yet achieved the effect of flow which he afterwards likened to a string of pearls. Klingspor

Although Victor Hammer was never a member of the Koch school, he was a close friend of both Rudolf and Paul Koch, and the latter cut his second type. His conception of the holiness of work, and the apprenticeship system, was similar to theirs, although he was a more solitary, less collaborative designer. His dedication to one letter form, the uncial, throughout his life, is remarkable, especially as he was well aware that the dedication was not widely shared. Nevertheless his types are of considerable beauty, especially when printed by himself; they have been used by others not widely but persistently, and have encouraged imitations.*

Victor Hammer, artist and printer, Anvil Press, 1981.

Sebastian Carter, 'Victor Hammer', *Matrix*, 7, 1987.

replaced it in their type repertoire in 1952 after the appearance of American Uncial.

In 1922 Hammer moved to Florence in Italy where he stayed until 1933, though he usually returned to St Martin for the summer months; and in 1923 he met Rudolf Koch for the first time, and formed a strong friendship. In 1926 Rudolf's son Paul, fresh from his work on the capitals of Peter Jessen Schrift, came to work in Florence and cut the punches of Hammer's next type, called Samson since it was used for an edition of Milton's *Samson agonistes* (1931), which was the first book printed by the Stamperia del Santuccio. This press, Hammer's first printing venture, was named after a small carved saint, or *santuccio*, at the doorway of his workshop, and here, using a reconstruction of a wooden hand press, handmade paper specially made by the Magnani mill at Pescia, and his own types, he set out to produce the sort of books he wanted.

After leaving Florence in 1933, Hammer began a period of wandering, to London, Kolbsheim in Alsace, Grundlsee in Austria, and Vienna; and then, after he was forced to leave his post as professor at the Vienna academy in 1939, to America. During this period he continued to print, and for his edition of

ABCDefghijklmnopqRstuvwxyzắő
ắchſfﬅtt1234567890

OF FOLLOWERS AND FRIENDS·
OSTLY FOLLOWERS ARE NOT TO
BE LIKED/LEAST WHILE A
MAN MAKETH HIS TRAINE
LONGER/HEE MAKE HIS
WINGS SHORTER/J RECKON
TO BE COSTLY NOT THEM
ALONE WHICH CHARGE THE
PURSE/BUT WHICH ARE WEARYSOME AND
IMPORTUNE IN SUTES·ORDINARY FOLLOW-
ING OUGHT TO CHALLENGE NO HIGHER CON-
DITIONS THEN COUNTENANCE/RECOM-
MENDATION AND PROTECTION FROM

*Hammer Unziale (1923), and
Samson (1931).*

ABER alle diese nuzBaRen Thiere
Lama aBgerechnet/Jahr
natürliche FReiheit Bewahrt·
von Milch und Käse ist/wie der
Kultur mehlreicher Grasarten/
teristisches Unterscheidungs
Nationen des alten Welttheils·
    Sind daher von diesen einige
nördliche Asien auf die West
Rika übergegangen/und haBen
Bend/den hohen Andesrücken
verfolgt/so muss diese Wande
gen geschehen sein/auf welche
Heerden noch Cerealien den
Ling Begleiten konnten·Sollte
Stamm der Hiongnu/welcher

Hölderlin's *Fragmente des Pindar*, finished in 1935 at Kolbsheim, he used the first type for which he cut the punches himself, having studied the technique of Schuricht and Paul Koch, with remarkable results. If one compares the delicacy and sophistication of the Pindar type with Neuland, the first attempt of that other virtually self-taught punchcutter, Rudolf Koch, it is plain that Koch chose a design in which it would be quite hard to go wrong, whereas Hammer took considerable risks. Pindar was the first of his uncials to have an accompanying fount of roman capitals, and thus marks an important step away from the doctrinaire one-case uncial; but it still kept the capital B form in what one must begin to call the 'lower case', as well as the R, which was never changed. Paul Koch had a fount of Pindar at the Haus zum Fürsteneck, although it was never issued commercially, and in the spring of 1938 the young Hermann Zapf used it for a visiting card, his first piece of printing.

In America, Hammer taught at Wells College in Aurora, New York state, until his retirement in 1948. Here between 1940 and 1943, after an uncompleted fount for American Type Founders, he cut American Uncial, his best known face, in which the forms of the letters are closest to roman – the lower case b is finally

These conclusions will/in a word/become val-
ueless just as soon as this new perception
develops further/and the practice of Kant's
successors of drawing new conclusions
from parts of Kant's conclusions is abandoned. If men had not clung one-sidedly to
the quality of appearance in reality/so
strongly emphasized by Kant/but rather
had tried to raise themselves to the great
free vision which had developed in Kant regarding the relations between the individual and the outer world; if men had been
able to lift themselves to the clear consciousness in which the ordinary opinion of the
outer world is extinguished and replaced/
not by conviction of/but by clear vision of/
the universal dependence of this world upon
the individual/then from this elevation a
wider view would have opened up. Whereas
the following of a single path could not keep
men from losing the way/a constantly rising and developing total view should have
led to progressive illumination of the darkness.— ¶ Not to searching reason but to
broadening/advancing vision it would have
become clear that the boundary which still
limited Kant's horizon was only a delusion

83   and

A page from 'Three fragments
from the posthumous papers of
Conrad Fiedler', Stamperia del
Santuccio (1951), set in
American Uncial (1945).

eva & zeno polycarp alexius quintilian

American Uncial titling (1953), and (right) Andromaque (1959).

decapitalised, though the R remains. The first casting was made by Charles Nussbaumer of the Dearborn Type Foundry in Chicago in 1945 and later ones by Klingspor, and the type was issued commercially in 1952 by Stempel, who had finally absorbed Klingspor, as Neue Hammer Unziale.

Hammer retired from Wells College in 1948, and went to live and work in Lexington, Kentucky where he completed his magnificent edition of Hölderlin's *Gedichte* in American Uncial, and many other books. In 1958 he cut his last type, Andromaque; it is a curious and original cursive uncial with several Greek forms, and was cast, though never released, by Deberny & Peignot in Paris in 1959. Hammer died in Lexington on 10 July 1967.

Victor Hammer's revival of uncial forms prompted others to follow: Goudy's Friar (Village, 1937), Libra by S. H. de Roos (Amsterdam, 1938), Česka Unciala by Oldřich Menhart (Grafotechna, 1948) and Solemnis by Günter Gerhard Lange (Berthold, 1952). The last three are one-case founts, and none overcomes the problems of rhythm and flow with the success of Hammer's.

VORUEBER! ach! VORUEBER!
geh! wilder knochenmann!
Jch bin noch jung! geh! lieber!
und ruehre mich nicht an.

gib deine hand! du schoen und zart gebild!
bin freund und komme nicht zu strafen.
sei gutes muts! ich bin nicht wild!
sollst sanft in meinen armen schlafen!

Stanley Morison

Stanley Morison's* strong personality influenced everyone with whom he came in contact, and his dominant position in English typography from the early 1920s up to his death in 1967 has excited admiration which ranges from the fulsome to the grudging. He corresponded vigorously with many of the leading typographers of his day; he was widely read and widely travelled; and he had a great gift of persuading influential people to do what he wanted. It would be impossible to write about type design in this century without mentioning him, and even though he himself designed only one typeface, and that in a somewhat once removed manner, that typeface was Times New Roman which, although figures are impossible to come by and compare, is arguably the most widely-used roman typeface in the world.

Morison was born on 6 May 1889 in Wanstead in Essex, between London and Epping Forest. The family moved to north London when he was seven or eight, and he always regarded himself a Londoner and a 'townee', so much so that he affected to regard Regent's Park as the country. His father, a travelling salesman of wild habits, deserted the family when Morison was in his mid teens, and, compelled to earn a living, Morison left school and began a series of jobs as first office boy and then clerk. At the same time he took after his strong-minded mother in continuing on a course of self-instruction which embraced philosophy as well as palaeography. From a free-thinking background he moved swiftly towards the influence of the Jesuits and was baptised into the Catholic Church in December 1908. Nonetheless, he always considered himself a rationalist, and this was acknowledged in the epitaph incised on his gravestone: St Thomas's submission to irrefutable proof,

'Quia vidi credidi' – 'Because I have seen I have believed'.

In his spare time he frequented the King's Library at the British Museum, where then as now manuscripts and early printed books were on display, and his nascent interest in book production was fired by the special printing supplement published by *The Times* on 10 September 1912. This influential publication contained both historical surveys and discussions of the work of the contemporary revival of calligraphy led by Edward Johnston and carried on by his pupils Eric Gill, Graily Hewitt and, in Germany, Anna Simons, as well as the work of the Insel Verlag and Count Harry Kessler in Germany and, in America, of Updike, Goudy and Dwiggins.

Amongst the advertisements in the printing supplement, Morison found one for a new monthly magazine of printing, *The Imprint*, whose first number was due to appear the following January.

When it was published, Morison bought it eagerly, and noticed in it an advertisement for an editorial assistant. He was then unhappily employed as a bank clerk, immediately applied to Gerard Meynell, and was accepted, in spite of his lack of qualifications. He contributed one article on liturgical printing, an abiding interest, to the penultimate August issue, but within six months the kindly Meynell, seeing the end of *The Imprint* coming, moved him to another of the family businesses, the Catholic publishers Burns and Oates. Gerard's uncle Wilfred, husband of the poet Alice Meynell, was managing director, and Wilfred's son Francis, then aged twenty-two, two years younger than Morison, was in charge of production. Together, Morison and Meynell produced some excellent trade books, using the talents of the best printers and the work of another recent convert to Catholicism, Eric Gill, whom Morison met here for the first time.

In August 1914 the first world war began. Both Morison and Francis Meynell were conscientious objectors on religious and political grounds, and both

Facing page: Stanley Morison (1889–1967), from a drawing by William Rothenstein, reproduced in 'The Fleuron' 3 (1924).

Nicolas Barker, *Stanley Morison*, London, Macmillan, 1972.

went to prison, Morison first. Meynell was released after a hunger strike, but Morison finished the war growing tomatoes for the government.

In 1916, while Morison was on bail and before his own arrest, Meynell left Burns and Oates. He had disagreed with his father on the question of women's suffrage and pacifism, but had won the support of Mary Dodge, an American heiress, who largely financed George Lansbury's left-wing, anti-war weekly *The Herald*. Meynell now began a new venture, the Pelican Press, as part of *The Herald*'s printing group and using its plant, with the intention of producing well designed work for the socialist cause. There he began to indulge his lifelong passion for printers' flowers, or fleurons, which Morison shared for a while but then renounced; he also bought three new American types, Benton's Cloister and Goudy's Kennerley and Forum titling.

At the end of the war, *The Herald* became a daily paper again, and the extra work took up all Meynell's time: among other things, he organised a celebrated poster campaign for the paper using McKnight Kauffer's famous Vorticist design of birds in flight. He therefore brought Morison in to supervise the day-to-day design work at the Pelican Press, though he himself kept a vigilant eye on what was going on there. The press now had Monotype machinery at its disposal, and Meynell had installed four faces, Old Face, Venetian, Imprint, and Plantin.

Morison's work at the Pelican Press, though it greatly widened his typographical experience, was very much under the influence of Meynell, and his time there came to an abrupt end in the autumn of 1920. Francis Meynell had been indulging in some cloak-and-dagger adventures which involved smuggling Russian diamonds into Britain to be sold in aid of *The Daily Herald*. George Lansbury knew nothing of the escapade, and when rumours began to circulate he denied them; when the story broke, Meynell had to resign from *The Herald*. He was still able to return to the Pelican Press, so that Morison was forced to look for another job.

He found one almost immediately, although it meant an unwelcome move out of London. In 1920 Charles W. Hobson, a Manchester advertising agent of enlightened tastes, decided to set up his own printing firm at nearby Heaton Mersey, to be called the Cloister Press. As general manager he engaged an outstanding printer, Walter Lewis (1878–1960), who had met Morison, approved of what he found, and recommended him to Hobson as the typographer they needed.

Morison went to the Cloister Press in May 1921, and for the first time found himself in sole charge of design; he was able to order type, including ATF Garamond, and issued a series of fine type specimens as well as indulging his penchant for grandiloquent copywriting. At the same time, Manchester bored him, and he made many expeditions to London, increasingly after the Cloister Press opened a London office at the start of 1922. It was now that he first met Oliver Simon, whom Harold Curwen had recently taken on at the Curwen Press. With Simon, Francis Meynell, Holbrook Jackson and Bernard Newdigate he formed the Fleuron Society, a modest publishing venture aimed at producing a book a year to show that books set and printed by machine could look as well as the productions of the private presses. Although the society broke up almost immediately because of Newdigate's disagreement with its basic aims, it had two important progeny: Meynell resolved to start his own publishing house to produce fine books using commercial book printers, which was called the Nonesuch Press, and Simon and Morison decided to work together on a typographical journal, *The Fleuron*. Simon edited the first four numbers, which came out between 1923 and 1925. They were printed at the Curwen Press, and appeared as substantial bound books. After Simon's money ran out, Morison took over the editorship, Cambridge University Press printed the volumes, the contents swelled and the pace of publication slowed down until the last number, the seventh, came out in 1930. In its combination of scholarly articles and lavish production, it is highly unlikely that *The Fleuron* will ever be equalled.

At the end of 1922 the Cloister Press, in spite of the admiration its work had aroused, went into liquidation. Walter Lewis went on to be University Printer at Cambridge, where he later brought Morison in as typographical adviser, and Morison began his new career as a freelance consultant, which off and on he stayed for the rest of his life. It was at this time that he began his formal relationship with Monotype, which was described in an earlier chapter, and with it his role as impresario of new faces. He did not turn to the design of type himself until the end of the decade.

Stanley Morison first came into contact with the management of *The Times* in 1929, when Edmund Hopkinson of their advertising department visited W. I. Burch of the Monotype Corporation to ask for a full-page advertisement in their forthcoming printing supplement. It was a curious coincidence that just as a similar supplement brought out by the paper in 1912 first interested Morison in printing, so this new one turned his attention towards his major achievement. Morison happened to be with Burch when *The Times* man called, and when he heard it explained to Burch as an added inducement that the paper could handle all the design and setting of the advertisement, he thumped the table, and suggested paying *The Times* a thousand pounds just to keep their compositors away from it. He then treated the dazed Hopkinson to a lecture on the iniquities of his paper's degraded design. Hopkinson reported back, and in August 1929 Morison was invited by William Lints Smith, the general manager, to discuss the appearance of what was then widely considered to be the best newspaper in the world.

Morison's interest in newspapers was a relatively recent one, and sprang from his researches into the work of John Bell. He immediately compiled a report on *The Times*'s types, beginning with their advertisement setting, and banished many old foundry faces. He also wrote an article for the printing supplement itself, which appeared on 29 October, on 'Newspaper types', in which he addressed the question of newspaper text setting. The following year, the text of the supplement was issued in book form, printed at *The Times*'s own private printing office, and set in Baskerville, one of the types undergoing trials as a possible face for the paper. The same printing office also produced Morison's most astonishing salvo in this, or any other, campaign for typographical reform: in June 1930 he prepared a unique copy (except that he kept a duplicate for himself) of a newspaper-sized folio, *The typography of The Times*, with forty-two full-sized reproductions of the paper from its earliest days to the present, bound in, and the text set in the largest possible composition size of Monotype Bembo, 24pt, for which the matrices were specially made. This book was presented to *The Times*'s chief proprietor, John J. Astor (later Lord Astor of Hever), who had bought Lord Northcliffe's shares after his death, and under whom the paper had returned to its normal dignified self after the turmoil of the Northcliffe interlude. It was a characteristic element in Morison's strategy: the authoritative historical survey culminating in the inevitable acceptance of his own solution.

[IONIC NO. 5] Prior to 1922 there is no recorded instance of a definitive study of the printing and reading qualities of small body types in relation to the specialized technique of newspaper printing processes. – C. H. Griffith

[EXCELSIOR] The essence of type design, as I get it now, is to hit a middle ground between mechanical exactitude and the flow of a written hand – suggesting some of the said flow and variety, but controlling it so the letter can be repeated.

Dear Griffith: Yessir. Keep away from news, sir. Anything else, sir? – W. A. Dwiggins

The Linotype Legibility Group. Ionic (1922), Excelsior (1931).

In March 1930 Ionic appeared in England in the restyled *Daily Herald* when it was taken over by Odhams, in conjunction with the practice, unusual in newspapers, of setting all its headings in one type family, Cheltenham. Most papers, including *The Times* before Morison, set their headings in a variety of styles chosen more for their suitability for a particular story than in accordance with any overall scheme.

This strategy was never pursued elsewhere in such a grand manner.

English newspapers at that time were mostly set in various evolutions of the modern face, which with faster running presses and consequently thinner inks were beginning to look grey on the page or, if the inking was increased, blotchy. Since almost all papers were set on Linotype or Intertype line-casters, it was natural that the seach for alternative faces should have been led by these companies. In 1922, C. H. Griffith of Mergenthaler Linotype brought out Ionic, a redrawn English nineteenth-century jobbing Egyptian, which became the first of the so-called 'Legibility Group' of faces which Griffith designed, being followed by Excelsior (1931) and others in the USA. Ionic took its almost monoline English model and gave it some extra stress to create a more lively look on the page, a process which went further with Excelsior; and although Morison dismissed it as making 'only slight progress' in the United States, it was in fact extremely successful very quickly, and was one of the most influential newspaper faces of all time. Its appeal was as much in its sturdy unpretentious appearance as in its practical merits of resistance to brutal stereotyping and fast press speeds, and these qualities were characteristic of the Legibility Group in general.*

Morison's analysis of desirable newspaper founts had, as John Dreyfus has pointed out, a strong bias towards book faces, especially Monotype ones.* He had begun his campaign at *The Times* by pointing out how badly the paper's design and printing compared with current standards of book production, and he impressed the management with a legibility study carried out by the Medical Research Council on Government printing, which was almost exclusively in Monotype faces. There was also the historical accident that some Monotype machines had been installed at *The Times* under Northcliffe, for reasons which remain mysterious, but in this it was almost unique among newspaper offices. The result was that after Morison's somewhat curt appraisal of Linotype Ionic and Intertype Ideal, all further trials were made with Monotype faces.

The trials were made both of the types in their freshly cast state, and after being subjected to stereotyping and fast running on the presses, to see how the image stood up to hard wear. Nevertheless, standards of presswork at Printing House Square were higher, and kinder to type, than elsewhere in the newspaper industry. *The Times* had an influential but not very large readership, so that runs were short, the machines ran slower, and a better than usual quality of newsprint was used.

The early experiments were made with Monotype Plantin, Baskerville and Perpetua, but by October 1930 Morison had so successfully played on the corporate pride of *The Times*'s management that he persuaded Lints Smith to set up a committee under the assistant editor R. M. Barrington-Ward (later editor) to consider the design of a new typeface for the paper. In a note to Lints Smith, Morison wrote, 'These new types, or type, since with minute variations they would all be of the same root design, would be

Allen Hutt, *The changing newspaper*, London, Gordon Fraser, 1973.

John Dreyfus, 'The evolution of Times New Roman', *The Penrose annual*, 1973.

selected *not* with a view to their being of striking, but rather of subtle allure. The face would be chosen for its effectiveness as much as for its "beauty"; the criteria of the effectiveness being a maximum of clearness in impression and a maximum of legibility to the reader who neither knows not cares, one way or the other, for the mysteries of typographical minutiae.' To put his case to the committee, Morison compiled a memorandum which was printed in an edition of twenty-five, and the first meeting had to be deferred for the members to digest it. In it Morison once again reviewed the historical background, but left the choices open. His conclusions, though they sound delightfully vague as befits a memo for a committee, actually define quite closely the type that eventually emerged: 'The new types proposed for *The Times* will tend towards the "modern", though the body of the letter will be more or less old-face in appearance.'

Two, if not three possible models were kept under review. Baskerville was dropped fairly soon as being too round and wasteful of space; trial cuttings were actually made by Monotype of Perpetua on a smaller body with reduced extenders; but Plantin remained the front runner.

At a meeting on 28 January 1931, the committee

PBRS

PBRS

Diagram comparing Plantin (above) with Times capitals.

instructed Morison to prepare specimens of 'modernised Plantin' and 'thickened Perpetua', and expressed a preference for Plantin. Morison followed the preference, since Perpetua suffered from the same disadvantage as Baskerville, of not being condensed enough. According to his own account, in *A tally of types* (1953), he sketched the outlines of the revised letters and gave them to Victor Lardent, a skilled draughtsman in *The Times*'s publicity department at Printing House Square, who prepared finished drawings. Lardent's story, told before he died in 1968 to James Moran, was that Morison gave him a photograph of 'a page of a book printed by Plantin' as a model. Most probably both accounts are true, and Morison gave Lardent photographic enlargements and also drew examples of the kind of adaptations he wanted made to them. Lardent was reportedly bitter that his contribution to the type was insufficiently recognised; but he was unfamiliar with type design, and Morison, who could sketch, but not make finished drawings, used him as an extra hand to put the image in his mind's eye down on paper, before taking the drawings to Monotype to be turned into working patterns. Even so, over a thousand punches had to be recut by the works before the type was right, an unusually high number.

It is characteristic of Morison that although he was producing a work-horse type, and had been empowered by *The Times* committee to adapt Plantin, he went back even beyond the model used by Monotype for Plantin in 1913. As we have seen, this was the type used for the 1905 *Index characterum* of the Plantin-Moretus Museum, Granjon's Gros Cicero (large face 12pt); the Moretus family, who bought this type after 1652, introduced wrong-fount sorts over the years, which were copied in the Monotype recutting. Nicolas Barker, in his life of Morison, demonstrated convincingly that he returned to the pure form of the Granjon type, probably in some sixteenth-century source.

Three sizes of Series 327 were cut in specimen form and at a committee meeting on 4 June 1931 the new type was recommended for acceptance. However, it was not put into use for another sixteen months, first because of obdurate opposition from some members of *The Times* board to Morison's other proposal, to romanise the mast-head, then set in an inline blackletter; then because of the 1931 general election; and then because of more argument about the mast-head, which was finally decided in Morison's

ABCDEFGHIJKLMNOPQ
abcdefghijklmnopqrstuvwxyz
ABCDEFGHIJKLMNOPQ
abcdefghijklmnopqrstuvwxyz
£1234567890

*Monotype Times New Roman
(1932).*

favour. *The Times* set in its new type finally came on the streets on 3 October 1932. Only one retired army officer complained.

Times is the most successful type of this century, and outsold its nearest rival in the Monotype list by very nearly two to one. Nevertheless, it was not exactly a Monotype face which other companies followed, since the original work had been done by Morison and Lardent as agents of *The Times*, and the paper reserved the use of the type for twelve months after its first use. Monotype did the development work, and printed a special issue of *The Monotype recorder* for September-October 1932 to celebrate its completion. *The Times* used Linotype and Intertype slug machines in harness with Monotypes, and indeed did much of its straight text setting on Linotypes, reserving Monotypes for complicated tabular work and advertise-

ment setting, as well as some text. The slug setters were fully equipped with the new face when the paper went to bed on 2 October.

Times New Roman was an ambitious undertaking for a newspaper at the beginning of the Depression, and its success was a tribute to the management's nerve and Morison's persuasive powers. The type exemplifies the way the best modern faces, though based on historical models, can leave their origins behind them and look completely of their age. Although it has strength of character, that character is not intrusive: as Morison put it, 'it has the merit of not looking as if it had been designed by somebody in particular'.

Morison's later years were spent on typographical scholarship and his unceasing quest for the cause of changes in letter forms. He died on 11 October 1967.

Newspaper types after Times

Times New Roman's curious genesis as a newspaper type in being developed by a single-letter composing machine manufacturer for principal use on line-casters led to one particular drawback. It was not only a condensed face, but was also closely set, in accordance with Morison's experience in book typography. Close setting had the disadvantage on slug casters that the matrix walls were very thin and wore out quickly, allowing the molten type metal to squirt up between them and make ugly vertical lines between the letters. Expensive matrix replacements were required more often than with other faces, and wider-set versions of the design were introduced, to Morison's disgust. Moreover, as press speeds rose to keep pace with rising circulation, Times was found to stand up less well to image degradation than other types designed with deeper understanding of newspaper conditions. As a result Times's greatest successes were in magazine and book setting rather than in the newspapers for which it had been intended.

But it was no longer true that a design had to be unlovely, or at best conspicuously unpretentious, to be a good newspaper face.* English Linotype's designer Walter Tracy (born 14 February 1914) showed with Jubilee (1953) that a rugged face suitable for newspaper conditions could retain some of the distinction of an old-face. Then in Telegraph Modern (1969), designed for *The Daily Telegraph*, he took the modern type style which had been largely exiled from newspapers by the Legibility Group and its followers, and Times, and restored it to its place in the repertoire by basing his design on Firmin Didot's 1784 type, and strengthening it for use under tougher printing conditions. In 1972 his expertise in the field was recognised when he was asked by *The Times* to design a new face to replace Morison's. Times Europa was a chunky and resilient type of considerable

sophistication,but itself was overtaken by technology when newspapers finally made the change from hot-metal composition and printing from stereos to computer setting and printing by offset lithography. Under the new conditions, *The Times* reprieved its eponymous face until 1991, when Aurobind Patel designed Times Millennium. This bouncy restructuring of the parent face illustrates well the perils of over-design in newspaper faces, in which the virtues of solid ordinariness should not be underrated or patronised. Walter Tracy died on 28 April 1995.

Contemporary with Times Europa, in the United States a new face was introduced, designed by Matthew Carter. Carter's work is described later, but

Jeff Level, 'Face to face with the daily news', *Fine Print*, 15, 1, 1989.

ABCDEFGHIJKLMNOPQR

12345 STUVWXYZ 67890

abcdefghijklmnopqrstuvwxyz

[LINOTYPE MODERN] The designer should not attempt to produce a "universal" type. Instead he should design for a particular class of newspaper and satisfy its particular requirements. So what seemed to be needed for modern newspaper work was a type in which the profiles of the letters are so clear in the original state that they can survive the destructive effect of production and still present a crisp appearance at the end.
– Walter Tracy

[TIMES EUROPA] Because of the particularly resolute adherence of the English newspaper industry to hot metal setting, particularly on Fleet Street, English Linotype under the direction of Walter Tracy went on producing designs for metal types into the 1970s.
– Sebastian Carter

[OLYMPIAN] It is astonishing to see how well Olympian survives so many constrictions, emerging as a subtly drawn, slightly old-face descendant of Ionic, Excelsior, and Corona, with better fit and rhythm, a distinction which, for all their merits, they lack.
– Sebastian Carter

Left and centre: three types by Walter Tracy. Top left: Jubilee (1953). Lower left: Telegraph Modern (1969). Centre: Times Europa (1972). Right: Matthew Carter's Olympian (1970).

Olympian, as a response to the specific demands made by newspapers, belongs here. Many American papers in the last decades of hot-metal setting made use of the teletypesetting (TTS) system, a primitive precursor of the on-line computerised composition of today. By TTS, syndicated material was sent to many papers by wire, producing punched tape which could be used on specially adapted line casters, so that rekeying was not required. The types used had to conform to a rigid system of unit widths which did not expand as the type size increased, so that with a general tendency in the United States for body sizes to get larger, the Legibility Group faces became excessively condensed, resulting in what Carter called a 'picket fence' effect. His solution was to design a narrow type with an old-face flavour, with the stress at a slight angle, which lessened the sense of crush. It is astonishing how well Olympian survives its

constriction, emerging as a spacious and subtly drawn face with excellent fit and rhythm.

Olympian straddled the ponderous shift of the newspaper industry from hot-metal to photocomposition by being produced for both methods. Subsequent faces have been primarily designed for the new technology, though the conservatism of the newspaper world has meant that designs such as Robin Nicholas's Nimrod (1980) for Monotype, a variation on Century, have predominated. Attempts by Gerard Unger and others to extend the repertoire with new varieties of type style have so far had only limited success. Only in the field of headline faces has this conservatism been less marked: the display type for *The Daily Telegraph* (1989–90), designed by Shelley Winter (born 1959), the first bold version in association with Walter Tracy, the regular on her own, was a welcome development.

Hans (Giovanni) Mardersteig

Mardersteig was the greatest scholar-printer of modern times, whose researches into Renaissance printing and lettering were published in magnificent books, printed at his Officina Bodoni in hand-set types on a hand press, together with literary classics and modern poetry. His typography was austere and immaculate, though never without a touch of sensuousness, and the types he used were often, though not exclusively, designed by himself. After World War II he also ran a commercial printing works, the Stamperia Valdonega, side by side with the Officina, using Monotype composing equipment and powered presses to produce work for the general market to standards equivalent to those of his fine work. And although originally hand cut and intended for private press work, his best type, Dante, was recut by Monotype and remains one of their most faithful adaptations.

Hans Mardersteig* was born in Weimar on 8 January 1892. His father was a lawyer, but his family was artistic, one grandfather having been a painter and the other a sculptor, and among the many visitors to the house was Count Kessler, who later set up his Cranach Press in the town. At university, Mardersteig studied law, and took his doctorate in it; but he attended some classes in art history, which was his abiding interest. After World War I, which he spent as a civilian because of tuberculosis, he joined the Leipzig publishing firm of Kurt Wolff, and with two colleagues started up and edited the art magazine *Genius* in 1919. *Genius* was well produced and well received, but short lived: Mardersteig's health forced

John Barr, *The Officina Bodoni, Montagnola-Verona, books printed by Giovanni Mardersteig on the hand-press, 1923–1977,* London, The British Library, 1978.

Giovanni Mardersteig, *The Officina Bodoni, an account of the work of a hand-press, 1923–1977,* edited and translated by Hans Schmoller, Verona, Edizioni Valdonega, 1980.

*Hans (Giovanni) Mardersteig
(1892–1977).*

him to leave Germany for the better climate of Switzerland, and it closed down. But his work on it had convinced him that his ideal books could be produced only by a private press of the classic kind, and he established his own at Montagnola near Lugano, calling it the Officina Bodoni. The name was taken from the types first used, which were those cut for the great Italian printer Giambattista Bodoni (1740-1813), one of the pioneers of modern face. Mardersteig did not find any of the recent Bodoni recuttings to his taste, since they were unsubtly and mechanically redrawn, and so he obtained permission from the Italian government for new castings to be made from the original matrices stored in the museum at Parma, where Bodoni had worked.

The early work of the Officina, which began publishing in 1923, consisted of a broad and multilingual selection of European classics, but Mardersteig's interest in Renaissance writing books soon brought him into contact with Stanley Morison in England, and their collaboration began with a series of books on calligraphy manuals. The first was a facsimile of Arrighi's 1522 *Operina* (1926), and Morison's introduction was set in Frederic Warde's new Arrighi italic, which Warde brought him when he arrived for a brief spell at the Officina. It was the first time Mardersteig had used a type not by Bodoni, and from then on many other faces were added to the Officina's repertoire, many of them Monotype faces cast in harder foundry metal for repeated hand setting. Also, Mardersteig began to concern himself with type design. His first experience was a simple liaison job. The Italian writer and bibliophile Francesco Pastonchi was planning a series of classics which Mardersteig was to print; he had supervised the design by Eduardo Cotti of a type for the purpose, and Mardersteig put him in touch with Morison so that Monotype could cut it.

Mardersteig printed a specimen of the type (1928), which was called after its initiator and became a house type at Mondadori, who were printing the series. Pastonchi also introduced him to Arnoldo Mondadori, who was organising a competition for the design and printing of an edition of the complete works of the poet Gabriele d'Annunzio, which Mardersteig won. The commission meant a move to the Mondadori headquarters in Verona, which coincided with Mardersteig's wishes, since his health had been greatly improved by his sojourn in Montagnola, and he wanted to be near the Italian libraries for his

Pour avoir trop aime votre bande inegale,
Muses, qui defiez, ce dites vous, le temps,
J'ai les yeux tout battus, la face toute pale,
Le chef grison et chauve, et je n'ai que

*Pour avoir trop aime votre bande inegale
Muses qui defiez ce dites vous le temps
J'ai les yeux tout battus la face toute pale*

researches. So in 1927 the Officina Bodoni moved to Verona (where, under the direction of Mardersteig's son Martino, it still is), and Mardersteig Italianised his name to Giovanni.

The labour of printing the forty-nine d'Annunzio volumes, all hand-set in Bodoni, consumed nearly ten years, and drastically reduced the publication of other editions. Towards the end, in 1935, Mardersteig took a break, and went to Scotland to advise the publishing house of William Collins on the printing at their Clear-Type Press in Glasgow. On asking to see their special 'clear type', and being told they had none, he set about designing one based on the Scotch roman of the Wilson foundry, which inspired Dwiggins's Caledonia three years later. The type was called Fontana, cut by Monotype, and released to the trade in 1961, but although attractive, it was too like Baskerville to be a commercial success.

His first essays in type design, however, began earlier. During the printing of the d'Annunzio edition it was found that some of the hair-line serifs of Bodoni's types were breaking during the long run on Mondadori's cylinder presses, to which the formes were transferred after the short hand-press run. Some sorts were needed with the same appearance as

DE
DIVINA
PROPORTIONE
DI
LUCA PACIOLI

MILANO · MCMLVI

*Title page from the Officina
Bodoni edition of Pacioli's
'De divina proportione' (1956),
showing Pacioli titling (1955).*

Foundry Dante, cut by Charles Malin (1955).

Bodoni's, but a slightly less delicate angle of cut. A skilled punchcutter was needed to make them, and Mardersteig was put in touch with Charles Malin, the Parisian craftsman who also cut some alternative sorts for Warde's Arrighi, and the foundry version of Gill's Perpetua. Malin became an occasional house punchcutter to the Officina Bodoni, working in Verona from time to time in a workshop set up for him. At Morison's suggestion Mardersteig commissioned him in 1929 to cut a new version of Francesco Griffo's *De Aetna* type (1495), which had recently been used as the model of Monotype Bembo. Morison had found that, as so often, the drawing office had tidied the design up too much for his taste, and was interested to see what Malin would make of it. The Griffo type was not used until 1939, and is a slightly amateurish performance by comparison with the later Dante. By the time it appeared, Mardersteig and Malin had collaborated on a more original face, Zeno (1935-6), inspired by a manuscript roman script by Arrighi. It is a dark, powerful face which was shown to splendid effect in Mardersteig's superb printing.

In 1932, while he was working on the early designs for Zeno, Mardersteig designed his first type for Monotype, Series 347, which was called after its creator, and also given the name Zarotto. It was a curiously crabbed face with a distinct whiff of Pastonchi about it; it had an odd stunted **k** with no ascender in either roman or italic. An advance fount was used to print the Mardersteigs' wedding announcement in April 1932, but though further modifications were made, both Mardersteig and Monotype judged it unsatisfactory, and it was never issued.

World War II curtailed, though it did not prevent, the work of the Officina, and after the war Mardersteig

gloria musarum, vulgo gratissimus auctor,
hic iacet, et fama pulsat utrumque polum.
Qui loca defunctis gladiis regnumque gemellis
distribuit, laycis rhetoricisque modis;
pascua Pyeriis demum resonabat avenis:
Amtropos heu letum livida rupit opus.
Huic ingrata tulit tristem Florentia fructum,
exilium, vati patria cruda suo;
quem pia Guidonis gremio Ravenna Novelli
gaudet honorati continuisse ducis.
Mille trecentenis ter septem Numinis annis
ad sua septembris ydibus astra redit.

XVIII

O ingrata patria, quale dementia, quale trascutaggine ti teneva, quando tu il tuo carissimo cittadino, il tuo benefactore precipuo, il tuo unico poeta con crudeltà disusata

was much concerned with the setting up of his general printing works, the Stamperia Valdonega. But nevertheless, between 1946 and 1952 he supervised Malin's cutting of the punches of Dante,* the supreme achievement of their collaboration. Although the *De Aetna* type may be glimpsed as its inspiration, and Griffo may be seen as a dry run for it, Dante is a fruitier type than either predecessor, and is in no sense a copy. Its robust elegance was well brought out in Mardersteig's printing: he first used it in an edition of Boccaccio's *Trattatello in laude di Dante* (1955), hence the name. A titling fount based on a constructed set of capitals by Pacioli, and called after him, was added to the family, and was the last work completed by Malin before his death in 1955.

Nevertheless, although conceived as a private type, Dante was at once seen to be suitable for wider application, and Morison suggested it be cut by Monotype. Morison was retiring from his position as adviser to the Corporation, and the work was overseen by his successor John Dreyfus, mostly at the Monotype works in Frankfurt, since the English

Zeno (1935-6).

E rat autem homo ex phari
mine, princeps Iudaeor
nocte et dixit ei: Rabbi,
nisti magister, nemo enim pot
quae tu facis, nisi fuerit Deu
Iesus, et dixit ei: Amen, amen

John Dreyfus, 'The Dante types', *Fine print*, 11, 4, 1985.

WHEN JOBS HAVE TYPE SIZES FIXED QUICKLY
THE MARGINS OF ERROR WILL WIDEN UNLESS
When jobs have type sizes fixed quickly
the margins of error will widen unless all
the determining calculations are based on
When jobs have their type sizes fixed quickly
the margins of error will widen unless all the
ABCDEFGHIJKLMNOPQRSTUVWXYZ *A*

THIS CLAIM IS QUITE VALID AND JUST ARE EXPECTING THE FULL PAYMENT ABCDEFGHIJKLMNOPQRSTUVWXYZ

Monotype Dante (1957), with its titling.

factory was over-burdened with non-roman scripts for the newly independent Commonwealth countries. Mardersteig made detailed criticisms of the trial sizes, but the work went through far more smoothly than Van Krimpen's Spectrum had done at Salfords shortly before. For the new semi-bold, Dreyfus had a few trial sorts cut by hand to establish details of weight and serif formation. (The punchcutter was Matthew Carter, who had trained at Enschedé with Rädisch – see p.170.) The only drawings Mardersteig made, which were of details of this semi-bold, were more geometric than even the Salfords drawing office would have produced, but in fact Monotype Dante is gracefully faithful to the subtleties of Malin's cutting.

After Malin's death, Mardersteig produced no more types (although some extra sorts for foundry Dante italic were cut by Ruggero Olivieri of Milan), but his other activities flourished more than before. In the aftermath of the war he had feared that the production of fine editions was a thing of the past, but he now, at the age many men retire, continued a series of books which for the beauty of their design, the craftsmanship of their printing and the scholarship of their contents will probably never be equalled. Giovanni Mardersteig, who had been banished to the top of a Swiss mountain at the age of thirty because of his health, decided that, in his own words, who wishes to be cured will be cured, and went on working until some months before his death on 27 December 1977, a few days before his eighty-sixth birthday.

Jan van Krimpen

Jan van Krimpen (1892–1958).
Engraving by S. L. Hartz.

Of the handful of designers of this century who have breathed new life into the classical letter forms, Jan van Krimpen* of Holland was the most austerely restrained. Although he studied and practised calligraphy, and had the most beautiful italic handwriting, his drawn lettering is not as calligraphic as Zapf's or Dwiggins's, and nor are his types. For, as he wrote, 'type and calligraphy are two essentially different things and . . . calligraphic influence in type should be no more than an underlying force'. His faces are increasingly refined recreations of letter forms inherited from the long development of European type design. Van Krimpen was a man whose culture was both wide and deep, but his work was far from being merely antiquarian; it was a constant process of reinterpretation, producing not new versions of old letters but fresh steps forward on the path of a living tradition.

Van Krimpen spent nearly all his working life at the great Haarlem printing house of Joh. Enschedé en Zonen. Founded at the beginning of the eighteenth century and still in the hands of the same family, the firm grew by absorption, adding a bookshop in 1724, a newspaper, the *Oprechte Haarlemsche Courant*, in 1737, and a type foundry in 1743. The punchcutters J. M. Fleischman and J. F. Rosart both worked there in the eighteenth century, and the acquisition of Ploos van Amstel's foundry in 1799 added to the growing collection of historic punches and types in the firm's possession, which now constitutes one of the greatest collections of such materials in the world. Fleischman's music type, cut for use in the Dutch Reformed Church psalters which were then the mainstay of

John Dreyfus, *The work of Jan van Krimpen, an illustrated record in honour of his sixtieth birthday*, London, Sylvan Press, 1952.

Jan van Krimpen, *On designing and devising type*, New York, The Typophiles, 1960. (Distributed in Britain by Sylvan Press.)

Enschedé's business, were considered so excellently done as to defy imitation, and this led to government contracts for banknotes and stamps, for which the firm became, and remains, renowned.

It was as a designer of lettering for stamps that the young Van Krimpen came to the notice of Dr Johannes Enschedé, the head of the firm, in 1923. A special issue of stamps was being prepared for the silver jubilee of Queen Wilhelmina, and the artist Van Konijnenburg was having trouble with the lettering. Van Krimpen's friend Van Royen was general secretary to the Dutch Post Office, and suggested he be asked to help.

Van Krimpen had been born in Gouda on 12 January 1892, and was then thirty-one, a freelance designer and calligrapher of literary interests, who had studied art at the Academy of Art in The Hague, and been deeply influenced by Edward Johnston's *Writing & Illuminating, & Lettering*. His friendship with poets had led to several small editions of their work, carefully designed and well printed by commercial firms; Van Krimpen published these himself, although in one case the royalties he paid amounted to one suit of civilian clothes for a poet who could not be demobilised from the army because he was too poor to buy them.

ABCDE

Typografien är för övrigt en säll kaleidoskop alltid te sig olika. Den gång häpnat över de relativt många

the quick brown fox over the lazy dog

Types by S. H. de Roos. Egmont Inline titling and Egmont italic (1933), and Libra (1938).

At the same time, Enschedé were looking for a designer. While the security printing side of the business was doing well, the letterpress and book printing side was at a low ebb, although the quality and scope of the typographic collections had been made known in Dr Charles Enschedé's monumental work* showing the firm's type holdings, much of it proofed from the original type or type recast from the original matrices. For Enschedé maintained their foundry, and were fortunate in having an excellent punchcutter in P. H. Rädisch, a German trained in Leipzig; and when Dr Enschedé and Van Krimpen met at the end of 1923 at the quincentenary celebrations of the work of Laurens Janszoon Coster (Haarlem's own rival to Gutenberg as the inventor of printing), Van Krimpen was asked to design a new type for the firm, to be cut by Rädisch and cast at the foundry.

The chief Dutch type designer at the time was S.H. de Roos (1877-1962), who had drawn Holländsche Mediäval (1912), the Zilver private press type (1915), and Erasmus Mediäval (1923), all cast by the Amsterdam type foundry. Van Krimpen criticised his types for self-consciousness and an excess of drawing, qualities which became even more prominent in his later faces Egmont (1933) and De Roos (1947), though they are less bothersome in his uncial Libra (1938).

But even in his first type Van Krimpen showed an unfussy clarity of form. He seemed to be so well prepared for Enschedé's commission that he quickly produced a finished drawing of the type he had in mind. This was approved, final drawings were made, and the type was hurried through the works, since Van Royen had suggested it be used in the official printing for the Dutch entries in the international exhibition of industrial design to be held in Paris in 1925. Because of this, the type was called after the Roman name for Paris, Lutetia.

Lutetia is a thoroughly assured first type, and established the collaboration of Van Krimpen with Rädisch as an almost perfect balance of inspiration and skill, both qualities being evident on both sides. Stanley Morison, reviewing the new face in *The*

Charles Enschedé, *Les fonderies de charactères et leur matériel dans les Pays-Bas du XVe au XIXe siècle*, Haarlem, Enschedé, 1908. (English edition edited and translated by Harry Carter as *Typefoundries in the Netherlands from the fifteenth to the nineteenth century*, Enschedé, 1978.)

Idem mon premier testament mon ciel brisé

Par-dessus les paysages et les ports de mauvaise mine

Idem les pavés échaudés et creusés de roues de buggys

THE GOSPEL ACCORDING TO SAINT JOHN
In the beginning was the Word, and the Word was with God, and the Word
was God. The same was in the beginning with God. All things were made by

ABCDEFGHIJKLMN
OPQRSTUVWXYZ

Lutetia (1925), roman, italic and open capitals.

Fleuron 6 (1928), recalled that the roman made a stir when it appeared because it was not copying an old design but was freshly drawn from reasoned canons of design. This was truer of Van Krimpen's later types: with the perspective of sixty years the roman seems to us to have something in common with the Doves type, particularly in the sloped cross-bar of the **e** and the exaggeratedly kicked-up-and-over dot on the **i** and **j**. These and other details were noticed by the American printer Porter Garnett when he ordered the type in 1929 for his Laboratory Press, and Van Krimpen co-operated with him in making revisions to several of the sorts, levelling the **e**'s cross-bar, bringing home the dots, and modifying the proportions of several other letters.

When in 1928 Burch and Morison asked Van Krimpen if he would allow Lutetia to be adapted for the Monotype, he at first refused, doubting that a version could be made that would satisfy him. However, as Burch offered him an unlimited power of veto over the trial cuttings, he reluctantly agreed, and in the end was as pleased as he was ever likely to be with the results. Of the type in general, he wrote characteristically darkly: '*Après coup* I think I knew what I wanted; and I am sure that, after a short time, I knew that I had wanted a number of things I did not want any longer'. The revisions that Garnett made went some way towards satisfying Van Krimpen's second thoughts, but he resisted making extensive changes to a type already in general use. The Monotype version was cut before the Garnett revisions, though the level-bar e was offered as a special sort.

If the unrevised roman looks a little quaint to today's eyes, the same cannot be said of the beautiful and original italic, of which Morison wrote, 'Perhaps the only serious criticism that need be made here is that Lutetia italic is so good in itself that it cannot combine, with the proper self-effacement, with its roman'. Walter Tracy, in his critique of Van Krimpen, considered this a serious flaw, though it has not prevented successful use of the italic on its own for poetry. A handsome set of inline capitals was also made by Rädisch, working with a graver on existing sorts under Van Krimpen's supervision, and called Lutetia Open.

After the success of Lutetia, Van Krimpen was asked by Enschedé to serve as their house designer, and he stayed with them until his retirement. Apart from types, he designed many books, beginning with handsome and literate specimen books of the firm's

SIGNATURE

THE GOSPEL
ACCORDING TO ST JOHN

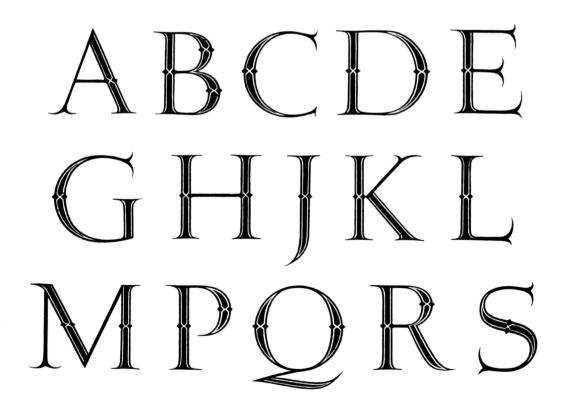

A B C D E
G H J K L
M P Q R S

Van Krimpen's lettering for 'Signature' (1947), Open Capitals (1928), and initials for the Curwen Press (1929).

type holdings, and continuing with many fine editions whose publishers were attracted by Enschedé's growing reputation. He also kept a friendly eye on other people's designs going through the press, such as the Nonesuch Press Homer for Francis Meynell. Frederic Warde visited Haarlem in 1927, and this led to commissions for the Pleiade and Pegasus Press publications in Paris, and later for the Limited Editions Club of New York. Van Krimpen also designed a lovely set of decorated capitals for Oliver Simon at the Curwen Press (1929), and an immaculate headline for Simon's periodical *Signature* (1947).

Meanwhile, his type designing work continued. He drew a Greek type, Antigone (1927), and the elegant Open Capitals, in both roman and Greek alphabets, which rendered in type the forms he had used often and well in his hand lettering. In passing, he later mentioned the remarkably similar Columna titling, designed in 1952 by the Swiss Max Caflisch and issued by Bauer. Neither Caflisch nor his foundry had seen Van Krimpen's capitals, and the similarity may be explained by a shared debt to Hubner's *Exempla scripturae epigraphicae latinae*.

Van Krimpen's next roman type had a most unusual *raison d'être*. Enschedé's 1768 specimen book showed a roman and italic, called Kleine Text No.2, attributed to the celebrated Dutch type designer Christoffel van Dijck (1606-69), although Van Krimpen came later to doubt the attribution when advising Monotype on the cutting of their Van Dijck. Punches survived for only the italic, and so in 1928 Van Krimpen produced a roman to accompany it. The search for a name for this type, helped along by a bottle of good Burgundy, yielded the name Romanée; it followed the seventeenth-century model quite closely, but so to speak Van-Krimpenised it. As a result, the roman and italic, though an interesting partnership, have different flavours, so that they were not often used together. Twenty years later, in 1949, Van Krimpen added an italic of his own design, which proved to be his last type: Romanée italic is a development of Spectrum, described below, but is even more upright in slant, so that it has no capitals of its own but uses roman ones, and has a somewhat obtrusive *f*, modelled on Arrighi.

In 1931, Van Krimpen produced his most successful face so far, called Romulus at the suggestion of Beatrice Warde. He smoothed out the quirkiness of Lutetia, made the proportions attractively four-square and the stress vertical, and drew a sinewy letter which

THE GOSPEL ACCORDING TO SAINT JOHN
In the beginning was the Word, & the Word was with God, & the Word was God. The same was in the beginning with God. All things were made by him; & without him was not any thing made that was made. In him was life; and the life was the light of men. And the light shineth in darkness; and the darkness comprehended it not.

THE GOSPEL ACCORDING TO SAINT JOHN

In the beginning was the Word, and the Word was with God, and the Word was God. The same was in the beginning with God. All things were made by him; and without him was not any thing made that was made. In him was life; and the life was the light of men. And the light shineth in darkness; and the darkness comprehended it not.

Light. That was the true Light, which lighteth every man that cometh into the world. He was in the world, and the world was made by him, and the world knew him not. He came unto his own, and his own received him not. But as many as received him, to them gave he power to become the sons of God, even to them that believe on his name: Which were born, not of blood, nor

Romanée (1928), and Romanée italic (1949).

THE GOSPEL ACCORDING TO SAINT JOHN
In the beginning was the Word, and the Word was with God,
and the Word was God. The same was in the beginning with God.
All things were made by him; & without him was not any thing

THE GOSPEL ACCORDING TO SAINT JOHN
In the beginning was the Word, and the Word was with God,
and the Word was God. The same was in the beginning with
God. All things were made by him; & without him was not any

OPEN KAPITALEN

&

Cancelleresca Bastarda

looks as fresh today as when it first appeared. The accompanying 'italic' has been criticised. Van Krimpen was influenced by his friendship with Stanley Morison, and particularly by Morison's essay 'Towards an ideal italic', in giving Romulus not a cursive italic but a sloped roman. This, thought A. F. Johnson writing in *Signature* (1940), 'may be logical, but results in a stiff and monotonous letter'. It is also less than wholly successful in its intended purpose of textual articulation since it is not quite distinct enough from the roman, and Van Krimpen later repented of it. The type seems nevertheless to have survived these criticisms with ease, and had it not been supplanted by Spectrum, would have been its author's major achievement.

Conversations with Morison on script types led to an alternative italic being designed, a hybrid version of chancery italic called at Morison's suggestion 'Cancelleresca Bastarda', a remarkably elaborate fount with a wide range of ligatures, swashes and alternative sorts. Because the calligraphic flourishes on the extenders needed more space than the relation of x- to body height of Romulus roman allowed, Cancelleresca Bastarda was cast on a larger body than the roman by a proportion of five to four, and Van Krimpen devised an elaborate and impractical scheme

of leading so that the types would line up when used together, which ensured that they virtually never were. Likewise the type's ungainly name, for which we must blame Morison, has helped make it a rarity.

Throughout the 1930s, Van Krimpen continued to design additions to the Romulus family, making it the first type intended primarily for book work to be so supplied: previous type families had been developed for jobbing work. To provide for the needs of learned printing, Romulus was given a companion Greek (less successful than Antigone), as well as various bolds and semi-bolds, and even a family of sans-serifs. Romulus was adapted for Monotype composition during the 1930s.

In 1939 Monotype cut Haarlemmer, which was designed for economy reasons to fit an existing die-case layout. The roman appeared more condensed and heavier than the italic, and Van Krimpen did not consider the type a success.

During World War II, Dutch printing went incommunicado as far as Britain and the United States were concerned. Under the occupation Van Krimpen and two colleagues, W. G. Hellinga and A. A. Balkema, produced fine work under the imprint of The Five-pound Press, called after the maximum

THE COMPLETE ROMAN ALPHABET

ABCDEFGHIJKLMNOPQRSTUVWXYZ
ÆŒ&
abcdefghijklmnopqrstuvwxyzæœfiflffifflff
1234567890   .,:;-!?''(*†‡§[£$ƒ—
1234567890 (F990)   / (S121)   % (S8416)
ÁÀÄÂÅÃÉÈËÊÍÌÏÎÓÒÖÔØÕÚÙÜÛÇÑ
áàäâåãéèëêíìïîóòöôøõúùüûçñ
ß ij fbfhfkfj

THE COMPLETE ITALIC ALPHABET

ABCDEFGHIJKLMNOPQRSTUVWXYZ
ÆŒ&
abcdefghijklmnopqrstuvwxyzæœfiflffifflff
1234567890   .,:;!?''([§   1234567890 (F991)

weight of paper allowed for unlicensed printing by the occupying forces. But these difficult years saw the birth of Van Krimpen's best type, designed originally for the Spectrum publishing company of Utrecht between 1941 and 1943, and later issued by Monotype in 1955. Drawn originally as a Bible type, demanding economy of width, large x-height and unobtrusive capitals, Spectrum transcends such constraints apparently effortlessly: there is no feeling of narrowness, but rather of comfortable fit and flow. The contrast between thicks and thins is increased from the earlier types, the stress is very slightly slanted, and the italic likewise. The beautiful capitals, especially in the larger sizes, retain much of the elegance of their designer's hand-drawn lettering.

Apart from a specialised Bible type, Sheldon, produced for the Oxford University Press in 1947, the Romanée italic already referred to, and a set of Romulus Open Capitals made in the same way as Lutetia Open, Spectrum was Van Krimpen's last type. He died in Haarlem on 20 October 1958.

Van Krimpen was a harsh critic of the work of others, and himself. It is hard to believe from reading his own short account of his work, *On designing and devising type*, that he was happy with any of his designs, and he is tantalisingly inclined drily to quote other opinions of his types rather than to give his own. An example of his idea of high praise is his conclusion on the Monotype version of Lutetia, about which he initially had misgivings: 'as a Monotype performance the rendering is quite good'. A warmer view of the austere passion which informed his work can be seen when he wrote, 'Of letters, however, – as Frederic Warde called them "the arbitrary signs of the alphabet" – it would be saying much too little to declare that I was interested in them: they have fascinated me from the very first time I saw a picture of a Roman inscription. And I can only explain this because of their being nothing but meaning: make them "pictures of things" instead of the "things" they are, according to Eric Gill, and their meaning is lost and they become just as stupid as ornament that has lost its sense.'

'Nothing but meaning' might be taken as Van Krimpen's motto, both in his type and his typography, which was without ornament, and derived its monumental effect from perfectly judged proportions and spacing. His drawn lettering was sensuous and occasionally adorned with flourishes which grew organically out of the letters, and I would place him with Oliver Simon and Jan Tschichold as the best of the formal classical typographers of this century.

Yet, as Walter Tracy* has pointed out, Van Krimpen's types, although original, refined and beautiful, have never been very widely used. Tracy's explanation is partly that each was flawed in some way: Lutetia had some quirky characters and an over-assertive italic, Romanée a too curious genesis, Romulus no usable italic at all, and Spectrum bad figures. Van Krimpen's figures were always poor, but could be replaced. The italic problems are more intractable, but do not affect Spectrum. Tracy makes a more serious point, that 'Van Krimpen thought like an artist, not a designer': that his types were approaches to an ideal in his head, and not a response to the practical needs of the printing industry. Van Krimpen himself admitted this, in an article on Dutch typography in *The Fleuron* 7 (1930), though he did not see it as a fault. 'I do not believe that it is possible to sit down and design a type to order,' he wrote, 'as it is attempted in Germany. The type which originates in such a manner may be tolerable in advertisements, but it cannot satisfy the requirements which experience demands for book printing. A satisfactory book type must be present in the mind and at the finger tips of the designer before he sits down to draw. Such a type does not require any added "personality" – either it is essentially personal or it is not.'

Van Krimpen's types were essentially personal, and for all their beauty they have given way to faces which may be less admirable, but work better. I hope their eclipse is a temporary one.

Walter Tracy, 'The types of Jan van Krimpen', *Fine print*, 7, 2–3, 1981.

S. L. Hartz

Juliana (1952–8).

The friendly qualities to some extent lacking in Van Krimpen's types are more conspicuous in those of his colleague and successor at Enschedé, S. L. Hartz (born on 28 January 1912). Primarily a portrait engraver, and stamp and banknote designer, Hartz has nevertheless produced typefaces of unaffected distinction. Emergo, drawn for Enschedé (1948–53) shows a lingering debt to Van Krimpen which he left behind when he came to design the excellent and underrated Juliana (1952–8) for English Linotype. His redrawing of a French engraver's letterform, Molé Foliate (1960) for Stephenson Blake, is exceptionally attractive.

ABCDEFGHIJKLMNOPQRSTUVWXYZ
abcdefghijklmnopqrstuvwxyz
1234567890
ABCDEFGHIJKLMNOPQRSTUVWXYZ
ABCDEFGHIJKLMNOPQRSTUVWXYZ
abcdefghijklmnopqrstuvwxyz
1234567890

Molé Foliate (1960).

Georg Trump

The life and work of Georg Trump is in many ways the epitome of the German type designer's: his professional career was spent in teaching, and he worked in his spare time for a foundry who energetically promoted his types, and produced a wide range of faces as they were needed, from smartened up Egyptians through a sans-serif and several romans, to scripts. Indeed, the Weber foundry of Stuttgart, who issued all but his first two types, had little need for a house designer, since he drew virtually all the range that they needed to offer.

That his types amount to more than the miracles of professionalism this would suggest is due to their calligraphic liveliness and beauty of form. This is natural enough in his favourite genre, the script, of which he drew rather more variations than one would have thought necessary, but even in types where freedom of form is usually suppressed, such as the Egyptian, his pen kept the letters dancing.

Trump* was born on 10 July 1896, in Brettheim, near Schwäbisch Hall in Baden-Württemberg. His ancestors had been farmers and brewers, and something of their hard-working nature was transmitted to Trump, who spent much of his energies in teaching rather than in the painting and designing which were his first love. At the age of sixteen he went to the school of arts and crafts at Stuttgart, but his artistic training was interrupted by World War I. He joined the army, and did not return until late 1919, with the rank of Lieutenant and several decorations; moreover, this was not the end of his military service, for he was of the generation who were old enough to fight in the first world war and still young enough to fight again in the second.

After World War I, Trump returned to the Stuttgart school, where he was fortunate in finding an inspiring teacher. Professor F. H. Ernst Schneidler

Vita activa, Georg Trump, Bilder, Schriften, und Schriftbilder, Munich, Typographische Gesellschaft, 1967.

(1882-1956) was later the designer of two well-known types, Schneidler Mediäval (1936) with its italic Amalthea issued in the year of his death, and Legend (1937), both cut by Bauer; but he also influenced the development of type design through his school and its pupils, who included Imre Reiner and Walter Brudi as well as Trump. A cornerstone of his teaching was that other graphic disciplines should be followed alongside lettering, and each would benefit the other. This certainly has remained the case with Reiner (1900-89), who was a highly distinguished wood-engraver as well as the designer of types such as Corvinus, and a bevy of scripts such as Matura (1938), Stradivarius (1945) and Pepita (1959). Trump too remained a talented illustrator, although his major work was in type.

After spending the years 1923-6 designing ceramics in southern Italy, Trump returned to Germany to start a graphics department in the school of arts and crafts in Bielefeld, in Westphalia, which rapidly established its own style and attracted attention. An exhibition in Cologne of the department's work in 1928 was noticed by Paul Renner (1878-1956), the designer of Futura, whose Meisterschule für Deutschlands Buchdrucker (advanced

Fashions change, and each
tastes. That is to say, of the
WHICH THE ARTIST CAN

HIJKLMNOPQRST
abcdefghijklmnopqrstuvwxyz
1234567890

Theodor Heuss

Das Buch
ist der Bote, der zum Gespräch
einlädt. Wir wissen: das gilt schon unter uns.

AABBCDDEEFGHIJ
OPQRRSSTTUVWX
abcdefghijklmnopqrstuvwxyz

school of book printing) had recently been established in Munich. He invited Trump to come to Munich in 1929 to teach lettering and typography, alongside the younger, and then considerably more radical, Jan Tschichold. The teaching of the school was outstanding, despite the harsh economic climate of the time, and was combined with much creative work by the staff. Renner was busy designing Futura, and Trump began work on his first faces, both for the Berthold foundry in Berlin: City (1931) was a mécane Egyptian taken to its ugly limits, much less attractive than the later Monotype Rockwell (1933), and Trump Deutsch (1935) was a blackletter. Meanwhile, Trump was appointed director of the school of arts and crafts in Berlin, to which he was able to devote his energies for only a brief period. For in 1933, with the rise of Hitler, Renner was dismissed from the Munich school, since the 'new typography' was now considered subversive. Renner, anxious that the directorship should not go to a Nazi appointee, persuaded Trump to take it on, and Trump thereby undertook the diplomatic and administrative burden of steering the school through the difficult years which followed. Under these circumstances it is surprising that he managed to design any typefaces at

ABCDEFGHIJKLMNOPQ
RSTUVWXYZ   ÄÖÜ
abcdefghijklmnopqrſstuvwxyz &

ABCDEFGHIJKLMNOPQRSTUV
WXYZÇÄÖÜ   1234567890
abcdefghijklmnopqrstuvwxyz

ABCDEFGHIJKLMNOPQRST
UVWXYZ ÄÖÜ ÆŒÇ $£
abcdefghijklmnopqrstuvwxyz&

Trump Deutsch (1935), City
(1931), Schadow (1937–45),
and Forum II (1952).

ABCDEFGHIJKLMN
OPQRSTUVWXYZ Ç

ABCDEFGHIJKLMNOPQRSTUVWXYZ

abcddefggghijklmnopqrstuvwxyz äöü chckß

ABCDEFGHIJKLMNOPQRSTUVWXYZ

abcdefghijklmnopqrstuvwxyz &»«

ABCDEFGHIJKLMNOPQ

abcdefghijklmnopqrstuvwxyz &

Above: Delphin (1951), Amati (1953) and Codex (1955). Right: Signum.

all, but he began his lifelong association with the C. E. Weber foundry in Stuttgart with the Schadow family (1937-45), a far more assured and attractive performance than City, which begins to show Trump's qualities of precision mixed with flair. The shaded capitals designed later for the family in two weights and called Forum I and II (1948-52) should not be confused with Goudy's capitals of the same name.

At the outbreak of World War II, Trump was again called up into the army, served as a company commander, and was wounded in the stomach during the last days of the war. Apart from the pain of his wound, the problem which faced him on his return was daunting. The Munich school had been almost completely destroyed by bombing in January 1944; rebuilding at a time of general shortages was slow; and the administration had to be reorganised as well. Nonetheless, Trump continued to produce typefaces: after the somewhat nondescript condensed modern face Amati (1951) he began work on a series of faces which owed their inspiration to his calligraphic skill and the lingering influence of Schneidler: the beautiful free italic Delphin, in two weights I and II (1951-5), Codex (1953), a roughly brush-formed roman, Palomba (1955), a chunky script close to Schneidler's

Signum

ABCDEFGHIJ

abcdefgghijkl

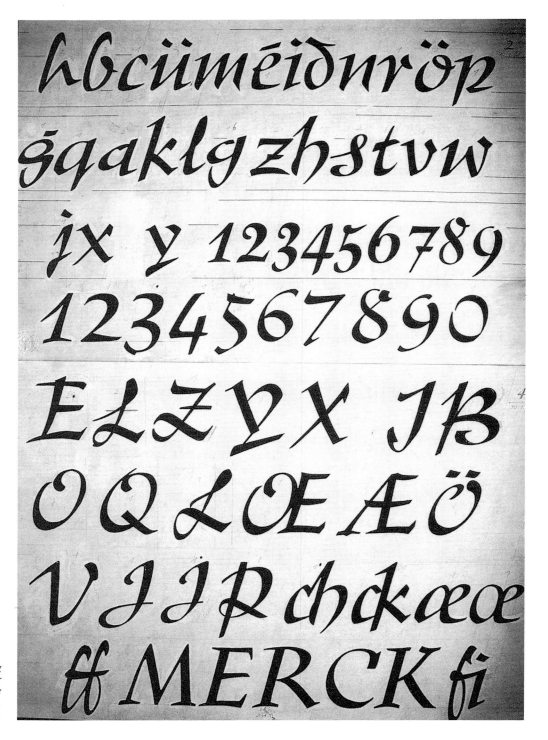

Georg Trump's drawing for a script type, Jaguar (1964). By courtesy of the Klingspor Museum, Offenbach. Photograph by Michael Harvey.

ABCDEFGHIJKLMNOPQRST
abcdefghijklmnopqrstuvwxyz &

ABCDEFGHIJKLMNOPQRST
abcdefghijklmnopqrstuvwxyz &

ABCDEFGHIJKLM

Above: Trump Mediäval (1954–60) and its decorated titling Trump Gravur. Right: A linocut by Georg Trump.

Legend, and the less successful, rather jumpy Time-Script (1956). At the same time he drew the completely uncalligraphic sans-serif Signum (1955).

Trump was able to produce more faces in the mid-1950s because in 1953 he resigned from the Munich school because of his war wound. In the peace and quiet of retirement he completed the designs already listed, and also his masterpiece, the Trump Mediäval family (1954-60), a vigorous and assured roman in several weights, with handsome shaded capitals called Trump-Gravur. Trump Mediäval manages to look original, harmonious and natural, and has been as useful in display work as it has been in book printing since Linotype cut it for mechanical composition.

Trump's last faces were a return to script, Jaguar (1964) and a redrawn old face, Mauritius (1968), which is good-looking but unoriginal compared with what had gone before.

Trump's last years were spent amidst increasing recognition, particularly in the United States, where his faces were highly popular. He died on 21 December 1985.

Joseph Blumenthal

Among the designers who appear in this book, there are very few who also managed general printing businesses. In many ways this is surprising, since such work makes one familiar with a wide range of types in daily use and, consequently, especially aware of what faces actually need to be designed. But the pressure of daily life leaves too little time for the more reflective labour of perfecting letter forms, and one of the few printers who have done so, Joseph Blumenthal,* produced his Emerson type during a sabbatical in Europe which he took after the temporary closure of his business.

Blumenthal was born in New York on 4 October 1897, the son of a German immigrant, who had prospered enough to send his three children to college: Blumenthal went to Cornell for one year before enlisting when America joined World War I in 1917. On his demobilisation he joined his father's business, but in 1924 he decided to follow his preference for the world of books, and got a job as a traveller for Ben Huebsch, who later founded the Viking Press. At this time he first became aware of the ability of fine printing to dignify great literature. He noticed in particular the work of Francis Meynell at the Nonesuch Press, of Bruce Rogers, and Updike. It is noteworthy that all these three produced their fine work not from private presses but at commercial workshops operating at the height of their powers; and of the three it was not Meynell the publisher nor Rogers the virtuoso designer that Blumenthal emulated, but Updike the master printer. However, Updike confessed that he could not set a line of type, whereas Blumethal ran his business from the shop floor.

After working with a few leading printers, including

Joseph Blumenthal, *Typographic years, a printer's journey through a half-century, 1925–1975,* New York, Frederic C. Beil, 1982. (Distributed in Britain by Hurtwood, Westerham.)

Rudge (where Bruce Rogers occasionally worked in the studio above the composing room, so that Blumenthal could claim that he had worked directly under Rogers), he set up his own workshop, the Spiral Press, in 1926, printing jobbing work for publishers and museums, all impeccably designed and printed, and the occasional book: his editions of Robert Frost's poetry for Random House led Frost to describe himself as the best-printed poet in America.

In 1930, with business badly affected by the Depression, Blumenthal sold his stock and machinery, but not the name Spiral, and went to Europe to travel, and also to design his own typeface. He made his drawings, and went to the Bauer foundry in Frankfurt, where the hand punchcutter Louis Hoell cut a 14pt from them. After several sets of smoke-proofs and refinement of the punches, Blumenthal was satisfied, and trial founts were cast by Bauer and proofed at the Bremer Press.

This foundry version of the type, first called Spiral, had no italic; but from Germany Blumenthal went on to England, where Stanley Morison offered to cut the type for Monotype composition, and for the Monotype version (1936) an italic was designed.

Emerson was not as successful in its Monotype cutting as it deserved to be, ranking fortieth among their text faces between Mardersteig's Fontana and Goudy Modern, for it is a strongly drawn and original face of a maturity remarkable in a first and only type. It was best used by Blumenthal himself, both in the brief period when the Spiral Press was working with a hand-press at Croton Falls up the Hudson River, and when he returned to New York as a general printer in 1934. Blumenthal closed the Press in 1971 and devoted himself to writing on typography and to mounting exhibitions, the most magnificent being 'The art of the printed book' at the Pierpont Morgan Library in New York in 1973. He died on 11 July 1990.

Fashions change, and each succeeding generation has its own tastes. That is to say, of the infinite variety of combinations which the artist can make of nature's ASPECTS, SOME GIVE GREAT PLEASURE TO

By that time the great green slope that rises away from the farmhouse garden is touched with shadow, and by the afternoon it lies wholly in the shade. Strollers from THE NEIGHBOURING TOWN SIT UNDER

Robert Hunter Middleton

Like Morris Benton before him, Middleton* was a modest man who spent his working life designing for one manufacturer, in his case the Ludlow Typograph Company of Chicago; he was also their design director, and made largely on his own the decisions that were needed about what faces to cut to keep up with a market which was hungry for type. Middleton and Ludlow mostly kept to the paths trodden by other manufacturers, but the faces they produced were of very high quality.

The Ludlow machine cast solid line slugs, but it worked from hand set brass matrices, and was used almost exclusively for advertising display work and newspaper headlines. One particular characteristic was that it sometimes used matrices slanted at an angle of seventeen degrees from the vertical, so that its italics gave the appearance of being kerned without in fact being so.

Middleton was born near Glasgow in Scotland on 6 May 1898, and emigrated to the United States at the age of ten, when his father went to manage a coal mine in Alabama. A few years later the family moved to Illinois, and Middleton went to the Chicago Art Institute with the intention of becoming a painter. However, he soon came under the sway of Ernst F. Detterer, a teacher greatly influenced by the European private press movement, who had studied briefly with Edward Johnston, and now set up a new curriculum at the Institute devoted to the printing arts. Detterer had been commissioned by the Ludlow Company, then only seventeen years old, to design a type using the same Jenson model that the other foundries had followed, with such faces as Benton's Cloister for ATF, after the example set by the private presses. Although Detterer took as his model the same book, Jenson's *Eusebius*, as Rogers had used for

Robert Hunter Middleton, the man and his letters, eight essays on his life and career, edited by Bruce Beck, Chicago, Caxton Club, 1985.

Centaur, and employed the same engraver, Robert Wiebking, his face, called Eusebius (1924) was far closer to the older Cloister. The young Middleton collaborated on the roman, designed the italic on his own, and so impressed Detterer with his abilities that the latter recommended him for a job with Ludlow. He began there in 1923, became director of type design in 1933, and retired in 1971; during that time he produced nearly a hundred faces.

The Ludlow machine was relatively cheap, and easy to operate, and was widely used, especially after its faces became known for their quality, in small shops which could not afford a Linotype. Huge numbers of matrices were needed, and Middleton was greatly helped to begin with by Robert Wiebking, who not only made punches and matrices but had designed his own pantographic machine for doing so, and taught him much about the technical requirements of matrices for practical everyday types.

The types Middleton produced were for the most part handsome workhorse faces which followed current fashion: Ludlow Black (1924) was modelled on Oswald Cooper's Black (1921) for Barnhart Brothers & Spindle, and Cameo (1927) was an inline roman like Tiemann's Narziss for Klingspor (1921).

Right: Eusebius (1924), the
roman designed by Ernst Detterer
with Middleton, the italic and
semi-bold by Middleton;
Delphian Open Title (1928).
Below: Record Gothic
(1927–61), and Tempo (1930).

ABCDEFGHIJ
abcdefghijklmno
ABCDEFGHIJK
abcdefghijklmnopqr
ABCDEFGHIJ
abcdefghijklmn

RHM

ABCDEFGHIJKLMNOPQRSTUVWXYZ&
abcdefghijklmnopqrstuvwxyz
1234567890$

ABCDEFGHIJKLMNOPQRSTUVWXY
abcdefghijklmnopqrstuvwxyz
1234567890

ABCDEFGHIJKLMNOPQRSTUVWXYZ
abcdefghijklmnopqrstuvwxyz

RENDERS THE LUDLOW
system particularly worthy of the

ABCDEFGHIJK
abcdefghijklm
ABCDEFGHIJ
abcdefghijkl
ABCDEFGHIJKLMNO
abcdefghijklmnop

Two sans-serif families, Record Gothic and Tempo, were cut sandwich fashion: Record, an excellent version of earlier German faces such as Venus and Akzidenz (Standard), was begun in 1927, but the cutting of the series was interrupted by Tempo (1930), modelled on the newer sans-serifs like Futura. Then, after World War II, with the return to the older style typified by Helvetica, designed by Max Miedinger for the Haas foundry of Basel in 1957, the Record family was completed. Middleton also produced a Garamond (1929), a mécane Egyptian Karnak (1931), and a Bodoni (1936); a vertically stressed sans-serif called Radiant (1938), a chunky one called Samson (1940), and a shadowed one called Umbra (1932), closely modelled on the Berthold foundry's Plastica (1929), as was Gill Shadow (1936). Middleton's Eden (1934) was very similar to Imre Reiner's Corvinus for Bauer (also 1934). He also produced many scripts, Mayfair (1932), Mandate (1934), Coronet (1937), Admiral (1953), Formal (1956), Florentine (1956), and Wave (1962), to satisfy a seemingly endless demand on the part of type users for this curious genre.

Middleton's most handsome display type was Delphian Open Title (1928), and in 1929 he designed the interesting 'serifless roman' Stellar, which while not being a conspicuous success foreshadowed in some respects Hermann Zapf's Optima of thirty years later.

Middleton was a highly respected craftsman, who in his spare time printed the wood-engravings of Thomas Bewick to a standard never achieved in Bewick's lifetime and contributed greatly to the revival of interest in the English artist in recent years. He died on 3 August 1985.

Jan Tschichold

Jan Tschichold (1902–74) in 1962. Photograph by Frank Bollinger.

Like Bruce Rogers, Tschichold was primarily a book designer who designed a few typefaces, one of which is well known. Like Rogers, too, he was a perfectionist, who made exquisite layouts, and worked in a variety of styles. But he was quite unlike him in the way he proclaimed his beliefs. Rogers on the whole kept his theories about his work to himself, for, as he pointed out, 'If you do that you can change them as often as you like and no one is the wiser'. Tschichold by contrast underwent two dramatic conversions in his career, and accompanied each with vigorous propaganda which condemned the style he had left behind. Yet his work was always immaculate, and even in his 'new typography' phase was distinguished by a fastidiousness not always shared by his contemporaries. As Ruari McLean* has observed, he was the only typographer of the modern movement whose training was not in architecture or the fine arts but in calligraphy, so that his feeling for letterforms was never completely suppressed.

Jan Tschichold was born on 2 April 1902 in the celebrated printing city of Leipzig, the son of a signwriter. He was interested in lettering from an early age, and much impressed at the age of twelve by the big printing trade fair BUGRA, which was reported by Bernard Newdigate as showing more signs of the influence of Edward Johnston in Leipzig than could be noticed in England. After a spell at a training college, Tschichold went to the Leipzig academy of graphic art and book crafts, whose director was the well-known type designer, Walter Tiemann. His professor Hermann Delitsch was a good teacher of calligraphy who encouraged his antiquarian researches, and his early work was a heady blend of Italianate and blackletter traditions. Tiemann, who appointed him an instructor in 1921,

Ruari McLean, *Jan Tschichold, typographer*, London, Lund Humphries, 1975. (Published in the USA by David Godine, Boston.)

Hand-lettered advertisement by Tschichold for a Leipzig trade fair (1922).

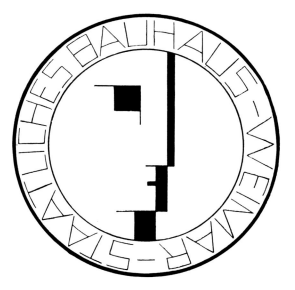

The Bauhaus seal, designed by Oskar Schlemmer (1922).

printers, and particularly by the Russian Suprematists, the Constructivists, and the Dutch De Stijl group. The early Bauhaus prospectuses by Feininger and Itten were Expressionist *jeux d'ésprit*, but with the arrival in March 1923 of the Hungarian graphic artist Lazlo Moholy-Nagy (1895-1946), the Bauhaus style as it is remembered today was introduced: rigidly rectilinear, using heavy sans-serif types and rules. This was the style of the publicity material for the 1923 exhibition, which so impressed Jan Tschichold.

The Bauhaus typographers were fortunate that many German printers were already equipped with well-designed sans-serif types (as opposed to virtually no well-designed romans). Sans-serif faces had first appeared in England, in a Caslon foundry specimen book of 1816, and by the end of the century were widely used for publicity printing in Britain, the United States and Germany: even in the nineteenth century its no-frills appearance was taken as especially suitable for countries in the vanguard of the machine age. By the first decade of the twentieth century, all the major foundries had families of sans-serifs, sometimes called Grotesque (or just 'Grot') in Britain, always called Grotesk in Germany, and confusingly named Gothic in the United States, and

designed for the Klingspor foundry, and Tschichold made a pilgrimage to Offenbach to meet Rudolf Koch, whose influence is perceptible in his work of the period.

However, in 1923 there occurred his first major conversion, which made him renounce everything he had so far done. He visited the first big exhibition of the Bauhaus at Weimar.

The Bauhaus was established by Walter Gropius at the capital of the new German Republic in 1919, by combining two existing schools of art in the city. Gropius was an architect, a pupil of Peter Behrens, and had already designed a handful of pioneering buildings before his army service in World War I; but although the new school's chief purpose was to train architects and industrial designers to abandon their classical training and rethink the structure and function of everything from a house to a chair, the teaching was very broadly based. Many of the staff were painters: Lyonel Feininger, Paul Klee and Wassily Kandinsky all taught there, and the basic drawing and design courses were immensely influential. The typographical ideas which were soon put into practice in the Bauhaus's publications were given impetus by the work of artists and poets rather than

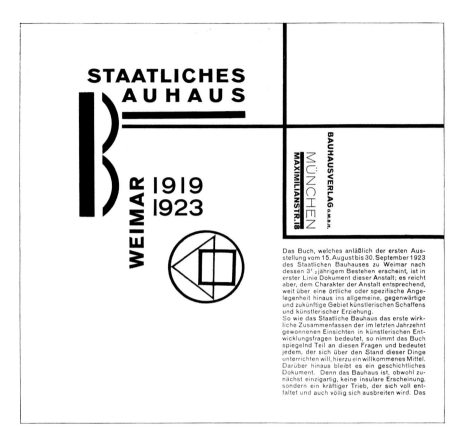

STAATLICHES
BAUHAUS

WEIMAR 1919 1923

BAUHAUSVERLAG G.M.B.H.
MÜNCHEN
MAXIMILIANSTR. 18

Das Buch, welches anläßlich der ersten Aus-
stellung vom 15. August bis 30. September 1923
des Staatlichen Bauhauses zu Weimar nach
dessen 3½ jährigem Bestehen erscheint, ist in
erster Linie Dokument dieser Anstalt; es reicht
aber, dem Charakter der Anstalt entsprechend,
weit über eine örtliche oder spezifische Ange-
legenheit hinaus ins allgemeine, gegenwärtige
und zukünftige Gebiet künstlerischen Schaffens
und künstlerischer Erziehung.
So wie das Staatliche Bauhaus das erste wirk-
liche Zusammenfassen der im letzten Jahrzehnt
gewonnenen Einsichten in künstlerischer Ent-
wicklungsfragen bedeutet, so nimmt das Buch
spiegelnd Teil an diesen Fragen und bedeutet
jedem, der sich über den Stand dieser Dinge
unterrichten will, hierzu ein willkommenes Mittel.
Darüber hinaus bleibt es ein geschichtliches
Dokument. Denn das Bauhaus ist, obwohl zu-
nächst einzigartig, keine insulare Erscheinung,
sondern ein kräftiger Trieb, der sich voll ent-
faltet und auch völlig sich ausbreiten wird. Das

*Prospectus designed by Lazlo
Moholy-Nagy for the
commemorative book of the 1923
Bauhaus exhibition.*

Antique in France. ATF issued Franklin, designed by Morris Benton (1904-13), Bauer the Venus family (1907-1927) and Berthold the Akzidenz/Standard group from 1896 on. There were many others, but it was the last two families that were mostly used by the Bauhaus typographers and then by Tschichold. What was new in their work was the almost exclusive use of a type style which had up to then been used as one among many, and the explicitly ideological choice of sans-serif as a type 'of our time'.

The Bauhaus delighted many observers, but horrified many more, particularly locally. A change of state government in Thuringia brought local hostility to a head, and in the spring of 1925 the Bauhaus moved to the more welcoming city of Dessau and the celebrated new building which Gropius designed for it. Here typography was taught by the Austrian Herbert Bayer (1900–85), who had been a pupil and assistant of Moholy-Nagy's. Bayer, following the theories of Walter Porstmann's *Sprache und Schrift* (1920), now formulated the much disputed and reviled doctrine of setting text without capitals, which became school policy. Early Bauhaus displayed typography had been almost all in capitals; Bayer now took the theory one step further. His design for a single-alphabet type (1925) is distinctly inelegant, while Tschichold's better looking one (1926-9) is ruined by its fidgety seagull **e**. Neither was cut. In one of the oddest cross-fertilisations in cultural history, a student from the Bauhaus went in the early 1930s to work with Victor Hammer in Florence, whose single-alphabet uncial types derived from a very different tradition. He did not stay very long.

Nor did the Bauhaus. Gropius resigned as director in 1928 (together with Moholy-Nagy, Marcel Breuer and Bayer) and, after a brief interregnum, recommended the architect Ludwig Mies van der Rohe as his successor; Mies directed the school during its final years, including a forced move to Berlin, until the Nazis closed it down in 1933.

Its effect was widespread, though stamped out in the short term in Germany. Most of the staff emigrated to the United States, Gropius via England, and in environmental design we are still living with the results of their work. But in typography, the designers who made the Bauhaus widely known, especially Renner and Tschichold, were never directly connected with it, but pursued its aims from outside. Apart from Bayer's experimental alphabet, the Bauhaus produced no type designs. It was left to

ABCDEFGHIJKLMNOPQRSTUVWXYZ
abcdefghijklmnopqrstuvwxyz

ABCDEFGHIJKLMNOPQRSTUVWXYZ
abcdefghijklmnopqrstuvwxyz

ABCDEFGHIJKLMNOPQRSTUVWXYZ
abcdefghijklmnopqrstuvwxyz

Old and new sans-serifs. The top two examples are Akzidenz, from the Berthold foundry: the condensed was introduced in 1896 and the medium a few years later. Below is Paul Renner's Futura (1928–).

others to create the simplified faces the new typographical style demanded.

Most of the nineteenth-century English sans-serifs were jauntier, and retained more details from roman faces (such as the eyeglass **g**), than the Venus and Akzidenz group, which took more seriously the implied constraints of block letters, that the strokes should always be of equal thickness. (Where strokes join, however, compromises are always made to counteract both the optical impression that converging strokes are thicker, and the danger of clogging with ink.) The German faces abolished the eyeglass **g**, and straightened the tail of **R**, which was usually curved in the English types; they tidied up many details, though they kept the double-bowled **a** and the curve in the tail of **y**, and chiefly the comfortable modern face proportions, in which the **O** is an oval, not a circle.

The new generation of sans-serifs, which began with the Ludwig & Mayer foundry's Erbar (1922-30), designed by Jakob Erbar, included Rudolf Koch's Kabel (1926–7), and culminated (1928 on) in the Futura design by Paul Renner (1878–1956) for Bauer; all took the circular O as their proportional norm, as Edward Johnston's London Transport face had done a decade before. All straightened the tail of

the **y**, though they varied in many other details. Futura went furthest in geometrical purity, and had a single-bowled **a**.

In the final analysis, the most constructed sans-serifs are vitiated by their own geometry, because the letters are isolated by it: they lack the sense of flow from one to the next which there is in the traditional letterforms and proportions. This onward movement is guided by details so subtle they go unnoticed, but they are the result of practical optics, not geometry.

After his first exposure to the Bauhaus in 1923, Tschichold changed his own style completely. He Russianised his name temporarily to Ivan, to identify himself with the left-wing stance of the new movement, he adopted an uncompromising 'new typographical' manner, and in a special number of the printing trade journal *Typographische Mitteilungen* in October 1925 he combatively announced his new ideas under the general title of 'elementare typographie' (all in lower-case on the cover), in company with Bayer, Moholy-Nagy, Kurt Schwitters and the Russian El Lissitzky. He then followed this up with a beautifully designed, rational yet radical, and above all practical series of manuals: *Die neue Typographie* ('the new typography', 1928), *Eine Stunde Druck-*

Tschichold's early types. Transito, and Saskia (both 1931).

gestaltung ('a lesson in design for print', 1930), *Schriftschreiben für Setzer* ('lettering for compositors', 1931), and *Typographische Entwurfstechnik* ('typographical layout method', 1932). These made the new style not just a broadside against the bourgeoisie and blackletter, but a comprehensive method capable of day-to-day application.

Much of Tschichold's writing was prompted by his activities as a teacher, for after a brief spell as a freelance designer in Berlin he was invited by Paul Renner in 1926 to join the Munich printing school of which Renner was director. He stayed there until 1933, when he was arrested and interned by the Nazis, and his teaching contract cancelled. (Renner was dismissed, it will be remembered, and his place taken by Georg Trump.) Tschichold decided to leave Germany, and moved to Basle, where he survived by teaching and some work for publishers; he became a Swiss citizen during World War II.

The discipline of designing books on a variety of subjects, not just typographical manuals, for conservatively minded publishers on whom he depended for a livelihood, began Tschichold's second, slower, conversion, to classicism. His style was becoming less doctrinaire before he left Munich, and two display

Two single-alphabet projects, by Herbert Bayer (1925) and Tschichold (1929).

Le Capital
FONDERIE

SASKIA

frohe Farben in das sonnige Bild des Sommers

zu tragen, und alle modischen Pastelltöne

finden die anderen, die für ihre Erscheinung

types he designed in 1931 are decorative rather than rational: Transito, for the Typefoundry Amsterdam, is a bold stencil letter, and Saskia for the Leipzig foundry of Schelter & Giesecke a calligraphic sans-serif. He also produced some faces for a photosetting system, Uhertype of Berlin, but the only one to have survived, Uhertype-Standard-Grotesk, is as near to Gill Sans as makes no difference. After his move to Switzerland he continued for a while to lay type-matter out in an asymmetric way, and showed a distressing penchant for mixing Georg Trump's unattractive type City with spidery script faces, as on the title page of his famous book *Typographische Gestaltung* (1935).*

In the same year he was invited to visit England by Lund Humphries, the firm who printed and published *The Penrose annual*; he restyled their letterheading, and later designed the 1938 *Penrose*, both in a clean asymmetric manner. But his experience in publishing gradually compelled him to adopt a more classical style, and he accompanied this shift with a running

abcdefghi
jklmnopqr
stuvwxyz

für den neuen menschen existiert nur das gleichgewicht zwischen natur und geist zu jedem zeit- punkt der vergangenheit waren alle variationen des alten ›neu‹·

Translated as: *Asymmetric typography*, translated by Ruari McLean, London, Faber & Faber, 1967. (In association with Cooper and Beatty, Toronto.)

Sabon Antiqua

ABCDEFGHIJKLMNOPQ
RSTUVWXYZÄÖÜ
abcdefghijklmnopqrstuvwxyz
ßchckfffiflft&äöü
1234567890 1234567890
.,:;-!?.'()[]*†‹›»«„"/£$

——

In Vorbereitung:

Sabon Kursiv
Sabon Antiqua halbfett

Facing page: Sabon (1966). The Stempel specimen. Right: Tschichold's design for the Penguin poets series (1949).

apologia which began by modifying his earlier pronouncements against centred layouts, and came eventually to the extraordinary conclusion that the 'new typography', in its insistence on certain styles of type and design, was inherently Fascist. Although they had little else in common, Tschichold was like Gill in being prone to rash, self-contradictory public utterances, but here he excelled Gill.

Tschichold's new classical style was perfected, and at the same time given its greatest scope, when after World War II Allen Lane, the founder of Penguin Books, invited him to come to England to restyle the Penguin list. Between the beginning of 1947 and the end of 1949, he established composition rules for printers, overhauled the standard paperback covers, designed many series styles, and individually laid out a formidable number of books, notably the attractive hard-bound King Penguins, which were modelled on the Insel Verlag's little picture books, and for which he had had some practice with the Birkhäuser classics in Switzerland. Tschichold's masterly use of subtly allusive type and ornament combined within a strictly formal overall scheme has never been bettered.

After he returned to Switzerland, leaving Penguin design in the good care of Hans Schmoller, he continued to design, but his reforming zeal seems to have spent itself. But it is from this period that his one significant typeface, Sabon (1966), dates. Its achievement was as much in what cannot be seen as in what can. In the early 1960s a group of German printers decided they needed a type which could be set on Monotype or Linotype equipment, or in a foundry version by hand, with no perceptible difference on the page. This meant that all the drawbacks of both composing machines, the Monotype unit width grid and the Linotype's inability to kern, had to be resolved in a design which should look, the specification said, like a Garamond made a whisker narrower for economy's sake.

Tschichold rose to the challenge with a professionalism which was astonishing in someone known better as a user than as a creator of typefaces. His task was helped by all the manufacturing being done in

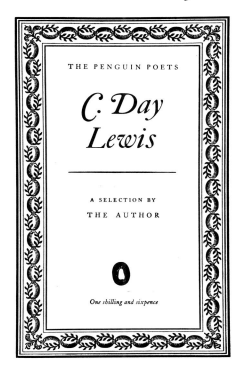

Frankfurt, where Monotype had a factory (which had cut Dante a decade before), and where Stempel, who made the foundry and Linotype versions, were based, but that does not diminish his success. Sabon is an admirable face, strong yet restrained, with only a hint of Garamond about it. (It is called after Jacob Sabon, a punchcutter from Lyon, who is thought to have brought some of Garamond's matrices to Frankfurt.) The roman capitals in particular are so handsome that one regrets that no titling fount was produced, and that Tschichold never designed any classical display letters.

Jan Tschichold died on 11 August 1974, a designer who had excelled in several different styles at different times, and whose only fault was that he disregarded Bruce Roger's advice about keeping his changes of mind to himself.

Berthold Wolpe

Berthold Wolpe (1905–89).
Photograph by Geoffrey Ireland.

Offenbach technical institute, where Koch had set up a workshop for students three years before; here he learned metal work, lettering, and later designed tapestries to be made in the workshop; and in 1929 he became a teacher in the school. He was involved in many collaborative ventures with Koch, notably the charming *ABC Büchlein* of 1934.

In 1932 he went to England, and finally made the decision to stay there in 1935. He worked for the Fanfare Press until 1939, and then from 1941 until his retirement in 1975 he designed jackets, bindings and some books for the London publishers Faber and Faber, where his hand lettering and bold layouts made their books instantly recognisable.

Wolpe had designed his first type in 1932; it was first called Matthias Claudius but later, because of the risk of confusion with Koch's Claudius, renamed Hyperion. It is a beautiful and unusual italic, for which punches were cut by Paul Koch in 12D only. The Bauer foundry then produced a full range of sizes, and used the type in two delightful books of Wolpe's designs, *Handwerkerzeichen* in 1936 and *Schmuckstücke und Marken* in 1938; but the type appeared commercially only after World War II.

His next, and best known type, Albertus, was designed for Monotype in England and begun in 1932. The titling appeared first in 1935, the roman upper and lower case followed in 1938, and the light and the bold in 1939-40. Albertus was based on Wolpe's lettering cut in metal, which Stanley Morison had seen and liked so much he commissioned the face, and its origins survive clearly in the shapes of the letters. Wolpe himself noted: 'On the bronze inscriptions the letters were not incised but raised; in other words the background was lowered and the outline only of the letters cut in. Such a metal inscription is cut with a chisel and not drawn with a pen, which gives it sharpness without spikiness, and as the outlines of the letters are cut from outside (and not from the inside outwards), this makes for bold

Of the designers who studied with Rudolf Koch, Warren Chappell and Berthold Wolpe have produced the most interesting types. Chappell's Lydian has already been mentioned, but he also created Trajanus, issued by Stempel in 1939, a handsome pen-formed roman. Wolpe's work was more independent, and was conditioned by his training in metal work rather than calligraphy, and his types are sturdily individual designs.

Berthold Wolpe* was born in Offenbach on 29 October 1905, the year before Koch began working at the Klingspor foundry there. In 1924 he went to the

Berthold Wolpe, a retrospective survey, London, Victoria & Albert Museum/Faber and Faber, 1980.

Warren Chappell's
Trajanus (1939).

simplicity and reduces the serifs to a bare minimum'.

In 1935, while he was working with the Fanfare Press, Wolpe designed Tempest for them, a vigorous sans-serif titling for use in display work, based on the freehand lettering he had developed for the jackets for the publisher Victor Gollancz, which Fanfare printed on the lines established by Morison. He also designed an attractive series of type ornaments for Fanfare about the same time.

In 1937, Monotype issued Wolpe's Sachsenwald, a bold calligraphic and simplified blackletter. In the Koch tradition, although the blackletter capitals are already considerably romanised for the English reader, Sachsenwald could be used with Albertus capitals, and was, in an edition of *The Rubaiyat of Omar Khayyam* printed at Fanfare in 1940.

Pegasus, Wolpe's only other type issued commercially, was designed for Monotype in 1937. Since it was cut on one size only it was unjustly neglected; but in the catalogue of a retrospective exhibition of Wolpe's work at the Victoria and Albert Museum in London in 1980, held to celebrate Wolpe's seventy-fifth birthday, the type was adapted with the help of Matthew Carter for composition on the Linotype VIP filmsetter; and with a new italic and bold by Wolpe, it

Albertus (1938).

Buchhändlerkonferenz in Eltville
Ferien in Holland

Kalkulationskursus für den Kaufmann
The medical research

ABCDEFGHIJKLMNOPQRSTUVW
XYZ £1234567890

abcdefghijklmno
pqrstuvwxyz!?&

ABCDEFGHIJKLMNO
PQRSTUVWXYZ

abcdefghijklmnopqrstuvwxyz

Der Grundcharakter einer Schrift wird von einheit
lichen Formmerkmalen aller Buchstaben eines Al

Hyperion (1932), and Pegasus (1937). Below: Decorata (1955).

was issued by Mergenthaler Linotype for digital setting in 1984. As Albertus was designed as a metal letter cut in relief, so the details of Pegasus are very much those of a letter incised in metal. It shows some signs of derivation from Koch's Marathon, but is a greatly superior design.

Wolpe also designed a handsome set of floriated capitals for the Westerham Press, called Decorata (1955), and an italic to be used with Edward Johnston's London Transport sans-serif in 1973. He died on 5 July 1989.

Roger Excoffon

Roger Excoffon, like Dwiggins, was above all a talented graphic designer, who ran a flourishing advertising design agency in Paris, called U&O, for many years. His posters for Air France and Bally shoes, done with a few economical yet eloquent brush strokes, were brilliant. His types were designed primarily for advertising, and belong to a category neatly defined by the critic Gérard Blanchard as *gestuel*, for which the English equivalent 'gestural' does not quite convey the full flavour of an image flowing naturally from the hand and spirit. Nevertheless, Excoffon's masterpiece, the Antique Olive family, is both completely original and a perfect balance between the *gestuel* and the typographic.

Excoffon was born in Marseille in 1910, and such artistic skill as he showed at school was chiefly in the drawing of maps. He went to university at Aix-en-Provence to read law, but found his heart was not in it, and went to Paris to study painting. Instead, he turned increasingly towards graphic art and letter forms. In 1947 he formed his own agency, and also became design director of the small Marseille type foundry, the Fonderie Olive.

For them he had already begun to design an elegant stressed sans-serif called Chambord (1945-51), whose capital alphabet was clearly modelled on that of A. M. Cassandre's Peignot (1937), drawn for the larger rival firm of Deberny & Peignot, but whose lower case was a far more restrained, less quirky performance. He followed Chambord with Banco (1951), a set of powerfully drawn sans-serif capitals which look like strips of bent sheet metal, and three scripts: Mistral (1953), a vigorous flowing brush letter which manages the difficult technical feat of joining letters with insouciant skill; Choc (1953), another brush script like the jottings of a Chinese calligrapher; and Diane (1956), a joined copperplate type which is the only serious rival to Zapf's Virtuosa in the field of formal scripts. The delightful Calypso (1958), aptly described by Blanchard as 'a game with orange

Roger Excoffon (1910–83) in 1960. Photograph by Roger Catherineau.

Choc

Mistral

Diane

ABCDEFGH

ABCDE
abcdefgh
VWXYZ
abcdefghi

Left: Choc (1953), Mistral (1953), Diane (1956), Banco (1951) and Calypso (1958). Right: Vendôme (1952), designed by François Ganeau.

peel', completed this astonishing dozen years' work, which gave French advertising of the next decade so much of its flavour.

In his rôle as art director of the foundry, Excoffon guided the production of Vendôme (1952), whose nominal author was François Ganeau, a theatrical designer and friend of Marcel Olive, the foundry's president. Vendôme was a spirited – one is tempted to say, theatrical – rendering of Garamond, and was an extraordinarily popular type.

Then, between 1962 and 1966, Excoffon designed Antique Olive (Antique being the French term for sans-serif). Although this was clearly planned as a family of sans-serifs to rival Haas's Helvetica and Deberny & Peignot's Univers (both began to appear in 1957 and both were designed by Swiss), the French had designed no formal 'mechanical' sans-serifs so far this century, and were not going to start now. Antique Olive was drawn with a subtlety normally reserved for classical romans and italics, and while the basic letter forms were in no way unusual, the shapes they took were totally new. Antique Olive was the most striking sans-serif since Futura and Gill, and is a more refined letter than either of them. Excoffon was fond of making an analogy between type

Spécialiste des voyages long-courriers

LE PLUS GRAND RÉSEAU DU MONDE

An example of Excoffon's graphic style. An advertisement for Air France (1964).

ABCDEFGHIJKL
MNOPQRSTUV
abcdefghijklm
nopqrstuvwx

ÉTOILES : elles sont séparées nous par des distances rables et lorsqu'elles paraisse très proches les unes des elles forment une grande blanchâtre appelée nébule

Si vous désirez partici différentes réunions, avoir l'obligeance de et retourner la carte que vous trouverez

designers and different drivers, more or less skilled, each of whom steers a slightly different route along the same road, or the same basic letter-form. Excoffon was a flamboyant and dangerous driver, but highly proficient, and a pleasure to watch.

Roger Excoffon died in 1983.

Display Types

It is inevitable in a book organised like this one into chapters devoted to the leading designers, that figures of considerable merit are neglected, especially if they are known chiefly for display types rather than text faces. I would like here to make amends in a small way by showing the display types of three such designers.

Oldřich Menhart was born in Prague in 1897, and developed a vigorous calligraphic style which seems quintessentially Czech. His uncial type has already been mentioned in the section on Victor Hammer. Menhart Antiqua was issued by the Bauer foundry in 1932, but he is probably best known outside his own country for Monument, cut by the Czech foundry Grafotechna, a delightfully robust shaded titling. He died in 1962.

John Peters*, born on 19 November 1917, spent most of his working life as a designer at the Cambridge University Press. When at the beginning of 1955 John Dreyfus took over Stanley Morison's position as typographic adviser at Monotype, his first commission was a titling fount from Peters, a hand-

some monumental shaded alphabet called Castellar, issued in 1957. Ten years later, another titling, designed to accompany Ehrhardt, and called Fleet, appeared. Earlier, Peters had also designed a small text face, Angelus (1954), for a Cambridge pocket Bible which never appeared, although Monotype cut the type. They also cut Traveller (1964), a chunky roman with a perceptible Eric Gill flavour, originally as a commission from the British Transport Commission, later released. John Peters, who had been wounded while in the RAF during World War II, later had a leg amputated, and died on 12 May 1989.

The Swedish designer Karl Erik Forsberg was born in 1914, and studied in Basel before returning home to work as a publisher's designer. His roman type Berling (1954), issued by the Berling foundry of Lund, first appeared in an admired Bible, but its reputation has suffered from a feeble redrawing when released in a dry transfer version by Letraset, by which it is best known outside Sweden. His calligraphic titling Carolus, on the other hand, is admirable.

Monument, Castellar and Carolus are shown on the next page.

John Dreyfus, 'John Peters', *Fine Print*, 16,1,1990.

ABC

DEFGHIJKLM

ABCDEF

GHIJKLMNO

ABC

DEFGHIJKLMNO

Top: Monument (1952) designed
by Oldřich Menhart.
Centre: Castellar (1957) by
John Peters.
Bottom: Carolus (1954) by
Karl Erik Forsberg.

New types for newer machines

All the designers who have appeared so far in this book saw their types first produced in metal, with the exception of Tschichold's few faces for the Uhertype photosetter in the 1930s. The next generation, those born in the decades after World War I, were transitional, beginning their careers designing metal type, then changing over in midstream to drawing faces which would never be cut and cast, but would go straight into film or, later, would be digitised. Later designers, those born in the 1940s and after, have worked entirely for cold composition. What these changes involved, and how they have affected type design, is the subject of this chapter.

The reader will remember that back in 1922 a group of designers proposed the foundation of the Fleuron Society to show that hot-metal composition, which was then still considered a new technology, could produce results comparable with those of traditional hand setting. It came to nothing because of the disagreement with this basic belief of Bernard Newdigate (1869–1944), the manager of the Shakespeare Head Press, an influential typographical journalist and a staunch believer in the values of the arts and crafts movement and the private presses. Yet in his brief essay 'Respice: prospice' in the first number of *The Fleuron* (1923), Newdigate referred to the bright future of offset lithography, then beginning to be used commercially, and, while noting that the type foundries were cheerfully sceptical of any threatened extinction, he looked forward to an equally bright future for photocomposition. He concluded, 'Whether the quality of the work is made better or worse by the invention or development of any ancillary art or method depends on the way in which the art or method is applied, rather than upon any inherent excellence or defect in the method itself. If the method is used for cheap and nasty work, it does not follow that the method itself is bad.' These words are just as apt now as they were then.

At the time when Newdigate was writing, the technology of typographical printing had been basically the same since Gutenberg: the surfaces of metal letters cast in relief were inked and pressed against paper. The way they were cast and assembled might have changed, and the way pressure was applied, but not the general principle.

An invention first made at the end of the eighteenth century was beginning to change this. The Bavarian Alois Senefelder (1772–1834) found that a drawing made with a greasy pencil on the smooth surface of a flat limestone slab could be damped, and then inked and printed: the water was repelled by the greasy image, and the ink by the water. The process was planographic, with no need for relief surfaces, and was called lithography, from the Greek words for stone and writing.

Throughout the nineteenth century, lithography was used for illustration, in books, on posters and ephemera, and for artist's prints; and also for the printing of music. Already by the 1850s, photographs were successfully transferred to lithographic stones and printed. But the process began to challenge letterpress for the printing of text only at the beginning of the twentieth century, when flexible metal plates were introduced to replace stones, and the image was transferred to the paper by way of a rubber blanket, which reduced wear on the plate and meant that the plate image could be the right way round. This adapted process was called offset lithography.

The advantages of offset were several. The presses were rotary (with both paper and plates on cylinders, by contrast with cylinder presses, where the printing surface was flat and the paper cylinder rolled over it), and could be run faster. The quality of the paper was less crucial for a good result, and half-tone photographs could be run together with text without needing shiny coated papers. All that was needed for reprinting a book was a set of plates or photographic film, instead of heavy, bulky pages of type which locked up capital in expensive metal.

Until after World War II the setting for books printed by offset was done on hot-metal composing machines as though for letterpress, cleanly proofed, and photographed on to the lithographic plates; but the illogicality of this procedure led engineers from the end of the nineteenth century to try to devise ways of setting text by photography, with the letters stored as master negatives, without the use of metal type at all.* The English pioneer of cinematography, William Friese-Greene, patented a simple line-composing machine in 1898, and over the next half-century, many methods were tried out. The Uhertype system (1925) already referred to worked by means of a master character cylinder which rotated to select the desired letters according to the instructions of a perforated tape, and exposed them in sequence on a ribbon of light-sensitive film. This in principle was typical of the first generation of photosetters, which all worked by the mechanical selection of characters in positive or negative form, and photographic exposure on film or paper through lenses.

For example, the Monophoto, introduced in 1955, worked in many ways just as the Monotype caster did. The tape from the keyboard unit was fed into the composing machine and determined the position of the diecase in a sequence of movements; but the diecase was made up not of matrices but of negatives of the characters, and a system of lenses was attached to adjust the size of type. Contemporary with the Monophoto, the Linofilm also employed mechanical matrix selection.

In theory there should have been no visible difference between hot-metal setting reproduced by offset, and photoset material in the same types; but in practice there was. The use of the same masters for several sizes of type, while it had obvious economic advantages, meant that the important optical adjustments in the type's design according to its scale could not be so rigorously applied. The fit between letters and their alignment were often imprecise at first; and there were often variations in the exposure and focus of the image. Corrections were more difficult. It is relatively easy to make small corrections to Monotype setting by hand, but early photoset corrections, however minor, had to be set line-by-line and spliced in,

and frequently the exposure of the corrected line was heavier or lighter.

The next significant step in photosetting was made almost contemporaneously with these machines, by two French engineers, René Higonnet and Louis Moyroud, who were working at the end of World War II. Their Lumitype machine, called the Photon in Britain and the USA, worked with stroboscopic light flashes through a continuously spinning disk with the type negatives arranged concentrically on it, and could achieve far greater speeds than mechanical setters. The first production model was installed at the *Patriot Ledger* newspaper in Massachusetts in 1954.

At the same time that photography and electronics were revolutionising character generation, the computer* was beginning to help with the preparation of the information which was fed from the keyboard to the composing unit, both in the initial setting and at the important correction stage. Firstly it helped with the justification of lines. On hot-metal machines, the keyboard operator tapped out the line, using a variable space key for the gaps between words. The Linotype word-space was an expanding mechanism which automatically filled out the line; the Monotype used a system of units to calculate the width of the cast spaces.

Decisions on whether to split words, and where, depended on the good sense of the operator and the standards set by the house; many typographers and master-printers spent a great deal of effort in improving standards of composition, especially in insisting on close word spacing. Because good setting requires thought, particularly over the decision about breaking words, compositors who were ignorant, or lazy, or in a hurry, tended to drive lines out, producing the loose word-spacing which was and remains all too common, especially in newspapers.

When computers were harnessed to the keyboards, they could make the spacing and hyphenating choices, so that the operator simply tapped out a paragraph as a single line and the machine did the rest. This obviously speeded up the keyboarding, though it made life dull for the operator; and because the line-breaking and other information could be added later, it also made it possible for decisions

Lawrence W. Wallis, *Typomania, selected essays on typesetting and related subjects*, London, Lund Humphries, 1993.

Computers and typography, compiled by Rosemary Sassoon, Oxford, Intellect Books, 1993.

Enlarged digital character, showing the stepping of curves. (Gerard Unger's Flora.)

about measure, and typeface design and size to be made or changed after keyboarding, which helped the designer. More recently still, developments in the compatibility of software has made it possible for authors to become their own keyboard operators, producing disks which a typographer can encode with the requisite design details, so that rekeying, with its extra expense and scope for error, is no longer necessary.

In theory, computers should have made bad setting impossible, because the result is no longer at the mercy of fallible compositors. In practice, of course, workable hyphenation programs have proved less easy to apply in all cases than the optimists believed, partly at least because programmers are fallible too, while inexperienced designers persist in devising typographical schemes, with excessively short lines or irregularly shaped type areas, which make acceptable spacing more a matter of luck than likelihood.

A surer benefit proffered by the computer was in correction. As we have seen, hot-metal Monotype setting could be corrected by hand, while on the Linotype new slugs had to be set. Whichever machine was used, it was quite easy for new errors to be introduced, and there was, moreover, no record kept of the corrections in machine-readable form: the Linotype kept no record at all, and the Monotype punched spool could reproduce only the original uncorrected setting in case of disasters. But computer tapes or disks can be continuously corrected and updated and, as the speeds of composing machines become even faster, it is relatively easy for whole books to be corrected and run through again.

Most recently, computers have come to be used not only as an aid to keyboarding, but in the design and production of typefaces. The generation of composing machines which followed the Lumitype/Photon, beginning with the pioneering Hell Digiset (1965), did not set with fixed images of the characters, whether on grids or circular bearers, photographically exposed in sequence, but stored the shapes of letters in digital form in their computer memories, and scanned them, whole lines at a time, using cathode ray tubes or, later, lasers. The storage of the letter forms has been either in the form of run-length coding, as in the Digiset, which builds the letters in a series of stripes, or as descriptions of the outlines, using mathematical expressions known as Bézier splines for the curves.

Digital setting made composition not only very much faster, but also much more precise: the image is less subject to irregularity of alignment, fit and exposure. However, it also meant that the outlines of letters are no longer smooth analog shapes, but are broken into steps, and this is more or less perceptible to the naked eye according to the fineness of definition at which they are printed out. Especially in the early days of the method, economies of space in the computer's memory, allied to coarse resolution in the print-out, led to visible staircases on curves, especially the subtle curves of faces designed for other means of production. Hermann Zapf's beautiful Optima suffered much in this respect. More recently, these problems have been reduced by better resolutions in the print-outs, and by devising barely visible flickers in the profiles of the letters, known as hinting.

Many types designed specifically for digitisation have developed strategies for avoiding such problems and for economising on computer memory, tending to simple curves and straight lines. But as the machines become more sophisticated, more becomes possible.

Digital setting has also made feasible a previously unimagined flexibility in the manipulation of letterforms. Before its introduction, the technology of cold composition affected the look of typefaces, aside from the first weaknesses of drawing in the adaptation of metal faces for the new medium, chiefly in the ability to kern. Type, since the invention of printing, had consisted of letters cast in relief on the end of rectangular columns of metal; but it had often reproduced the shapes of more fluid manuscript letters. Italics and scripts always presented a problem to type founders because their inclination and calligraphic flourishes tended to spread beyond the rectangles on which the characters sat. A few script types were cast on lozenge-shaped bodies with triangular infills to even up the ends of the lines, but generally such overflowings could be accommodated only by casting the letters with projecting parts, called kerns, which sat on the shoulders of the letters next door. Where these kerns were likely to hit parts of the neighbouring letters, as in the **fi**, **fl** or **ff** combinations, special double sorts called ligatures were supplied.

When type came to be cast by machine, the Monotype could cast kerned letters without difficulty, but slug machines like the Linotype, which assembled all the matrices in a row before the line was cast, could not. The Linotype drawing office therefore had to restructure every character which might project outside its body, producing, particularly in italics, a characteristically crabbed **f** and **y**. In the English Linotype Granjon (1924), designed by George W. Jones to compete with Monotype Garamond, the flourish of the roman **f**, usually bent back in Linotype faces, was kept by including no less than twenty-six different sets of ligatures, which were intended to cover all eventualities. When Beatrice Warde, Monotype's publicity manager, reviewed the type in *The Fleuron*, even while commending the type's beauty, she could not resist pointing out that as there was no **fg** ligature it could not set 'Afghanistan'. (She did not mention that it could not manage 'Kafka' either, but the writer was not yet well known – and neither could the Monotype: a space had to be inserted.) The only slug caster which could produce italic characters of a kerned appearance was, as we have seen, the Ludlow, which occasionally adopted the lozenge-shaped script method, and had inclined matrices for some faces.

With the arrival of photosetting, the problem no longer existed, and letters could overlap the notional rectangle occupied by their neighbours without difficulty. They could even join up. The ingenuity of a metal script type such as Roger Excoffon's Mistral, which appears to be a continuous flow, was no longer required, and scripts such as Matthew Carter's Snell Roundhand for the Linofilm (1966) could be designed like copper-plate. Also, because there was no longer a technical reason for ligatures, they have tended to disappear as an extravagance, although their Renaissance elegance is missed by many, and the overlaps which replace them are often clumsily handled. Ligatures linger, together with other attractive relics such as ampersands, paragraph marks and swash characters, in many of the more historically-minded faces.

While kerning as a technical term attached to the manufacture of metal type has become obsolete, the word has expanded to take in the spacial relationship between letters, what used to be called their fit. 'It is difficult to appreciate without seeing a demonstration', wrote Harry Carter in 1937, reviewing Monotype Van Dijck in the journal *Signature*, 'how completely a letter is altered by having more or less space about it. The success or failure of a type is very much a question of getting a good balance of white inside and outside the letters.' When type occupied metal rectangles, this fit was established by the type founders and composing-machine manufacturers. Capitals could be spaced out or even, by careful trimming, closed up in individual cases; but the space between lower-case letters was for all practical purposes fixed. But cold-composed type is far more flexible, and the space between letters is easily adjusted. Such freedom can be dangerous in the hands of people with no sense of the natural rhythm of a typeface, and unfortunately they seem at present to be in the majority. Even the manufacturers do not always, it seems, take enough account of the effects of type size on the closeness of fit. Many large sizes are too widely spaced, or when closed up by typographers, often squeezed too far in the opposite direction. On the bonus side, however, programs have been developed for spacing pairs of lower-case letters according to their individual profiles, which permit fitting of a sophistication previously given only to capitals.

Computer storage of letterforms has also made it easier for type users to distort them. The commonest faults in the hands of careless designers have been the automatic slanting of roman founts to save the expense of a true italic, and the condensing and expanding of letters beyond tolerable limits. Yet this mistreatment of type is the price that is paid for a

```
Oranupitbold IK                                    28-02-1990 12:56
                        H: 60.0 p
```

The Carters
The Carters

printed by IKARUS M at GUM

A working print-out of type created on Ikarus M software.

technology which also yields great benefits. The manipulation of outlines, for example, is of considerable use in developing different weights of type from a basic design, the kind of laborious work which, when done by hand, absorbed much of the working life of Morris Benton and his kind. Using Peter Karow's Ikarus program, introduced in the early 1970s, the outline of the face could be plotted and fed into the computer, and then rearranged by the type designer according to the weight required, as well as manipulated in other ways. The most recent advance in this field has been the Multiple Master technology introduced in 1992 by Adobe Systems in California, which gives the user a far wider choice. Here the type designer creates two or more designs at the limits of various axes, for weight, width, style or optical scaling, and the user can select one of many gradations between them. The optical scaling axis is of particular significance, since it confronts the problem of correction for size which has bedevilled type manufacture since the introduction of the Benton engraving machine in the 1880s. The Multiple Master scaling subtly alters the profile of the letters from small to large, reproducing the traditional practices of hand punchcutters in computer language.

The Adobe design staff mostly use proprietory software in the creation of their types, but several forms of software are currently available, including Fontographer, FontStudio or Ikarus M. Using them, designers can either scan in drawings before manipulating them on screen, or can create designs directly on the computer. The faces can be fitted and put into PostScript format at speeds which would have been inconceivable a few years ago.

The development of type designs has traditionally been a territorial matter, promoted by foundries or machine manufacturers who jealously guarded their exclusive creations. While this is commercially understandable, it has always been frustrating for designers who have been broadly tied to the faces available from the printing works or typesetting house who are doing the work in hand, and the typesetters were limited in the choice they offered by the machines they had.

Type development in the early years of photosetting was dominated by the mechanical typesetting manufacturers Monotype and Linotype, and by some of the traditional foundries, who quickly developed photosetting systems in competition, such as Deberny & Peignot with the Lumitype/Photon, and Berthold with the Diatype and its successors; but new firms rapidly joined in. One common factor was that advances in engineering tended to outstrip the ability of the drawing offices to keep up; for while it was relatively easy to adapt existing faces for the new machines, doing it well took longer, and the kind of typographic subtleties which had become commonplace in the days of hot metal were often forgotten.

The ease of adaptation tempted some of the newer manufacturers to adopt a somewhat piratical attitude towards other people's designs, and it was not uncommon to see copies – often quite rough copies – of well-known faces such as Palatino or Optima appearing under different names in different catalogues, with no fee paid to Hermann Zapf or Stempel, the designer and original manufacturer. It was partly to stop this abuse that the Association Typographique Internationale (usually abbreviated to ATypI) was set up in 1957 under the presidency of Charles Peignot of Deberny & Peignot, and later John Dreyfus of Monotype. The aim was to work towards an international convention on typeface protection. An agreement was reached in 1973 at the Vienna Congress on Industrial Property, when ten countries signed an Arrangement on Typeface Protection, but ratification has been delayed by the necessary modifications in the signatory countries' internal laws. Meanwhile, the problem of piracy has become enormously greater, with the ease of copying of software. This time the illegal use comes from users rather than rival manufacturers, and is sometimes a matter of ignorance rather than intention. Typeface software is licensed for use by customers: they are not at liberty to reproduce it and pass it on at will. FAST, the Federation Against Software Theft, is supported by the major type companies, and FontWorks have published an excellent short booklet outlining the legal situation. Unless software piracy is checked, the smaller digital type foundries will not survive, and it will not be worthwhile to create new designs.

As had happened when hot-metal typesetting was introduced a century ago, the earliest typefaces to be released for photosetting were adaptations of existing faces, but quite soon new designs were commissioned. We shall see in the section on the work of Adrian Frutiger that in the mid-1950s he was invited by Charles Peignot to oversee the transfer of Deberny & Peignot's classic metal faces for the Lumitype/Photon machine, and then designed Meridien and Univers for both the Lumitype and for metal foundry type. Univers was quickly recognised as an important face by John Dreyfus at Monotype, and adapted for Monotype composition both on hot-metal machines and the Monophoto. Then in 1962, Dreyfus commissioned Frutiger directly to design Monotype's first face freshly conceived exclusively for film composition, Apollo.

This pattern was broadly representative of the industry in general, and the profiles of designers which follow will show it in more detail. The other foundry, aside from Deberny & Peignot, who took the challenge of photocomposition seriously was the Berlin firm of H. Berthold AG. Founded in 1858, it first showed its Diatype photosetter at the DRUPA printing exhibition in its centenary year, and it also adopted an enterprising design policy under its type director Günter Gerhard Lange (born 1921). Lange's uncial Solemnis (1952) has already been referred to, and he is the author of Concorde (1969), a clean, no-nonsense roman. His adaptations of the classic faces such as Baskerville, Caslon, Garamond and Walbaum are particularly sensitive, and he has commissioned many outside designers to design faces, including a number from Friedrich Poppl (1923–82), Hermann Zapf's Comenius (1976), and Gudrun Zapf-von Hesse's Nofret (1986).

At the same time as the older firms were adjusting to the changed conditions, newer ones were appearing to market photosetters and CRT machines. Not all had pretensions to typographic distinction, but among those who did was the Swiss company Bobst Graphic, set up in 1972 and ten years later absorbed by Autologic. Two types by Team 77, consisting of André Gürtler, Christian Mengelt and Erich Gschwind, were produced for Autologic, Media (1976) and Signa (1978), and others included Robert Norton's Else and Bram de Does's Trinité, both in 1982.

However, as typesetting machines proliferated, the inconvenience to typographers grew. However excellent the types available on any one device, what was needed was the ability to set a range of favourite faces on a variety of machines. To try to secure this, the International Typeface Corporation of New York was founded in 1970 by Aaron Burns, Herb Lubalin and Ed Rondthaler. ITC set about commissioning new designs, reviving and redrawing old ones or licensing existing ones; they promoted these designs vigorously through their lively house magazine *U&lc*, and sold them to subscribing manufacturers as finished fitted artwork ready for adaptation to the individual typesetting machines. ITC were extremely successful for many years, responsible for many revivals such as Franklin, Century and Californian/Berkeley (and some horrors best not revived, such as Souvenir), and many new designs such as Avant Garde Gothic, by Lubalin and Tom Carnase (1970), and three by Hermann Zapf, called Zapf Book, Chancery and International.

For all the ubiquity of ITC faces, the work of adaptation still had to be done for each composing machine, and slight differences remained between the versions from different machines. What was needed was system of digital description of typefaces which would operate on all machines, and this finally appeared in 1983, when Adobe introduced the PostScript language. Apple's similar TrueType followed. Typefaces issued in PostScript format are not only usable on a wide variety of typesetting equipment, they can also be shown at any resolution, either on screens at 75–100 dots per inch, or printed out on paper from the 300 dots per inch of office laser-printers to fine-detail imagesetters at around 3000 dots per inch. PostScript has enabled the major type libraries to become widely and interchangeably available for typesetting at any level.

abcdefghijklmnopqrstuvwxyz
ABCDEFGHIJKLMNOPQRSTUVWXYZ
1234567890 &£$.,:;!?"

abcdefghijklmnopqrstuvwxyz
ABCDEFGHIJKLMNOPQRSTUVWXYZ
1234567890 &£$.,:;!?"

Lucida Bright (1987), designed by Charles Bigelow and Kris Holmes.

It has also encouraged the spread of small independent digital type foundries. These had existed before, though they were not common. The partnership of Bigelow and Holmes, begun in San Francisco by Charles Bigelow (born 1945) and Kris Holmes (born 1950), had drawn a titling alphabet for the Arion Press letterpress limited edition of *Moby Dick*, called Leviathan (1979), which was reproduced by line blocks. Their first digital design was Lucida (1985), with an on-screen version called Pellucida, which has now expanded into a family, with a sans-serif version, and Lucida Bright, designed for the magazine *Scientific American*. Bitstream, set up by Matthew Carter and Mike Parker in 1981, worked from the start as a digital foundry, and countless small business have followed suit*.

Many have produced designs very far removed from the sober creations with which this book has been largely concerned. The magazine *Emigré*, started in Sacramento by Rudi VanderLans and Zuzana Licko (born in Czechoslovakia in 1961), was a showplace of Licko's designs, and in 1985 they set up Emigré Fonts to market them, as well as others by like-minded designers. Emigré faces arouse both enthusiasm and detestation, but cannot be ignored. FontShop International's *Fuse* operates in much the same area.

The separation of typeface production from the manufacture of typesetting machines has affected even Monotype. In March 1992, following financial troubles at the main company, the type design section which had been trading as Monotype Typography detached itself and became an autonomous business under the control of René Kerfante. Both before this and since, Monotype has continued with the pattern established at the beginning of the cold composition era, making its extensive type library available to the next generation of machines – in this case, converting them to PostScript format – and issuing new designs, many of them by staff designers. Robin Nicholas's Nimrod has already been mentioned. Ron Carpenter (born in Dorking in 1950) has produced Cantoria, a reworking of a pair of bizarre early Monotype faces (1986), Calisto, a roman with a Dutch flavour (1987), and Amasis, a pared-down slab-serif (1990). Monotype celebrated the Columbus bicentenary in 1992 with a face named after the explorer, designed by Patricia Saunders and based on types used in Saragossa early in the sixteenth century.

The most notable commission from an outside designer has been Michael Harvey's Ellington (1990), called after the Duke. Harvey, a distinguished stone carver and lettering artist, was born in 1931 and worked with Reynolds Stone before setting up on his own. Ellington is a condensed type, descended from the lettering style he has developed over many years of producing book-jackets, which is too lively to work well as a text face, but makes a good display letter.

This brief survey of the post-war explosion of typesetting methods has referred several times to Hermann Zapf, the senior designer of the period. His career, and those of younger designers who have followed him, will be described in the sections which follow.

Gerald Lange, 'Opening the floodgates: digital type foundries on the rise', *Bookways*, 9, October 1993.

It is the reader's famil
with typefaces that a
for their legibility; rea
read best what they re
most! It is the reader'
with typefaces that a
It is the reader's fam
with typefaces that a
for their legibility; re
read best what they r
most! It is the reader
with typefaces that a

It is the reader's familiari
typefaces that accounts f
It is the reader's familiar
with typefaces that acco
It is the reader's famili
with typefaces that acc

The rough and the smooth.
On the left-hand page are two
Emigré faces. Left: Template
Gothic, designed by Barry Deck.
Right: Modula by Zuzana Licko.
On the facing page: three
Monotype faces. Top: Calisto
(1987) designed by
Ron Carpenter.
Centre: Columbus (1992) by
Patricia Saunders.
Bottom: Ellington (1990) by
Michael Harvey.

in the daylight; and, if I must add the truth, night is kinder in this respect than day, which too often destroys an air-built castle at the moment of its completion, without the least ceremony or remorse. Night is generally my time for walking. *That constant pacing to and fro, that never-ending restlessness, that incessant tread of feet wearing the rough stones smooth and glossy – is it not a wonder how the dwellers in narrow ways can bear to hear it!*

U ndoubtedly the most momentous of all voyages of discovery: this is the verdict given in *Printing and the Mind of Man* (London, 1967), on the voyage described by CHRISTOPHER COLUMBUS in his own

Introducing

Ellington

A **Jazzy** new typeface designed for Monotype by Michael Harvey, letterer and jazz lover, in tribute to Duke Ellington.

Ellington is a condensed design that combines the lively, calligraphic features of the broad-edged pen with the clear-cut sparkle of a modern typeface. **Ellington** is now available in four weights with italics in Type 1 format for use with all PostScript language printers.

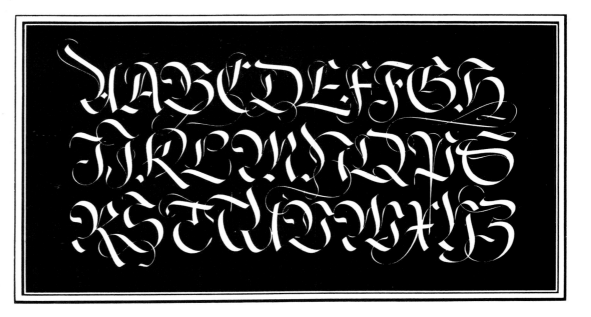

Die Buchstaben haben dann Anmut,
wenn sie nicht mit Unlust und Hast,
auch nicht mit Mühe und Fleiß, sondern
mit Lust und Liebe geschrieben sind

BODONI

Facing page: Hermann Zapf (born 1918).

Two plates from 'Feder und Stichel' by Hermann Zapf (1949).

The designers – 2
Hermann Zapf

At the end of World War II, German printers and type founders had lost a high proportion of their plant and typographical material as the result of bombing, and faced the formidable task, along with most of industry, of rebuilding and re-equipping their factories. Moreover, they had to do so almost exclusively with roman faces, since one of the few useful legacies of the Third Reich was the adoption of roman as the standard alphabet, or *Normalschrift*, for German, in place of blackletter. The decision to change had been taken in 1941; before then blackletter had been promoted by the Nazis with considerable effort as the quintessentially German script, and afterwards was condemned as a Jewish invention.

Those printers who before the war had used roman types the most had been the book houses, largely concentrated in Leipzig and therefore now in the eastern zone. The foundries of the Federal Republic had to work almost from scratch, and sought designs for the new romans and italics that were needed. Chief among those who came forward to provide them was the young Hermann Zapf.*

Zapf was born on 8 November 1918 in Nuremberg, the birthplace, almost exactly forty-two years earlier, of Rudolf Koch. He left school (where his reports gave him a B in penmanship) in 1933. In that year his father, who as a trade union official in a large car factory had become, with the rise of the Nazis, politically undesirable, was sacked from his job, and as a result Zapf was debarred from further education and therefore the career in electrical engineering he had hoped for. Instead, he began a four year apprenticeship as a retoucher at a local printing firm, Karl Ulrich & Co.

In 1935 an exhibition of the work of Rudolf Koch, who had died the previous year, was shown in

Hermann Zapf, and his design philosophy, Chicago, Society of Typographic Arts, 1987.

Top: An example of Zapf's
calligraphy, from 'Feder und
Stichel' (1949).
Below: Gilgengart (1941).

Nuremberg, which inspired Zapf to become a calligrapher. He bought Koch's instruction book *Das Schreiben als Kunstfertigkeit* ('the skill of calligraphy'), and Edward Johnston's *Writing & Illuminating, & Lettering*, and began a course of self improvement which resulted in his becoming one of the great modern masters of the art. His apprenticeship with Ulrich ended in 1938, and he went to work at Paul Koch's workshop at the Haus zum Fürsteneck in Frankfurt, where he began to learn something of the craft of printing with the hand press, as well as punchcutting and related skills. In the autumn he was introduced by the printing historian Gustav Mori, whose legendary library he was able to use, to the Stempel foundry in Frankfurt, for whom he designed many of his best types. Here he met the superlative punchcutter August Rosenberger (1893-1980), with whom he collaborated on several magnificent books.

Early the following year Zapf began work on his first type for Stempel, a Fraktur blackletter called Gilgengart. As he had to learn as he went along, the type developed slowly, and suffered further from the disfavour into which blackletter fell after 1941. As Zapf wrote later, 'A new printing type has a long, often thorny way to completion. Before a type has come far enough to please outsiders, it adds grey hairs to its co-producers.' Gilgengart was cut in two forms, the second narrowing the capitals of the first, and also omitting some decorative flicks on the bottom of the letters.

Concurrently with Gilgengart, Zapf designed for the Bärenreiter-Verlag of Kassel a music type, Alkor, which was destroyed during the war, and began work on his early masterpiece of book production, *Feder und Stichel* ('Pen and graver'), a book of twenty-five calligraphic alphabets. The drawings were finished in 1941, and the plates hand cut in lead by August Rosenberger in his spare time. The book first appeared as a limited edition from Stempel's own private press in 1949.

In 1941, Zapf was called up, and served as an army cartographer in France, first in Dijon and later Bordeaux, where he began a set of flower drawings which were used in *Das Blumen-ABC* ('flower alphabet'), again cut by Rosenberger and published by the Stempel press in 1948. His war service ended as technically a French prisoner in various military hospitals, but he was quickly released.

On his return he took up the design direction of Stempel, and began the enormous task of rebuilding

House of Representatives

Pictures of the week

Manual of modern advertising

Brunswick Map Printers

Palatino (1949).

its repertoire of faces after the devastation of the war. Already in 1946 he had begun work on a pen-formed roman called Novalis, which was not dissimilar to Warren Chappell's pre-war Trajanus for the same foundry, but was never issued. This work was quickly overtaken by a new face based on Renaissance forms for which the first drawings were ready in 1948, and which made its first appearance in the introduction to *Feder und Stichel* the following year. It was called Palatino.

Palatino has proved so universally popular that its remarkable qualities tend to be taken for granted. Zapf himself wrote in *About alphabets,** 'The studies and sketches of my Italian visit were converted into the Palatino type family, their very names suggesting their Italian models', and certainly the type's classical sense of proportion seems to show signs of the strong impact made by the experience of his first visit to Italy on an impressionable young man who had hitherto been working in the Koch tradition. Palatino is so completely unlike such characteristic pre-war German

Hermann Zapf, *About alphabets, some marginal notes on type design*, New York, The Typophiles, 1960. (Revised edition, MIT Press, 1970.)

roman types as Weiss Antiqua and Koch's Marathon that the direct influence of Italian lettering seems needed to explain it. Nevertheless, the fact is that Zapf did not go to Italy until the Autumn of 1950, by which time Palatino and Michelangelo, those miracles of Renaissance grace, were already cut. Only Sistina, the more robust titling fount, was based on sketches actually made in Italy.

Together with this extraordinary and apparently instinctive absorption of classical letter forms, Palatino still shows beneath its surface the stirrings of penmanship learned from Koch, which leaves small but vital traces on the contours of the letters. While this is never allowed to dominate the shapes, it gives the type its crispness, and prevents it ever becoming bland. The earliest cuttings were more calligraphic in some details, such as the absence of serifs on the tails of p and q, but these were added later.

Palatino was immediately adapted for Linotype composition, since Stempel had held the contract for making matrices for the German branch of Mergenthaler Linotype since 1900, and it has since been adapted for virtually every typesetting system in the West. As it was found somewhat heavy in weight for text setting in the smaller sizes, Zapf designed a lighter version, called Aldus, for Linotype composition sizes (1952-3).

At the same time as Palatino, Zapf was at work on a newspaper face, called Melior, a modern and sophisticated addition to the Ionic family with the curves drawn on a principle which foreshadows the super-ellipse, a mathematical construction described fifteen years later in *Scientific American*. At the same time, the details of Melior were carefully designed to withstand as far as possible the various processes, rotary letterpress, offset and gravure, which would use it, and Zapf was able to study the technical requirements of such types at Linotype's Brooklyn headquarters during his first visit to the United States in 1951.

Melior appeared in 1952, and its originality can be gauged by comparing it with Zapf's far more conventional Mergenthaler Antiqua of two years later, which was intended for specialist scientific work, and presented technical rather than aesthetic challenges.

We can get an idea of the amount of work Zapf produced in these years when we realise that between 1948 and 1954 he designed not only Palatino, Aldus and Melior, with their titlings and bolds, italics and swashes, but also many other faces. There were the

Melior (1952).

elegant Virtuosa scripts (1952-3), and several Greek alphabets, some made to accompany existing Stempel faces such as the sans-serif Neuzeit, but including the beautiful Phidias (1953) to partner Michelangelo, Frederika (1953) to go with Virtuosa, and the excellent all purpose Heraklit (1954). He drew the Mergenthaler Antiqua already mentioned, as well as handling the drawings for the German Linotype Janson (1952), based on the Stempel Janson types (which have already made their appearance in connection with Monotype Ehrhardt), and for Stempel's cutting of a missing 24pt and a new 48pt. He designed the attractive Saphir decorated capitals (1952) and the vigorous jobbing face Kompakt, and a successful Persian script as well as many ornaments. And as if this were not enough, he began work on a new type which at its development stage was called significantly Neu-Antiqua ('new roman'), but was later christened, as a linguistically logical successor to Melior, Optima.

Optima is in many ways Zapf's most original design, in that it established virtually on its own a new type category, which its creator was careful to call a 'serifless roman', to distinguish it from stressed sans-serif. He tells us that it was inspired by Florentine lettering he had seen on his Italian visit, which

Inks for Quality Printing

Italian Architecture

Famous Painters of Italy

Horse Race at Ascot

ABC
DEFGHIJKLMNO
PQRSTUVWXYZ
1234567890

FAHRENHEIT

KINGDOM

BERNARD SHAW

EDINBURGH

Saphir (1952), and the two titlings for the Palatino family, Michelangelo and Sistina (both 1950).

ABCDEFGHIJKLMMNN
abcdefghijklmnopqrstuvwx

ABCDEFGHIJKLMNOPQRSTUVWXYZ
abcdefghijklmnopqrstuvwxyz 1234567890

Optima (1958).

dispensed with serifs; it is also more originally an extension of the development of roman book types, taking the comfortably round proportions of a transitional face such as Baskerville's and shedding the serifs with no distortion of its essential nature and no sense of anything missing.

Although Optima was not originally conceived as a book face, because of the widespread opposition to sans-serif for text setting, Zapf's conversations with Monroe Wheeler of the New York Museum of Modern Art convinced him that its roman inflections made it legible enough for continuous reading. Time has proved Wheeler right. Optima appeared at the DRUPA printing trade fair at Düsseldorf in 1958, and has been extremely popular ever since. A serifless italic defies imagination, and so in common with most sans-serifs a sloped version was produced to accompany the roman. Various bolds followed, with the boldest forms growing vestigial serifs on some letters to help with their articulation.

The logic of producing Optima at this time was confirmed by the almost contemporary history of Zapf's 'straight' sans-serif, Magnus, designed without much enthusiasm for English Linotype, of which the trial size was cut in 1957. The project was abandoned in 1960 after the appearance of Adrian Frutiger's Univers.

At the end of 1956, Zapf resigned from the type directorship of Stempel, although he kept very close links with the foundry. The administrative burden was threatening to outweigh his creative work, and he wanted to develop his talents in book design, calligraphy and other graphic techniques. The portfolios and books of typographical design and lettering he produced over the years have been outstanding. Beginning with *Feder und Stichel*, already described, and continuing with the magnificent landscape-format *Manuale typographicum* of 1954, *Typographische Variationen* of 1963, the second upright volume of the *Manuale* in 1968, and the privately issued *Orbis typographicus* of 1980, the books are an extraordinary outpouring of graphic creativity.

It is unfortunate that the projected *Manuale phototypographicum* of the late 1960s was abandoned for financial reasons: the first two *Manuale* volumes were set in metal, the first by hand and the second with some additional mechnical composition, and it would have been suitable to produce a third with photosetting to represent Zapf's continuing and passionate involvement in the developing technology of type

The Rampant Lions Press salutes Hermann Zapf, designer Jack Stauffacher, first mover George Lawrence, patron & the Stempel foundry, makers of the Hunt Roman

Hunt Roman (1962).

composition. For although he has continued to value metal type and design for it, he has at the same time both overseen the transfer of his faces to film and digitisation, and also given his attention to designing for the new typesetting systems.

Nevertheless, three of Zapf's best designs for cold composition, Comenius for Berthold, Zapf Book for the International Typeface Corporation, and Marconi for Hell Digiset, all dating from 1976, are children of what must be one of the last instances of a type commissioned for private use and cast in metal by a commercial foundry. In 1960, he was invited as visiting professor of design to the Carnegie Institute of Technology at Pittsburgh, and the following year was commissioned by the Hunt Botanical Library there to design a face for use in the Library's publications, chiefly as a display letter to use with their standard text type, Monotype Spectrum. He developed his design from a pen letter he had occasionally used, in which the stress was almost vertical, and drew an alphabet which was transitional in origin but of its time in appearance. Hunt Roman was intended for hand setting only, and so Zapf was able for once to design without having to worry about the unit systems of mechanical composition, and

because it was to be used in the United States it did not have to conform to the standard base-line of German types. With this freedom he produced a beautiful face, with enough calligraphic crispness to make it lively, and enough strength to discipline that liveliness. It was cut in four sizes by Stempel, and the 18pt pilot size was completed in May 1962.*

The only disadvantages of Hunt were that it had no italic, and was unavailable to the trade. Comenius, Zapf Book, and Marconi, of fourteen years later, were by no means exact adaptations, but they bear a close family resemblance, and made good these deficiencies. Comenius is the superior version, but all lack the sharpness of Hunt, possibly in unconscious recognition of the softness of the medium for which they were designed, by contrast with metal. In Zapf International, which ITC brought out the next year, 1977, the absence of sharp-edged features was actually required in its design brief.

One other typeface for ITC should be noticed: the popular italic Zapf Chancery (1979), which turned

Hunt Roman, the birth of a type, commentary and notes by Hermann Zapf and Jack Werner Stauffacher, Pittsburgh Bibliophiles, 1965.

the arguments about italic versus sloped roman by providing a slightly inclined italic in place of 'roman', and an italic of greater inclination for emphasis. As Kris Holmes* has pointed out, Zapf Chancery has distinctly more bite, almost a touch of blackletter, by comparison with most faces for cold composition (including Zapf's two earlier designs for ITC), though if, as she says, tongue-in-cheek, the *x* 'has the vigour of Gene Kelly in his prime', Gene Kelly is about to fall over. Zapf Chancery's first extended showing was in a catalogue designed by Carl Zahn for the Boston Museum of Fine Art, but its chief rôle is clearly as an advertising display face.

In 1966, Zapf was appointed a typographical consultant to Hallmark International, the makers of greetings cards. Here he devised training schemes and manuals for their lettering craftsmen, collaborated on an educational film called *The art of Hermann Zapf* (1968), and also designed a handful of proprietory faces, covering most of the stylistic range from scripts to roman. Between 1967 and 1972, there appeared at roughly annual intervals: Jeanette, a script, Firenze, a chancery italic, Textura, a blackletter, Hallmark

Uncial, Missouri, a calligraphic roman, Scriptura, another script, and, also in 1972, Crown, a roman book type for use in Hallmark's own Crown Editions. The types could also be used in combinations: for example, Winchester used Uncial Capitals with Textura lower case, and Charlemagne mixed Uncial capitals with lower case from the Shakespeare designed by Zapf's wife Gudrun Zapf-von Hesse.

After leaving Stempel in 1956, Zapf also became a consultant to Mergenthaler Linotype in New York. For their Linofilm typesetter he designed in 1969 the script Venture and the italic Medici. (The latter was also the name of Palatino during the development stage, but the two types should not be confused.) At the end of his advisory term in 1974, he drew Orion, a deliberately neutral text face.

For the Digiset digital typesetter manufactured by the Rudolf Hell company of Kiel, he has designed Marconi (1976), another variation on the Hunt theme done in the same year as Comenius and Zapf Book, Edison (1978), a chunkier workhorse type for newspapers and technical publications, Vario (1982) and Aurelia (1983). (Aurelia was also the provisional name for Sistina, and as with Medici the two should not be confused.)

Comenius (1976). Kris Holmes, 'Zapf Chancery', *Fine Print on type,* 1988.

regularComeniusnormal
abcdefghijklmnopqrstuvwxyz
ABCDEFGHIJKLMNOPQRSTUVWXYZ
äåæöøœßüÆÄÅÖØŒÜ1234567890%
(.,-;:!i?¿ –) · [''„""»«]+—=/$£†*&§

italicComeniuskursiv
abcdefghijklmnopqrstuvnvxyz
ABCDEFGHIJKLMNOPQRSTUVWXYZ
äåæöøœßüÆÄÅÖØŒÜ1234567890%
(.,-;:!i?¿ –) · [''„""»«]+—=/$£†&§*

Given the unexciting typefaces that have come from the interregnum of metal and phototype, one might wonder why Zapf Chancery has suddenly appeared out of the fog of undistinguished designs. *Kris Holmes*

Zapf Chancery (1979).

Zapf's lifelong concern with non-roman types has continued, with Greek and Cyrillic versions of many of the faces so far mentioned. For the University of Wisconsin, at the suggestion of Walter Hamady, he produced a Sequoia alphabet (1984-7), and in 1983 he began to work on a roman-based Pan-Nigerian type to accommodate the nine chief languages of that country.

In 1977, Zapf was appointed Professor of Typographic Computer Programs at the Rochester Institute of Technology in New York State, and in 1983 his work with the Metafont design program developed by Professor Donald Knuth at Stanford University produced the Euler type family for the American Mathematical Society. The basic roman is, like Zapf Chancery, really an upright italic, with rounded contours rather in the manner of Goudy; and there are script, italic and even Fraktur versions, as well as many mathematical sorts. At the same time as this design, drawn on a screen without the aid of even a pencil and paper, Zapf has recently returned to an earlier technique of making type, and designed a Civilité script for which matrices were made by Paul Hayden Duensing and cast at his private foundry at Kalamazoo, Michigan.

In 1985–6 Scangraphic issued Zapf Renaissance. Although this is described as a 'new interpretation' of Palatino for setting on the Scantext 1000, it is a more fragile creation with substantial differences. After a number of more or less utilitarian designs, even if their patrician styling marks them as unmistakeably by Zapf, Renaissance is a return to the beauty of earlier years, with a delicacy which is attainable only with digital setting.

Thus Zapf's first ambition to become an electronic engineer has been realised by the most round-about route imaginable. Unquestionably we are the richer that the political barriers put up against his early training in electronics forced him into printing, where he experienced, compressed into one career, the whole history of type manufacture so far, from hand punchcutting at the Haus zum Fürsteneck, through the industrialised foundry at Stempel, mechanical and film composition at Linotype, to the computerised design and character generation of today. We are doubly fortunate that he had both the technical ability to make the new machines work for him, instead of relinquishing control to the engineers, and also the graphic genius to make them work to such advantage.

155

Zapf Renaissance Antiqua leicht Zapf Renaissance Roman light

Zapf Renaissance Roman book & Zapf Renaissance Antiqua Buch

ZAPF RENAISSANCE KAPITÄLCHEN & ZAPF RENAISSANCE CAPS BOOK

Zapf Renaissance Roman bold Zapf Renaissance Antiqua fett

Zapf Renaissance light italic Zapf Renaissance leicht Kursiv

Zapf Renaissance Buch Kursiv & Zapf Renaissance book italic

ZAPF RENAISSANCE CAPS BOOK ITALIC & ZAPF RENAISSANCE KAPITÄLCHEN

Zapf Renaissance Kursiv mit Zierfiguren Zapf Renaissance / Italic plus Swashes

Zapf Renaissance (1986).

Gudrun Zapf-von Hesse

The early editions of Zapf's *Das Blumen-ABC*, *Feder und Stichel* and *Manuale typographicum*, issued in the late 1940s and early 1950s, were beautifully bound by a young Frankfurt binder called Gudrun von Hesse (born 1918), who had learned bookbinding with Otto Dorfner in Weimar. In 1935 she began to teach herself lettering using the Edward Johnston and Rudolf Koch manuals which were an inspiration to so many calligraphers, and in 1941 studied in Berlin with Johannes Boehland, the designer of the spirited brush script Balzac (1951) for Stempel. In 1952, Stempel issued her beautiful Diotima* roman and

Diotima (1952), Smaragd (1953) and Nofret (1986).

italic, which had been tried out in the wedding invitation for her marriage to Hermann Zapf the previous year. (He jokingly referred to this as trying to neutralise the opposition.) Gudrun Zapf later added to the Diotima family an open titling alphabet, Smaragd (1953), and a set of swash italic capitals, Ariadne (1954).

In 1968 she designed Shakespeare roman and italic for Hallmark, and in 1986, Nofret for Berthold, which is like a condensed Diotima semi-bold.

Paul Hayden Duensing, 'Diotima', *Fine Print on type*, 1988.

RSTUVWXYZabcdefghijklmn

ABCDEFGHIJKLM abcdefghijklmn

ABCDEFGHIJKL
MNOPQRSTUVWXYZ

abcdefghijklmnopqrstuvwxyz
ABCDEFGHIJKLMNOPQRSTUVWXYZ

abcdefghijklmnopqrstuvwxyz
ABCDEFGHIJKLMNOPQRSTUVWXYZ

Aldo Novarese

Aldo Novarese (1920-95).

Aldo Novarese was Italy's most prolific designer of this century and one of the most prolific ever. Born on 29 June 1920 at Pontestura Monferrato in Piedmont, he studied in Turin at the G.B. Paravia printing school, where he later returned to teach, and in 1936 joined the type design office of Italy's leading type foundry, Nebiolo, also in Turin. He became type director of Nebiolo in 1950. His predecessor in this office was Alessandro Butti (1893–1959), with whom his earliest types were designed. These included the classical titling Augustea (1951), and the square sans-serif Microgrmma (1952). Novarese added lower-case founts to both of these, creating the sans-serif Eurostile (1962), and Nova Augustea, which has idiosyncratic letter forms quite similar to those of his Novarese (1978), designed for the Haas foundry but licensed to ITC. Side by side with these, he produced a classic Garamond, called Garaldus (1956), and a huge number of advertising display faces, of which the most original is Stop (1971).

Novarese left Nebiolo in 1975 after an internal reorganisation and became a freelance type designer, without reducing his output. In addition to his type designs he worked as a graphic designer, written booksonthe subject, taught, and produced a type classification system based on serif formation.

He died on is September 1995.

ABCDEFGHIJKLMNOPQRST
UVXYZWÇÆŒ 1234567890

ABCDEFGHIJKLMNOPQ
RSTUVXYWZÇÆŒ&
1234567890

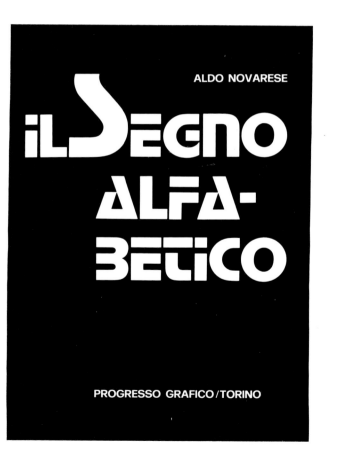

ALDO NOVARESE

IL SEGNO
ALFA-
BETICO

PROGRESSO GRAFICO/TORINO

abcdefghijklmnopqrstuvwxyz
ABCDEFGHIJKLMNOPQRSTUVWXYZ
1234567890 &£$.,:;!?"

abcdefghijklmnopqrstuvwxyz
ABCDEFGHIJKLMNOPQRSTUVWXYZ
1234567890 &£$.,:;!?"

José Mendoza y Almeida

*José Mendoza y Almeida
(born 1926).*

Two of the designers of the generation after Roger Excoffon who have contributed most to French type design have been to some extent outsiders. Adrian Frutiger, whose work is described in the next section, is Swiss, while the slightly older José Mendoza y Almeida, while born in France, is fiercely proud of his Spanish descent.

José Mendoza was born in Sèvres, on the outskirts of Paris, on 14 October 1926. His maternal grandfather was a decorative craftsman at the porcelain works for which Sèvres is famous, and his Castilian father was an advertising lettering artist, who first encouraged the young José to start drawing alphabets. Mendoza's schooling was interrupted by World War II, when the family took refuge in the Auvergne, and then by the early death of his father in 1944. Forced to earn a living, he worked in the graphic design studio in the photo-engraving firm of Clichés Union in Paris, specialising like his father in lettering. In 1954 he spent a year working with Maximilien Vox, and there met Roger Excoffon, who invited him to join the Fonderie Olive, where he stayed for five years, producing drawings for Vendôme and many of Excoffon's faces. He left in July 1959 to work as a freelance. His first type, Pascal, appeared the following year, cut by the Typefoundry Amsterdam. It is a sort of country cousin to Optima, which had recently been issued in Germany; more condensed and with a lift in its step, it is a most attractive face. It was the only Mendoza type to be cut in metal, and for the next ten years he worked on a series of photo-titling alphabets. His next major commission came in 1971 from Monotype, for another in the series of designs by distinguished international designers for the Monophoto which had begun with Apollo. Photina (1972) is a roman of original conception with a particularly juicy italic, now widely available in PostScript form.

Although his designs have been digitised, Mendoza himself is resolutely committed to drawing by hand, and has spoken eloquently on the subject. For

ABCDEFGHIJKLMNOPQRSTUV
WXYZÆŒ

abcdefghijklmnopqrstuvwxyz
1234567890£&æœ

Morris and the printed book

A reconsideration of his views on type and book design in the light of later computer-aided techniques

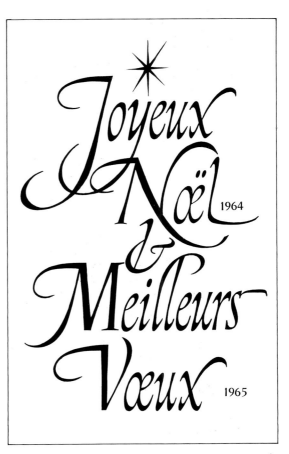

many years he made beautiful New Year cards cut in wood and this sense of craftsmanship informs all his work. He has designed a handsome italic, Sully-Jonquieres, and a calligraphic script, Fidelio, both of which were issued in 1980 by Mecanorma; both are now available from FontShop International. In 1990 ITC brought out his Mendoza, a gutsy roman and italic.

Top: Pascal (1960).
Above: Photina (1972).
Right: a greeting card with Mendoza's woodcut lettering.

Adrian Frutiger

Adrian Frutiger (born 1928).

Although born and educated in Switzerland, Frutiger* has spent all his working life in France, where he went at the invitation of Charles Peignot of the Paris foundry Deberny & Peignot.

Like most foundries, Deberny & Peignot had grown by amalgamation, the result of a merger between the enterprise which took its name from Alexandre de Berny (the son of Balzac's mistress), and later under the direction of Robert Girard, the designer of Astrée (1921), with the concern founded by Gustave Peignot in the 1860s. Gustave Peignot died in 1889, and his son Georges initiated a spirited programme of type designs by contemporary graphic artists. Eugène Grasset designed an ugly type which bears his name (1898), which was followed by those of Georges Auriol (1863-1938). Auriol (1901-4) is the only *art nouveau* face which can be read in long texts, and combined with the ornaments from the same hand in the books on typography by François Thibaudeau still looks fresh and lively. After this, Georges Peignot's later commissions were a disappointment, typified by Naudin (1913-20), based on the lettering of the illustrator Bernard Naudin. But he was responsible for the revival of the eighteenth-century Cochin and Moreau-le-Jeune types which were enthusiastically taken up in England and the United States, and for the first of the modern recuttings of the Imprimerie Nationale 'Garamond' (1912).

The Peignot dynasty was shattered in World War I when Georges and his three brothers were all killed. The management was taken over by Georges's son Charles (1897-1983), who reacted against the eighteenth-century revival style in the direction of *art déco* modernism. The foundry was committed to Naudin and Astrée, and Peignot was too young to persuade it to change course overnight; but in the late 1920s he commissioned the eminent poster artist A.

Adrian Frutiger, *Type, sign, symbol,* Zurich, ABC-Verlag, 1980.

les feuilles éparpillées 1234567890
ABCDEFGHIJKLMNOPQR

NE LE RENDS PAS ILLISIBLE

lequel je préférais, du Télémaque, du Racine, ou du Boil
J'ai avoué que tous me semblaient également beaux.
Monsieur, vous ne voyez pas le titre du Boileau! J'ai

SUPERBE

M. Cassandre (1901-68) to design the wonderfully eccentric Bifur (1928) and in 1936 the even more peculiar Peignot, as well as the more conventional two-tone sans-serif Acier Noir of the same year. These types are so redolent of their period that description is superfluous.

Charles Peignot was a type founder of vision, and he saw foundry type threatened not so much by mechanical hot metal composition as by filmsetting and dry transfer techniques. After World War II Deberny & Peignot anticipated the second challenge with a range of adhesive alphabet sheets called Typophane, for which Charles's son Rémy Peignot drew the attractive titling Cristal (1957), and the first by securing French distribution rights to the Lumitype photosetting machine (called the Photon in Britain and the United States), developed by two French telephone engineers, Higonnet and Moyroud.

In 1947 Charles Peignot and Cassandre collaborated on Touraine, a normalised version of Peignot made about the same time as Excoffon's Chambord, but increasingly Peignot turned his attention to faces for the Lumitype, which meant a repertoire of faces not just for the Francophile 'Gauloise' market, but for the world. With great foresight, he spotted in 1952 the

talents of the young Swiss designer Adrian Frutiger, and invited him to Paris.

Frutiger was born on 24 March 1928 at Unterseen in Switzerland, the son of a weaver. As a child he used to help his father, and has always been concerned with the way graphic techniques are grounded in the crafts, and the shapes of letters in the way they were scratched, incised, written or cut in metal. He showed an early interest in painting and sculpture, but his teachers at school prudently suggested he put his lettering talents to use in the printing industry, and in 1944 he began a four year apprenticeship with the firm of Otto Schaeffli in Interlaken. At the same time he attended courses at the Zurich school of arts and crafts, where his professors were Walter Käch and Alfred Willimann, and produced as a school project an astonishingly accomplished synopsis* of the development of the western alphabet, with the specimen scripts cut in the side grain of planks of wood. The work won a prize from the ministry of the interior, and an edition was printed from the wood. And while still

Adrian Frutiger, *Schrift/écriture/lettering,* Zurich, Bildungsverband Schweizerische Buchdrucker, 1951.

MIHIQVIDEMNVMQV
AMPERSVADERIPOTVIT
ANIMOSDVMINCORPI
ORIBVSESSENTMORT
ALIBVSVIVERECVMEX

Nec tamen omnia inchoatiua
habent primam profitionem.
Albefco enim nō habet albeo
licet figuranter Virgilius enim

*Two sections from Frutiger's
student project
'Schrift/écriture/lettering' (1951).*

164

at the Zurich school he also began work on a sans-serif type which later resurfaced as Univers.

After his move to Paris in 1952, Frutiger soon produced three faces for Deberny & Peignot which he later came to regard as practice work only, though many designers would be happy to rate them higher: they were a sharp-seriffed Latin titling fount, Président (1953), a shadowed sloped roman, Phoebus (1953) and a calligraphic script, Ondine (1954). Then, for the Lumitype, he supervised the adaptation of the classic repertoire, Garamond, Baskerville, Bodoni and the rest, to the matrix disks, and also designed his first major face, Méridien (1955), a sharp yet sensuous classical type which shows clearly both its creator's abiding feeling for the incised origins of roman lettering, and the curious seriffed y which appears in several of his faces. Méridien was simultaneously cut in metal, in roman only.

When Peignot decided to add a sans-serif family to the Lumitype range, Frutiger persuaded him to allow the development of the design he had begun at the Zurich school, rather than adapt an existing type. Trials were made and approved, the production went ahead, and Univers appeared in 1957 in both film and foundry metal for hand setting; shortly afterwards

Méridien (1955).

Monotype produced it in both hot metal and film, and most typesetting systems followed.

The type's phenomenal success was due to its skilfully unobtrusive detailing. It eliminated virtually everything but the essential forms of the letters, and was carefully and sweetly drawn. It was the most rational and basic of the post-war sans serifs. Max Miedinger's almost exactly contemporary Helvetica for the Haas foundry in Basle (1957) returned to the Berthold Akzidenz/Standard family of the beginning of the century, which was still extremely popular among Swiss typographers, and polished it up. Antique Olive, designed a few years later by Roger Excoffon, took the basic letters and gave them a strong dose of Gallic panache. Herman Zapf's 'serifless roman' Optima (1958), as the description suggests, pared away the serifs from a roman alphabet; and Syntax (1968), by another Swiss designer, Hans Meyer, is a curious hybrid, taking some of the shapes of old styles and giving them a modified monoline treatment. Frutiger worked geometrically, but his geometry is more complex and humane than that of the pre-war constructed round-O sans-serifs such as Futura, and Univers runs more comfortably along the line as a result.

La terre de France est remarquable par la netteté de sa figure, par les différences de ses régions et l'équilibre général de cette diversité de parties qui se conviennent, se groupent et LA TERRE DE FRANCE EST REM

ABCDEFGHIJKLMMNOPQRSTUVWXYZ
1234567890 abcdefghijklmnopqrstuvwxyz

England in the seventeenth century

Standard system of shorthand

Permit for exportation

ABCDEFGHIJKLMNOPQRSTUVWXYZ
abcdefghijklmnopqrstuvwxyzæœ
ABCDEFGHIJKLMNOPQRSTUVWXYZ
abcdefghijklmnopqrstuvwxyzæœ
£1234567890

végétal précieux **compact** *léger*
fort faible *rapide* **lourd** stable

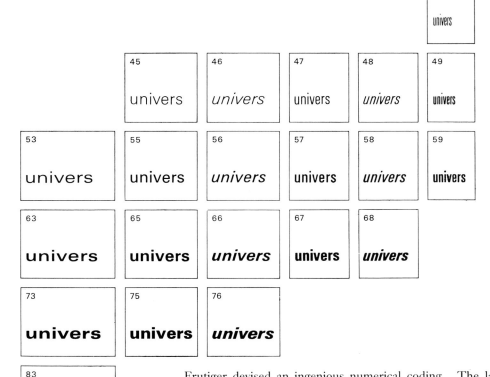

Frutiger devised an ingenious numerical coding system for the twenty-one members of the Univers family, to replace the often confusing fount nomenclature of weights and widths usually adopted in type families. Monotype, in making their version, took no notice, and kept to names and their own series numbers: thus Deberny & Peignot Univers 83 appears as Monotype Univers Ultra Bold Expanded, Series 697. However, Frutiger used his system again with his later sans-serif, called after him.

The success of Univers led to many commissions, including a modified version of the face for use in signs at Orly airport at Paris. (A decade and a half later, this process worked in reverse, with airport lettering inspiring the typeface Frutiger.) In 1959 the face Opéra was designed for the slug-setting Sofratype machine, and the following year Egyptienne for Deberny & Peignot, the first of several versions of the mécane Egyptian letters. In addition, Frutiger worked on many book design and lettering jobs, largely for scientific publications, but he also produced a magnificent set of abstract woodcut illustrations to the book of Genesis (1962), published as a fine edition by Pierre Bérès. In 1962 he set up his own studio, in association with Bruno Pfaffli and André Gürtler.

The latter has since left to set up Team 77 with Christian Mengelt and Erich Gschwind, responsible for Media (1976), Signa (1978), Haas Unica (1980) and Basilia Haas (1982), as well as publishing much detailed analysis of typeface design.

Frutiger's next major face was commissioned by Monotype in 1962. After a transitional period adapting metal types for use on the Monophoto, the Corporation asked for a new design, which was not cut in metal. Apollo is an historically interesting face, but not altogether a success: the italic is fidgety and the roman lacks a sense of flow. Frutiger has always been at his best not when he is designing classical alphabets but when taking normally unremarkable faces like sans-serifs and mécane Egyptians and imbuing them with unexpected elegance.

This elegance can be seen in muted form in Serifa, designed for Bauer in 1967, and in the rather similar Glypha (1979); it is even apparent when he was given the thankless task of designing an alphabet which could be read by optical character recognition machines, and still looked reasonably pleasant to humans. The result is OCR-B.

Iridium, designed in 1975 for Linotype, is a particularly handsome example of Frutiger's ability to

In 1784, 'The Marriage of Figaro' (*Mariage de Figaro*), by Beaumarchais, came out at Paris, where it was acted with astonishing success. Thomas Holcroft no sooner received notice of this piece, than he formed the instant resolution of going over to France to procure a copy of it, in order to translate and adapt it to the English stage.

He arrived in Paris the latter end of September, 1784, and proceeded to the lodgings of his friend Bonneville, to whom he immediately communicated the object of his journey. They both set about the accomplishment of it directly; but they found it attended with greater difficulty than they had expected. The comedy had not been printed: therefore, their first plan was to procure a manuscript copy, either at the theatre, or through some friend of the author. This attempt, however, they found fruitless, from the jealousy with which the managers of the French theatre prevented any copies from getting abroad. The only resource now remaining,

Zeichen erkennen
Zeichen gestalten

breathe life into a conventional form. If it is possible for a transitional face to dance, then Iridium dances, yet it always remains in formation.

At the same time as his work on Iridium, Frutiger was at work on lettering for directional signs at the new Paris airport, Charles de Gaulle, at which the first terminal opened in 1975. Much of his work has been in the non-typographical but related field of sign alphabets, notably for Electricité de France and Gaz de France. For Charles de Gaulle a sans-serif was chosen as being practical and sensible, and a deliberate choice was made of a design that would not look as 'clinical' as the sans-serifs of the previous decades, such as Univers, and also would echo the curves of the terminal's architecture. The result was code-named Roissy, after the village where the airport was built, and when adapted by Linotype as a typeface was called after its creator. Frutiger (1976) is an efficient but cheerful face which shows that it is still possible to draw new forms of sans-serif. Yet, paradoxically, in spite of its origins in a modern airport, it has something of the timeless about it, of the lettering scratched in stone at the dawn of script, and the universal sign language which Frutiger has studied so carefully. It is his concern with the larger concept of

abcdefghijklmnopqrstuvwxyz
ABCDEFGHIJKLMNOPQRST
1234567890 .,;:''«»&!?

Håmbûrgefönstiv iam admodum mitigàti raptarum d earum parentes tum maxime sordida veste

abcdefghijklmnopqrstuvwxyz
ABCDEFGHIJKLMNOPQRST
1234567890 .,;:''«»&!?

Håmbûrgefönstiv iam admodum mitigati raptarum d earum parentes tum maxime sordida veste

Adrian Frutiger

Below: Frutiger (1976).
Bottom: Avenir (1988).

The basic character in a type design is determined by the uniform design characteristics of all letters in the alphabet.

The basic character in a type design is determined by the uniform design characteristics of all letters in the alphabet.

graphic communication, combined with his sense of the craft of lettering, which gives his work such quality.

Icone, which Linotype issued in 1980, took his interest in the glyphic formation of lettering a stage further: but here the details which transformed a sans-serif became the letter itself. Versailles and Breughel were both designed for Linotype in 1982; the first is based on lettering cut in metal, and the second is like nothing so much as a spirited calligraphic rendering of Apollo, with chunkier serifs.

In 1986, Linotype's centenary year, Frutiger designed Linotype Centennial, a modern face, and in 1988 an oddly restrained sans-serif, Avenir, combining the forms of Futura and Gill Sans. He recently returned to live in his native Switzerland.

'The great stroke of luck in my life', Frutiger wrote in 1964, 'is to have been blessed first with an artistic feeling for shapes, and second with an easy grasp of technical processes and of mathematics'. Since he wrote that, the need for such a grasp has become ever more pressing. Like Zapf's, Frutiger's understanding of the technical problems posed by the changes from pantographically cut metal type to film, and then to digitised faces, has ensured that his aesthetic vision has been realised with a minimum of loss by the way.

▌▌ Looking back on more than forty years of concern with sans serif typefaces, I felt an obligation to design a 'linear' style of sans serif in the tradition of Erbar, Futura** and to a lesser extent of Gill Sans**. These have 'constructed' characters from which the element of a handwriting movement has been removed.

Constructivist typefaces, such as Futura and Gill Sans, have come back into fashion, but most of the new faces in this style have been limited to display uses and are difficult to read in long texts.

Avenir is intended to be nothing more or less than a clear and clean representation of modern typographical trends, giving the designer a typeface which is strictly modern and at the same time human, i.e. suitably refined and elegant for use in texts of any length. **▌▌** ADRIAN FRUTIGER

Matthew Carter

Matthew Carter (born 1937).

*Facing page: Comparative settings
showing Bell Gothic (1938),
designed by C. H. Griffith,
and Matthew Carter's
Bell Centennial (1978).*

Matthew Carter's early training included learning how to cut punches by hand with Enschedé's great craftsman Paul Rädisch, and he has occasionally undertaken punchcutting jobs such as the guide sorts for Dante bold (see p.100) and a set of figures to accompany Monotype Van Dijck. Although all his own types have been drawn for cold composition, the discipline of metal, combined with an unerring elegance, informs all his work.

Carter was born on 1 October 1937 in London, the son of the typographical historian Harry Carter, translator and editor of the English edition of Charles Enschedé's *Typefoundries in the Netherlands*. After leaving school, he went to Enschedé in 1955 for a year and then returned to London to work as a freelance lettering and type designer, later joining Crosfield Electronics, to work on designs for the Lumitype/Photon. Here he designed Auriga, a mécane rather like Trump's Schadow, but with curious blocky details; he took this design with him when in 1965 he moved to New York to work with Mergenthaler Linotype, who released it in 1970. For Linotype he designed three scripts which availed themselves of the overlap kerning offered by film and digital composition – Cascade and Snell Roundhand (both in 1966), and Shelley (1972), and the newspaper type Olympian, conceived for both metal and film composition. (See 'Newspaper faces after Times', p.94.) He also produced a very handsome unquirky sans-serif, Video (1977).

In 1978 came Galliard. For some time Mike Parker, who had succeeded Jackson Burke as Mergenthaler Linotype's type director, had felt the lack of a distinguished old-face type designed specifically for photosetting, and Galliard was intended to fill that gap. It was based on the types of the French punchcutter Robert Granjon (1513–89), which had already been the starting point of two classics of the twentieth century, Monotype Plantin in 1913 and Times New Roman in 1932. Carter's Galliard is, as its name

Vaught Donald L 542 39th St Short Wylam – –780-8608
Vaught Ernest
   65 Merrimont Rd Hueytown – – – – – – –491-6244
Vaught J C 625 Barclay Ln – – – – – – – – –836-2436
Vaught Joe Jr Stertt – – – – – – – – – – – –672-2919
Vaught Ralph L 700 77th Wy S – – – – – – –836-8452
Vaught Susan A 2109 46th Pl Central Pk – – –787-4227
Vaultz Eva 1543 Dennison Av SW – – – – – –925-1752
Vause S F 603 Huckleberry Ln – – – – – – –979-5289
Vause Stephen F 445 Shades Crest Rd – – – –823-2662
Vautier Harold G 204 Killough Sprngs Rd – –853-5626
Vautrot Ruby L Mrs 2021 10th Av S – – – – –933-2265
Vazquez Norberto
   Old Jasper Hwy Adamsvie – – – – – – –674-3370
Veach J L 5725 Belmont Dr – – – – – – – – –956-3990
Veach Loren Aldrich – – – – – – – – – – – –665-1831
Veal Ad 450 21st Av S – – – – – – – – – – –251-9049
Veal Ad rl est 1711 Pinson – – – – – – – – –841-7380
Veal B Evan atty 1711 Pinson – – – – – – – –841-2789
Veal Clarence E Garndle – – – – – – – – – –631-3856
VEAL CONVENTION SERVICES—
   1711 Pinson – – – – – – – – – – – – – – –841-2789
   2109 10th Av N – – – – – – – – – – – – –322-6102
Veazey W B Vincent – – – – – – – – – – – –672-9506
Veazey Wilbur E 1541 53rd St Ensley – – – –923-1960
Veazey William A 287–A Chastaine Cir – – – –942-4137
Veazey Willie J 3084 Whispering Pines Cir – –823-5795
Vebber Mark H 5216 Goldmar Dr – – – – – –956-1661
Vebco contr 1900 28th Av S Homewood – – – –879-2259
Vedel Dental Technicians Inc lab
   1116 5th Av N – – – – – – – – – – – – –322-5475
Vedel George C 3848 Cromwell Dr – – – – – –967-2832
Vedel George C Jr 744 Saulter Ln – – – – – –871-8234
   Resf 34744 Saulter Ln – – – – – – – – – –870-9758
Vedel Murrey B 612 Oakmoor Dr – – – – – –942-3619
Vedell Collen J Daisy City – – – – – – – – –674-7772
Vedell William L 8830 Valley Hill Dr – – – –833-9915
Veenschoten & Co mfrs agts 2930 7th Av S – –251-3567
Veenschoten L A 1919–D Tree Top Ln – – – –822-7109
Veenschoten W E 3240 Pine Ridge Rd – – – –871-8883
Vega Abraham 915 16th S – – – – – – – – – –933-7619
Vega Delores 2–B Watertown Cir – – – – – –836-5980
Vega Edwin 2116 Rockland Dr Bluff Park – – –823-0403
Vegetable Patch Number 1 The
   Highway 31 S Alabstr – – – – – – – – – –663-7618
Vegetable Patch Office Alabstr – – – – – – –663-7378
Vegetable Patch The Number 2 Dogwood – – –665-4179
Veigl Patrick B Pawnee – – – – – – – – – – –841-1238
Veitch Beulah 1172 Five Mile Rd – – – – – –853-3361
Vest W L 4708 Lewisbrg Rd – – – – – – – – –841-7402
Vest W T 4737 N 68th – – – – – – – – – – –836-6371
Vesta Villa Exxon Self Serve
   1500 Hwy 31 S – – – – – – – – – – – – –823-5008
VESTAVIA AMOCO SERVICE
   1456 Montgomery Hwy – – – – – – – – – **823-1213**
VESTAVIA BARBEQUE & LOUNGE
   610 Montgomery Hwy Vestavia – – – – – **822-9984**
Vestavia Barber Shop
   610–A Montgomery Hwy – – – – – – – – –823-1974
VESTAVIA BEAUTY SALON
   710 Montgomery Hwy – – – – – – – – – –823-1893
Vestavia Beverage Co
   623 Montgomery Hwy – – – – – – – – – –822-9847
VESTAVIA BOWL
   Montgomery Hwy S Vestavia – – – – – – –979-4420
Vestavia Church Of Christ
   2325 Columbiana Rd – – – – – – – – – –822-0018
VESTAVIA CHURCH OF GOD
   2575 Columbiana Rd – – – – – – – – – –**823-1895**
Vestavia Church Of God Day Care day
   nursry 2575 Columbiana Rd – – – – – – –823-1895

VESTAVIA CITY OF---See Vestavia
   Hills City Of

VESTAVIA COIFFEURS
   617 Montgomery Hwy Vestva – – – – – –**823-1104**
Vestavia Country Club—
   Shades Mountain – – – – – – – – – – – –823-2451
   Golf Shop Shades Mountain – – – – – – –822-8300
   On Mondays & Before 8:30 AM Dial
     As Follows:—
     Stable Shades Mountain – – – – – – – –823-2451
     Accounting Dept Shades Mountain – – – –823-2979
     Golf Course Supt Shades Mountain – – – –823-2019
     Tennis Shop Shades Mountain – – – – – –823-2689
     General Manager's Ofc – – – – – – – – –823-2139
     Building Maintenance Shop
       Shades Mountain – – – – – – – – – –823-2349

Vaught Donald L 542 39th St Short Wylam – – –780-860S
Vaught Ernest 65 Merrimont Rd Hueytown – – –491-6244
Vaught J C 625 Barclay Ln – – – – – – – – – –836-2436
Vaught Joe Jr Stertt – – – – – – – – – – – – –672-2919
Vaught Ralph L 700 77th Wy S – – – – – – – –836-8452
Vaught Susan A 2109 46th Pl Central Pk – – – –787-4227
Vaultz Eva 1543 Dennison Av SW – – – – – – –925-1752
Vause S F 603 Huckleberry Ln – – – – – – – –979-5289
Vause Stephen F 445 Shades Crest Rd – – – – –823-2662
Vautier Harold G 204 Killough Sprngs Rd – – –853-5626
Vautrot Ruby L Mrs 2021 10th Av S – – – – – –933-2265
Vazquez Norberto Old Jasper Hwy Adamsvie – –674-3370
Veach J L 5725 Belmont Dr – – – – – – – – – –956-3990
Veach Loren Aldrich – – – – – – – – – – – – –665-1831
Veal Ad 450 21st Av S – – – – – – – – – – – –251-9049
Veal Ad rl est 1711 Pinson – – – – – – – – – –841-7380
Veal B Evan atty 1711 Pinson – – – – – – – – –841-2789
Veal Clarence E Garndle – – – – – – – – – – –631-3856
VEAL CONVENTION SERVICES—
   1711 Pinson – – – – – – – – – – – – – – – –841-2789
   2109 10th Av N – – – – – – – – – – – – – –322-6102
Veazey W B Vincent – – – – – – – – – – – – –672-9506
Veazey Wilbur E 1541 53rd St Ensley – – – – –923-1960
Veazey William A 287–A Chastaine Cir – – – –942-4137
Veazey Willie J 3084 Whispering Pines Cir – – –823-5795
Vebber Mark H 5216 Goldmar Dr – – – – – – –956-1661
Vebco contr 1900 28th Av S Homewood – – – – –879-2259
Vedel Dental Technicians Inc lab
   1116 5th Av N – – – – – – – – – – – – – –322-5475
Vedel George C 3848 Cromwell Dr – – – – – – –967-2832
Vedel George C Jr 744 Saulter Ln – – – – – – –871-8234
   Resf 34744 Saulter Ln – – – – – – – – – – –870-9758
Vedel Murrey B 612 Oakmoor Dr – – – – – – –942-3619
Vedell Collen J Daisy City – – – – – – – – – –674-7772
Vedell William L 8830 Valley Hill Dr – – – – –833-9915
Veenschoten & Co mfrs agts 2930 7th Av S – – –251-3567
Veenschoten L A 1919–D Tree Top Ln – – – – –822-7109
Veenschoten W E 3240 Pine Ridge Rd – – – – –871-8883
Vega Abraham 915 16th S – – – – – – – – – – –933-7619
Vega Delores 2–B Watertown Cir – – – – – – –836-5980
Vega Edwin 2116 Rockland Dr Bluff Park – – – –823-0403
Vegetable Patch Number 1 The
   Highway 31 S Alabstr – – – – – – – – – – –663-7618
Vegetable Patch Office Alabstr – – – – – – – –663-7378
Vegetable Patch The Number 2 Dogwood – – – –665-4179
Veigl Patrick B Pawnee – – – – – – – – – – – –841-1238
Veitch Beulah 1172 Five Mile Rd – – – – – – –853-3361
Vest W L 4708 Lewisbrg Rd – – – – – – – – – –841-7402
Vest W T 4737 N 68th – – – – – – – – – – – –836-6371
Vesta Villa Exxon Self Serve 1500 Hwy 31 S – –823-5008
VESTAVIA AMOCO SERVICE
   1456 Montgomery Hwy – – – – – – – – – – **823-1213**
VESTAVIA BARBEQUE & LOUNGE
   610 Montgomery Hwy Vestavia – – – – – – **822-9984**
Vestavia Barber Shop
   610–A Montgomery Hwy – – – – – – – – –823-1974
VESTAVIA BEAUTY SALON
   710 Montgomery Hwy – – – – – – – – – – –823-1893
Vestavia Beverage Co 623 Montgomery Hwy – –822-9847
VESTAVIA BOWL
   Montgomery Hwy S Vestavia – – – – – – – –979-4420
Vestavia Church Of Christ
   2325 Columbiana Rd – – – – – – – – – – –822-0018
VESTAVIA CHURCH OF GOD
   2575 Columbiana Rd – – – – – – – – – – –**823-1895**
Vestavia Church Of God Day Care day
   nursry 2575 Columbiana Rd – – – – – – – –823-1895

VESTAVIA CITY OF---See Vestavia
   Hills City Of

VESTAVIA COIFFEURS
   617 Montgomery Hwy Vestva – – – – – – – **823-1104**
Vestavia Country Club—
   Shades Mountain – – – – – – – – – – – – –823-2451
   Golf Shop Shades Mountain – – – – – – – –822-8300
   On Mondays & Before 8:30 AM Dial
     As Follows:—
     Stable Shades Mountain – – – – – – – – –823-2451
     Accounting Dept Shades Mountain – – – – –823-2979
     Golf Course Supt Shades Mountain – – – – –823-2019
     Tennis Shop Shades Mountain – – – – – – –823-2689
     General Manager's Ofc – – – – – – – – – –823-2139
     Building Maintenance Shop
       Shades Mountain – – – – – – – – – – –823-2349
     Swimming Pool Shades Mountain – – – – –822-2559
Vestavia Country Club Employee's
   Lounge Shades Mountain – – – – – – – – –822-9840
Vestavia Hardware & Home Supply

---

suggests, a far more dancing interpretation of the Granjon letter, based on no particular size but 'an anthology'. Granjon's italics were celebrated, and Carter's is drawn with particular verve. Galliard has since become a modern classic, seeming better as time goes by. Its marketing was helped by licensing to ITC, and Carter has done some tinkering with the details over the years both at Bitstream and at the business he set up with Cherie Cone in 1992, Carter and Cone.

The bolder weights of the Galliard family are a model of the kind of subtlety which can be achieved by the Ikarus program in the hands of a sensitive craftsman. As Charles Bigelow wrote in his review of the type,[*] 'Most bolds for historical seriffed faces are too flabby – the bone of the strokes is obscured by the fat that was larded on by later hands – but the Galliard bolds manage to maintain a more muscular appearance. The Ultra roman is especially jolly and athletic; it reminds this reviewer of Fatty Arbuckle in his best silent comedies.'

In the same year as Galliard, Carter also produced a complete contrast, Bell Centennial. This arose from a very specific design brief for a type for American telephone directories, and is a textbook example of highly skilled if inconspicuous type design. Up to 1937, such directories had been printed locally in whatever type the printer chose; but in that year the Bell company asked C. H. Griffith of Mergenthaler Linotype to design a type for use in all their directories. Griffith came up with a condensed sans-serif which was christened Bell Gothic, and this served well until the printers switched their composition over from hot-metal Linotypes to CRT setters in the early 1970s. The coarser resolution led to loss of detail and complaints of illegibility from subscribers. Linotype's brief was to adapt the design for the new conditions, and Carter managed to make the type more legible, larger on its body and yet more economical of space. It managed to do this while remaining graceful; as Gunnlaugur Briem puts it, 'Carter created a bullet-proof rhinoceros that could dance Swan Lake'.

Meanwhile Carter had returned to London in 1971 for ten years, during which time he continued to work for Linotype, producing many of his best-known faces, as well as being typographical adviser to Her Majesty's Stationery Office. In 1981 he returned

Charles Bigelow, 'Galliard', *Fine Print on type*, 1988.

Snell Roundhand

❦ ɪᴛᴄ Galliard ᴄᴄ ❧

QRSTUVWXYZ&ABCDEFGH

abcdefghijklmnopqrst

vuwxyz

❦

Bitstream Charter: abcdefghijklmno

abcdefghijklmnopqrstuvwxyz

MATTHEW·CARTER'S
MANTINIA
A·NEW·DESIGN
WITH·CAPITALS
TALL·CAPITALS
ALTERNATIVES
SUPERIORS·&
LIGATURES

to the USA where he and Mike Parker both left Mergenthaler Linotype and set up Bitstream in Cambridge, Massachusetts, one of the first digital type businesses. Bitstream Charter (1987) was the first type produced there, intended as a no-nonsense roman for both laser-printers and high-definition typesetters, its proportions based on those of Fournier, but with thickened up serifs.

In 1992 Carter left Bitstream to set up Carter and Cone. A new digitisation of Galliard has been produced there with expert sets. As a titling face to accompany Galliard, he has produced Mantinia (1993), which has a dangerously generous selection of tied sorts and ligatures which could be over-used by undisciplined designers. The same is true of the early-Christian-looking Sophia (1993).

SOPHIA

Gerard Unger

Gerard Unger (born 1942).

The Dutch are a patriotic people and justifiably proud of their superiority in type design. Indeed, Gerard Unger claims that there are more type designers per head of population in the Netherlands than anywhere else on earth. In the period after the deaths of Jan van Krimpen and De Roos, the flame was carried forward by S. L. Hartz (see p.109), Dick Dooijes (born in Amsterdam on 6 May 1909), Chris Brand (born in Utrecht on 16 September 1921), and Bram de Does (born in Amsterdam on 19 July 1934).*

Dooijes trained with De Roos, and worked for Enschedé's rival the Typefoundry Amsterdam, formerly called the Tetterode foundry. For them he designed a sans-serif, Mercator (1958), an open display face Contura (1964), and Lectura (1969), a

Mathieu Lommen, *Letterontwerpers*, Haarlem, Enschedé, 1987.

handsome roman book face which subsequently became available from Scangraphic.

Chris Brand, a distinguished calligrapher, is best known for his book face Albertina (1965), for the Monophoto.

Bram de Does was for some years the head of design at Enschedé, the position occupied by Van Krimpen, and his predecessor's influence is detectable, though not overpowering, in his work. The commission for his type Trinité (1982) came after Bobst Graphic approached Enschedé for permission to adapt Van Krimpen's Romanée for photosetting. De Does's advice was that since the conversion of a design from metal to film was as complicated a matter as designing afresh (an opinion which Van Krimpen would have endorsed, as we have seen), a completely new type was preferable. As a result, he was asked to design Trinité as a joint venture with Enschedé and Bobst/Autologic. The name reflected an unusual feature of the type, that there were three alternative lengths of extenders, allowing the appearance of both compact and spacious leading. Trinité is a handsome face in the tradition of excellence associated with Enschedé, and while the italic lacks a degree of bite, the roman is admirable. (At the time of writing, the Enschedé Font Foundry is at work digitising the original Romanée.)

All these designers show a refinement of form which is quintessentially Dutch. By contrast, the early types of Gerard Unger can be seen in many ways as a reaction against this pervasive good taste. Unger was born on 22 January 1942, in Arnhem. His father was publicity director of a large Dutch textile manufacturing firm, working with a number of internationally known designers including Moholy-Nagy, so that the young Gerard was brought up in an atmosphere in which modern design was highly valued. He studied typography and type design at the Gerrit Rietveld Academy in Amsterdam between 1963–7, and afterwards became an assistant to Wim Crouwel (born

The sun's on the pavement,
  The current comes and goes,
And the grey streets of London
  They blossom like the rose.

Crowned with the spring sun,
  Vistas fair and free;
What joy that waits not?
  What that may not be?

green-grocery at the corners. Enchanted Covent Gardens of the Hesperides; and great in order to scatter chests of them on the early sunbeams in the London dawn cross a time, the clearness of Italian air; and by its stranded barges and glidings of red sail, Lucerne lake or Venetian lagoon – by Thames'
  With such circumstance round him in what necessary effects followed upon the have had Giorgione's sensibility (and more

1928), the author of one of the most notoriously reductive single-alphabet designs, followed by a period combining work in an advertising agency, two days a week at Enschedé, where he designed Marqueur (1972), a utilitarian alphabet for engraved signs, and an increasing amount of freelance work.
  At this period he began his association with Dr Rudolf Hell's organisation, developers of the Digiset, for whom several of his early faces were designed. The first three were conceived as a loose grouping. Demos (1975), a workhorse roman, and Praxis (1977), a sans-serif, were both designed to resist coarse CRT rastering, and are square-cut and robust, and a deliberate move away from the delicate and bookish Dutch tradition. Flora (1984), called after Unger's daughter, can be used as the italic for Praxis or on its own and, although its idea sprang from Schneidler's Grafik (1934), it is by far the most original design of the three. In it the sans-serif form comes as close to a true cursive as is possible. Although its axis is vertical, it gives a remarkable impression of movement and calligraphic flow.
  Unger's more recent faces form another cohesive group, with strong horizontal stress (which he has ascribed to the flat Dutch landscape as seen in thou-

In former days the
shape a new book

In former days the
shape a new book

In former days the
shape a new book

In former days the shape
a new book was to take

In former days the shape
a new book was to take

In former days the shape
a new book was to take

Above:
Albertina, designed by Chris
Brand (1964).

Below:
Bram de Does's Trinité (1982).

White space is not a
mere residue. It is an
active force. It is vital
in the detail of text
White space is not a
mere residue. It is an
active force. It is vital
in the detail of text

White space is not a
mere residue. It is an
active force. It is vital
in the detail of text

White space is not a
mere residue. It is an
active force. It is vital
in the detail of text

White space is not a
mere residue. It is an
active force. It is vital
in the detail of text

White space is not a
mere residue. It is an
active force. It is vital
in the detail of text

sands of paintings)* promoted by pronounced wedge-shaped serifs. Also characteristic of these faces is the high spring point of the curves of the lower-case **m** and **n**, which they share with faces such as Van Krimpen's Romulus and Dwiggins's Electra. Hollander (1983), influenced by seventeenth-century Dutch types like those of Van Dijck, is a sharply drawn book face with generous x-height. The cuneiform flavour of its serifs was intensified, and at the same time made chunkier, in Swift (1985). Although designed initially as a newspaper type, Swift works well in book setting, and both Paul Luna's excellent *Understanding type for desktop publishing* (1992) and the *Rookledge Handbook of type designers* are set in it.

Swift marked the end of Unger's association with Hell, and his next face was designed for Bitstream. Amerigo (1987) moves the wedginess noticeable up to now in the serif formation of his types into the swollen terminals of the letters' strokes, rather in the manner of Berthold Wolpe's Albertus. Both it and

Gerard & Marjan Unger, 'Dutch landscape with letters', *Gravisie* 14, Utrecht, 1989.

Oranda (1988), a variation on Swift, were designed for low-resolution laser-printers. Argo (1990), for URW in Hamburg, is a subtly drawn sans-serif with many of the characteristic Unger features. Interviewed by Robin Kinross* Unger has described the early versions as dangerously close to a 'souped-up Helvetica'; he revised it to something more like an Ungerised Frutiger.

All these faces were drawn by hand before being scanned into the computer. With Gulliver (1993) Unger has moved towards creation directly on screen, and it is the first type he is marketing himself. Billed as the world's most economic typeface, it is aimed at the kind of utilitarian work, such as encyclopaedias and newspaper classified setting, where character count is critical. As the name suggests, its design is linked with that of Swift. (Although the earlier type was named after the bird, for its grace in flight, rather than the author, Unger has noted the ambiguity and used the name of Swift's hero, who visited the lands of very small and very large people, for his type.)

Robin Kinross, 'Technology, aesthetics and type' (article on Unger), *Eye*, 3, 1991.

abcdefghijklmnopqrstuvwxyz
ABCDEFGHIJKLMNOPQRSTUVWXYZ

abcdefghijklmnopqrstuvwxyz
ABCDEFGHIJKLMNOPQRSTUVWXYZ

Swift

Bitstream Amerigo von Gerard Unger

Rigid was something of an eccentric: he invariably spoke English to his

Rigid was something of an eccentric: he invariably spoke English to his

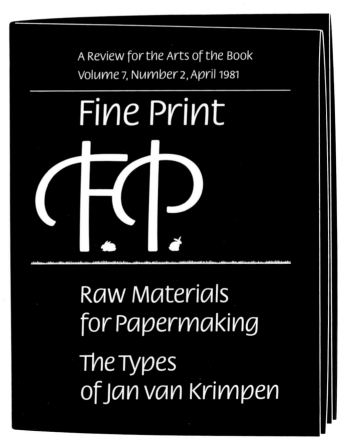

A Review for the Arts of the Book
Volume 7, Number 2, April 1981

Fine Print

F.P.

Raw Materials
for Papermaking

The Types
of Jan van Krimpen

Top: Oranda (1988).
Centre: Argo (1990).
Bottom right: A cover designed by
Gerard Unger for 'Fine Print',
showing an early version of Flora.

Gulliver

Gulliver regular

Gulliver

Gulliver italic

Gulliver

Gulliver book

Gulliver

Gulliver book italic

Gulliver

Gulliver semi bold

Gulliver

Gulliver semi bold italic

Gulliver

Gulliver bold

Gulliver

Gulliver bold italic

However, the serifs are given more conventional brackets than Swift's and the earlier type's gutsy individuality is toned down.

As well as a gifted designer, Gerard Unger is an articulate critic of type design, and has written a perceptive article on Dwiggins in the Dutch journal *Quaerendo*.* Dwiggins advocated what he called the 'M-factor', which he derived from his marionette making: details of modelling which seemed exaggerated close to were inconspicuous when seen from the stalls, but nevertheless essential for delineating form and character. The same factor could be applied to types to give them visual sparkle and help their legibility and flow, what Dwiggins called that 'something that gets all the animals under one "top" and brands them as A Circus'. In practical terms, conspicuously in Electra and more restrainedly on Caledonia, this meant certain angularities and emphases of the horizontal which have had a considerable influence on Unger's work.

Gerard Unger, 'Experimental No.223, a newspaper typeface designed by W. A. Dwiggins', *Quaerendo*, 11, 4, 1981.

Sumner Stone

The Stone family* of typefaces consists of a classically graceful roman and a particularly attractive italic, called Stone Serif, with a Sans and a more idiosyncratic simplified roman and sloped roman called Informal, all designed with related bolds, to be used together, and to look well in laser-printed versions as well as high-definition setting. The family, or clan, as Stone calls it, was designed while he was director of typography at Adobe Systems, and afterwards licensed to ITC.

Sumner Stone was born on 9 June 1945 in Venice, Florida. While at high school he edited the school paper and fell under the spell of the hot-metal Linotypes at the local printer's. When he went on to Reed College in Portland, Oregon, he was taught by the calligrapher Lloyd Reynolds who encouraged his interest in letter-forms, and he was also inspired by the Hallmark film made by Hermann Zapf, which led to his working for two years with Hallmark in Kansas City. He then moved to California, where he set up a lettering studio in Sonoma, and at the same time went back to school at Sonoma State University to study mathematics. There he became interested in the design of typefaces on the computer, which led him to move first to Autologic and then, in 1985, to Adobe.

At the end of 1989 Stone left Adobe to set up his own Stone Type Foundry in Palo Alto, where he has produced Stone Print (1991), a condensed roman designed for the American graphic design magazine *Print*, and Silica (1993), a lively slab serif. These have been created by a combination of drawing on paper and screen using FontStudio and Fontographer.

Above: Sumner Stone (born 1945).
Facing page:
Top: The Stone Family (1987).
Centre: Stone Print (1991).
Bottom: Silica (1993).

Sumner Stone, 'The Stone family of typefaces: new voices for the electronic age', *Fine Print on type*, 1988.

Sumner Stone, *On Stone, the art and use of typography on the personal computer*, San Francisco, Bedford Arts; London, Lund Humphries, 1991.

The Stone Family of Typefaces: New Voices for the Electronic Age

AaBbCcDdEeFfGgHhIiJjKkLlMmNnOoPpQqRrSsTtUuVvWwXxYyZz

AaBbCcDdEeFfGgHhIiJjKkLlMmNnOoPpQqRrSsTtUuVvWwXxYyZz

AaBbCcDdEeFfGgHhIiJjKkLlMmNnOoPpQqRrSsTtUuVvWwXxYyZz

AaBbCcDdEeFfGgHhIiJjKkLlMmNnOoPpQqRrSsTtUuVvWwXxYyZz

AaBbCcDdEeFfGgHhIiJjKkLlMmNnOoPpQqRrSsTtUuVvWwXxYyZz

AaBbCcDdEeFfGgHhIiJjKkLlMmNnOoPpQqRrSsTtUuVvWwXxYyZz

ABCDEFGHIJKLMNOPQRSTUVWXYZ
abcdefghijklmnopqrstuvwxyz
ABCDEFGHIJKLMNOPQRSTUVWXYZ
abcdefghijklmnopqrstuvwxyz

The truth is that

Typography

is an art in which violent revolutions can scarcely, in the nature of things, hope to be successful. A type of revolutionary novelty may be extremely beautiful in itself; but, for the creatures of habit that we are, its very novelty tends to make it illegible...

TYPOGRAPHY FOR THE TWENTIETH-CENTURY READER, ALDOUS HUXLEY 1928

Robert Slimbach

Robert Slimbach (born 1956).

By one of the ironies of design history, Robert Slimbach, who seems to have been creating original and mature faces from the moment he began, fell into type design almost by accident. He was born in Evanston, Illinois, on 15 December 1956, the son of a photo-engraver and printer; but as a keen gymnast he went to the University of California at Los Angeles on an athletics scholarship. After university, he worked producing silk-screen posters and prints, many incorporating hand lettering. In 1983, mainly to supplement his income, he joined Autologic, where he began to study classic typefaces and the designs of Hermann Zapf and Georg Trump.

He moved in 1985 to Ventura as a freelance type designer. He produced two highly assured faces for ITC, a squareish roman and italic called Slimbach (1987) and Giovanni (1988), a cleaned-up old face.

In 1987 Sumner Stone invited him to Adobe, where he designed Utopia, a Transitional face, and the much admired Adobe Garamond (both 1989). The next year came the extraordinarily assured Minion, which already looks like becoming a modern classic. It has features in common with Sabon, but is sharper and more condensed. Although it was designed and first issued before the introduction of Multiple Master technology, it was subsequently reissued as a three-axis face in 1992. In the same year, Slimbach collaborated with Carol Twombly on the lively sans-serif Myriad, and his chancery italic fount Poetica appeared. Sanvito, the following year, is a freer italic, and shows Slimbach's growing interest in scripts, the latest of which is Caflisch Script (1993), based on the handwriting of Max Caflisch (born 1916), the eminent Swiss designer.

Although Slimbach is enthusiastic about the creative control offered by the computer to the designer, his preparatory work is done on paper, and his calligraphy is highly accomplished.

At the Gates of the Forest
At the Gates of the Forest

At the gates of the for-
est, the surprised man
of the world is forced
to leave his city esti-
*mates of great and
small, wise and foolish.
The knapsack of cus*

abcdefghijklmn
ABCDEFGHIJKLMN

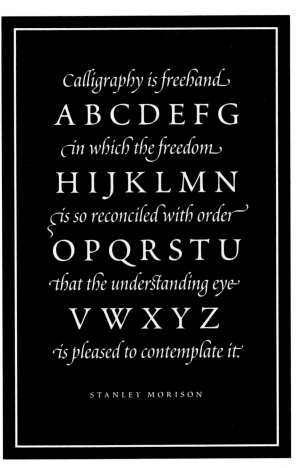

Calligraphy is freehand
A B C D E F G
in which the freedom
H I J K L M N
is so reconciled with order
O P Q R S T U
that the understanding eye
V W X Y Z
is pleased to contemplate it.

STANLEY MORISON

Carol Twombly

opqrstuvwxyz
OPQRSTUVWXYZ

Carol Twombly's work for Adobe has admirably complemented Robert Slimbach's. Her designs have been largely for display faces, with the exception of her sophisticated version of Caslon, and when they collaborated on Myriad the work seems to have been preternaturally even-handed, with each partner working on sets of drawings and then exchanging them.

Twombly was born in Concord, Massachusetts, on 13 June 1959, and studied at the Rhode Island School of Design, where she was taught by Charles Bigelow, who directed her artistic interests towards type design. She was influenced, too, by Gerard Unger, who taught digital typography there for a term. She did some freelance work for Bigelow and Holmes, and attended a course in digital typography at Stanford set up by Bigelow with support from Donald Knuth. Her first type was an accomplished one, a sharply-drawn, slightly inclined informal face called Mirarae (1984), which won first prize in a typeface competition sponsored by the Japanese typesetting firm of Morisawa. She began working part-time for Adobe, and joined the staff full-time in 1988.

For Adobe she has designed three display types, which all appeared in 1989. Lithos is based on the kind of monoline early classical inscriptional lettering shown in Adrian Frutiger's lettering book on page 164, although Twombly's immediate models were Greek. In Lithos they are given a distinctly balletic look. Trajan is a pure version of the famous Roman incised letter, and Charlemagne is a regularised interpretation of the large drawn capitals of the Carolingian period. All three combine sensitive drawing, a respect for their models, and yet a practical attitude to the needs of typographers. After an interlude in which she produced her version of Caslon (1990), and the two years spent on Myriad, her latest design is an open-ended shaded display alphabet with a curious bulgy white inline, called Viva (1993).

Margery Cantor, 'Carol Twombly, type design and other sports', *Fine Print*, 16, 3, 1990.

ABCDEFGHIJKLMNOPQRSTUVWXYZ
abcdefghijklmnopqrstuvwxyz&

ABCDEFGHIJKLMNOPQRST
ABCDEFGHIJKLMNOPQRST

ABCDEFGHIJKLMN

ABCDEFGHIJKLMN

ABCDEFGHIJKLMNOPQRSTUVWXYZ abcdefghijklmnopqrstvvwxyz

ABCDEFGHIJKLMNOPQRSTUVWXYZ *abcdefghijklmnopqrstuvwxyz*

Facing page, top:
Myriad (1992) in collaboration
with Robert Slimbach.
Below: Carol Twombly
(born 1959).

This page:
Mirarae (1984).
Lithos, two weights (1989).
Trajan (1989).
Charlemagne (1989).
Caslon (1990).
Viva (1993).

ABCDEFGHIJKLMNOP
abcdefghijklmnopqr

Epilogue

The skeleton shapes of the letters of our alphabet change hardly at all. Why then do skilled type designers devote so much time, sometimes their whole lives, to drawing different versions of their outlines?

To the question put at the beginning of this book, the case histories in it return a wide variety of answers. Rudolf Koch, whose exalted view of the craftsman's task was quoted in the Introduction, and Eric Gill, were both artist-craftsmen for whom type design provided a clear solution to their doubts, which were widespread at the time, about the rôle of the arts in society: letters were not a luxury but a necessity; their form followed their function; they were, in Van Krimpen's words, 'nothing but meaning', and in Gill's, 'things, not pictures of things'. The making of letters has for many designers a strong mystical significance, whether they take the religious view that the word preceded the flesh, or the anthropological one that the making of graphic signs was one of the first activities that distinguished men from beasts.

Such a dedication to the writing, drawing or cutting of letters does not, however, explain what makes the letters different in outline. The study of the vast subject of the cultural influences on letter forms absorbed the last years of Stanley Morison and has occupied many scholars before and since, and is far from complete; but the practical point is that designers, not being cameras, change what they copy. In the course of an interesting essay on the subject, Charles Bigelow* neatly summed up the question. 'This is the crucial paradox of type design imitation, and the force which drives type design evolution. A designer skilled and knowledgeable enough to perceive and render all the subtle nuances of another master craftsman is really too good to do a slavish copy. A master designer will inevitably transform an imitation into a creative act, which will give the new design true individuality.'

Bram de Does made the sensible observation which led to the design of Trinité, that the adaptation of an existing type for a new typesetting system is in any case so skilled and laborious a process that a new design is preferable. Yet the question of what a 'new' design is remains a difficult one: it remains equally true that all type designs are new, and that none is. Goudy wrote, 'It is hardly possible to create a good type face that will differ radically from the established forms of the past', and yet his types are more individual than many drawn by designers who probably imagined that they were working with their own unaided wits. The creations which broke most abruptly with the forms of the past were probably the constructed sans-serifs of the late 1920s, and yet that break proved a dead end.

In all this, type design is like the composition of music, in which themes are reused openly or covertly, and new material developed according to formal rules. No one would dream of censuring Brahms or Rachmaninov for writing works based on a theme of Paganini's, nor of claiming that Paganini was therefore the greater composer. Although the antecedents of a type may be interesting and revealing, the type must be judged for what it is. The student should learn to discriminate between a copy and a reconstruction – in musical terms, between an arrangement and a set of variations – while bearing in mind that the copy may work better on the page than a more original but awkward type.

As we have seen, most theorists have taken the view that a text typeface should be quiet and unassuming, without details which cry out; that, in Keats's words, 'Heard melodies are sweet, but those unheard / Are sweeter'. And yet to type-conscious readers this is an impossibility: inevitably we become aware of what a book is set in, and how well or badly it is set. Quite apart from the larger question of whether readers are

Charles Bigelow, 'Technology and the aesthetics of type', *The Seybold report*, 10, 24, 1981.

aware of the qualities of book design and production as a whole (most of the evidence says not, but I cannot believe it), the legibility and beauty of the typeface in which a book is set has a melody, which may be sweet or grating, but can no longer be unheard. The loss of the state of innocence in which Baskerville looks like Bembo, and Helvetica is indistinguishable from Univers, has the compensating advantage that we become more aware of the tiny details and the 'subtle allure' which go to make up the best faces. It is some small acknowledgement we can make of the labours of the designers.

And then there is the perennial question, What is the best typeface? By this, the questioner usually means, What is the best type for my purposes? The answer can only be one of several classic favourites. If the question has a larger ambition, suggesting some kind of search for an ideal face, there can be no answer. As Robert Bringhurst has written, 'The ideal typeface, like the ideal string quartet, or the ideal tragic drama, is a figment of the theorist's imagination. Such a face will be found not by perfecting a set of letters, but only by limiting what we ask of it. There are better and worse types, and there are types which seem perfect for certain contexts and occasions. But no ideal, all-purpose typeface exists, and, what is more, *none is desirable*. Like the quest for the ideal commercial apple or wheat or potato . . . the search for the ideal typeface is, at its best, a blinkered and simplified version of the urge to nurture and improve. In its more invidious forms, that quest amounts to a concerted depletion of the gene pool.'

For this reason, the wise student of type design will be a tolerant critic, quick to welcome new designs and slow to condemn them. Cheltenham, so detested by Stanley Morison, has shown astonishing resilience, which must mean it has some merit which is not immediately apparent. Most people's tolerance runs out faced with the loathsome Souvenir, but it will probably not disappear finally until a stake is driven through its flabby heart at some nocturnal crossroads. A collection of essays by typographers from around the world, edited and published in 1993 by Robert Norton, called *Types best remembered/Types best forgotten*, gives an entertaining view of a variety of eccentric loves and hates which only serves to underline how subjective such matters can be.

Every designer has a mental shortlist of types which perform well under particular circumstances, are economical of space, and beautiful without being showy; yet there is another requirement which sounds paradoxical, that the type should not be hackneyed. For all the declarations of the more puritanical theorists, most type-conscious people feel that a typeface which has become very familiar runs the risk of becoming boring. Even Adrian Frutiger, who designed his sans-serif Univers for wide acceptance and use because of its carefully detailed unobtrusiveness, confessed that its very success made it seem dated twenty years later.

Finally, we should always remember that well-designed type is only the first step towards readable texts and handsome pages: bad setting and thoughtless layout can ruin the best-looking typeface. I hope that this account of the labours of some of the creators of type will increase the respect among users and consumers for these small miracles of art and skill.